INTRODUCTION TO ARBITRATION

To Donald Harmer

My pupil master

INTRODUCTION TO ARBITRATION

BY

HAROLD CROWTER
FRICS, FCIArb, FHKIArb, FFB

FOREWORD BY
THE RT. HON. LORD JUSTICE
ANTHONY EVANS

|L|L|P|

LONDON   HONG KONG
1998

LLP Reference Publishing
69–77 Paul Street
London EC2A 4LQ
Great Britain

EAST ASIA
LLP Asia
Sixth Floor, Hollywood Centre
233 Hollywood Road
Hong Kong

First published in Great Britain 1998

British Library Cataloguing in Publication Data
A catalogue record for this book is
available from the British Library

ISBN 1–85978–883–1

Are you satisfied with our customer service?

These telephone numbers are your service hot lines for questions and queries:

Delivery: +44 (0) 1206 772866
Payment/invoices/renewals: +44 (0) 1206 772114
LLP Products & Services: +44 (0) 1206 772113
e-mail: Publications@LLPLimited.com or fax us on +44 (0) 1206 772771

*We welcome your views and comments in order to ease any problems
and answer any queries you may have.*

LLP Limited, Colchester CO3 3LP, U.K.

Text set in 10/12pt Plantin by
Selwood Systems, Midsomer Norton
Printed in Great Britain by
WBC Limited,
Bridgend, Mid-Glamorgan

FOREWORD

The author of this new book is a distinguished arbitrator, currently chairman of the Chartered Institute of Arbitrators and with a wide international practice. He states in the Preface that his intention is twofold: to give an introduction to arbitration that is readily understandable to those with little or no previous knowledge of the subject, and to provide "a simple practice manual to more serious students".

It seems to me that both of these objects are triumphantly achieved, and I would add a third. He has also produced a work which will be useful for the practising arbitrator, for whom a convenient summary of the main provisions of the Arbitration Act 1996, combined with a perceptive commentary based on the author's long practical experience, will be of daily value. I have found this for myself. I have used the chapter on "Court assistance and intervention", and it explains the provisions of the Act clearly, effectively and with the minimum of words and analysis.

This is a book whose simplicity deserves to be called brilliant, and I commend it not only to students but also to practising arbitrators and lawyers, as their companion and guide.

June 1998   ANTHONY EVANS

PREFACE

New legislation always spawns a range of new books. This has been true of the English Arbitration Act 1996 which has, to some extent, radically changed the statutory framework of arbitration having its seat in England, Wales or Northern Ireland.

Arbitration in England has been well served by advanced legal texts and books with a more practical content for many years. These books have, with few exceptions, been aimed at the practitioner, the lawyer and the serious student. Books on arbitration specifically written for those with little or no knowledge of the subject are rare and it is primarily for such latter readers that this text is intended.

The book is intended, as its title suggests, to give an introduction to arbitration under the Arbitration Act 1996 that is readily understandable to those with little or no previous knowledge of the subject. I hope it may also be of assistance as a simple practice manual to more serious students of the subject.

The chapters follow a logical sequence, from a brief history and general introduction to the subject through each stage of the arbitral process in turn culminating in the award, enforcement and appeals. There is a final short chapter on special types of arbitration such as consumer schemes and arbitrations under statute. The text is illustrated by examples where appropriate. I have tried hard to avoid legal language wherever possible and I have intentionally made very few references to case law.

I have tried to cover comprehensively all of the important provisions of the Arbitration Act 1996. Inevitably the text reflects my own practice and philosophy but I have made a particular effort to take a mainstream view on all controversial areas of practice.

Even though I am an arbitrator in the construction industry, this is not a book for the construction industry alone. There are relatively few examples from construction and the book will be just as relevant to those practising in shipping, commodities, commercial rent review, consumer matters or any other area of arbitration.

It is hoped that this book will find a place on the shelves of those coming to arbitration for the first time, either on an entry level training course or as part of a university or college course covering the subject of arbitration as part of its syllabus.

My sincere thanks go to my wife Ruth for her forbearance and support during the writing of this book, which has disrupted our precious holidays on more than one occasion. I am also grateful to Chris Linnett from my office and to John Cane, one of the most experienced arbitrators in the country, for reading drafts of the text and for their comments, suggestions and criticisms which, for the most part, I have been delighted to accept.

Finally I dedicate this book to my pupil master Donald Harmer, now enjoying retirement in Spain. Without his help and the highest quality of his training and example, my own practice would be much the poorer. He was in the vanguard of arbitral training at the introductory level and above, both with the Chartered Institute of Arbitrators and the Diploma in Arbitration at the College of Estate Management at Reading University. Donald was my inspiration in arbitration and I publicly acknowledge and salute his unique contribution.

April 1998   HAROLD CROWTER

CONTENTS

4. APPOINTMENT

5. THE ARBITRATOR

9. COURT ASSISTANCE AND INTERVENTION

13. OTHER TYPES OF ARBITRATION

TABLE OF CASES

TABLE OF STATUTES

TABLE OF STATUTORY
INSTRUMENTS

TABLE OF INTERNATIONAL CONVENTIONS

CHAPTER 1

A BRIEF HISTORY OF ARBITRATION IN GREAT BRITAIN

WHAT IS ARBITRATION?

General principles

Arbitration is a process where, by agreement, parties to a contract submit their differences or disputes to the consideration and decision of one or more independent persons. Arbitration has the force of law and generally an arbitrator's decision, called an award, can be enforced in the courts just as a judgment of the court.

Arbitration is a private procedure. Only the parties to the arbitration agreement and their representatives can attend any arbitration meeting or hearing. The press and public are excluded. This characteristic of privacy is very important in commerce and trade. If the dispute went to court there might be a risk that trade secrets and customs could become public knowledge because of the public nature of the procedure.

Choosing the arbitrator

In most arbitrations there is only one arbitrator. Some trades, such as shipping, have historically used tribunals of three arbitrators. In international arbitration it is normal to have three arbitrators; commonly, but not invariably, one will be chosen by each side and the third, who will be the chairman, will be chosen by the other two.

Generally the parties are free to choose the arbitrator by agreement; it will be someone in whom they both have confidence. Commonly the arbitrator will possess a great deal of technical knowledge relevant to the general subject matter of the particular

dispute and therefore will have technical rather than legal qualifications and experience. Particularly in international disputes, the
parties may wish to appoint lawyers to the arbitral tribunal.

If the parties are unable to agree on an arbitrator, they generally
look to someone else to appoint an arbitrator for them. This
appointor will normally be named in the contract providing for
arbitration; usually it will be the president of a professional institution or the president or chairman of a trade association, for
example the President of the Chartered Institute of Arbitrators or
the President of the Grain and Feed Trade Association (GAFTA).
The court can also appoint an arbitrator.

Flexibility and cost

Arbitration is a very flexible procedure and can be adapted to suit
the particular dispute. Because of its flexibility it can and should be
cheaper and quicker than going to court. If, however, an arbitration
is allowed to mirror court procedure it may take just as long and
may be just as expensive. In a court case the parties only have to
pay a modest fee for the services of the judge and the use of the court
facilities; most of the true cost is met by taxpayers. In arbitration the
arbitrator has to be paid and accommodation often has to be rented
and paid for. In this respect arbitration is more expensive than court
procedure.

Use of arbitration as a method of dispute resolution

In the twentieth century there has been an enormous growth in
the use of arbitration. Perhaps the majority of international trade
contracts incorporate an arbitration clause. Few foreign companies
wish to be subject to the idiosyncrasies of national courts, particularly one which might be biased in favour of the party residing
within its jurisdiction. Arbitration is truly international and parties
can be confident that at least one member of the arbitral tribunal
will be sympathetic to their culture and trade practices.

In the United Kingdom arbitration has been the preferred
method of dispute resolution in many trades and industries and in
commerce. Shipping, insurance, banking, commodities (tea, coffee,
edible oils, grain, timber etc.), construction, commercial rent
review, metals and consumer contracts are all areas of activity which

use arbitration as their normal method of dispute resolution.

Certain disputes cannot be arbitrated; they are most criminal matters and civil matters which are reserved to the courts as a matter of public policy, for example a battle over the custody of a child.

Training and certification of arbitrators

Since 1980 enormous strides have been taken, primarily by the Chartered Institute of Arbitrators, to train and examine arbitrators and to set very high standards of ability and achievement before a person can be admitted as a member of the Chartered Institute's panels of arbitrators. This drive to quality has now extended to many corners of the world; regular training courses are run in North America, Latin America, Asia, Australia, Africa and throughout Europe. The future success of arbitration depends on the quality of arbitrators and their ability to adopt procedures appropriate to the individual case. Happily, other appointing bodies are also now insisting on training and demonstrated ability before an arbitrator is appointed.

The party who commences the arbitration is called the **claimant** and the other party is called the **respondent**. The arbitrator or arbitrators are sometimes called the **arbitral tribunal**. In Scotland the arbitrator is known as the **arbiter**.

HISTORY

General

In the Middle Ages, and even before, when merchants fell into dispute in connection with their trade, they would often refer it to another merchant of high esteem for his decision and the disputing parties would agree to abide by his decision. They needed quick simple justice with readily understandable procedures. The customs of merchants developed over the years into legal rules.

Eventually the practice of arbitration was given a statutory basis. In England, Parliament passed the first Arbitration Act in 1698.

At one time there was great resentment between the courts and arbitration as the courts regarded arbitrators as people who were taking their business away. Those times have changed, and in modern times the courts and arbitrators have enjoyed a close working relationship. So many disputes are decided by arbitrators that if the courts were to hear them, they would be swamped with work and would need many more judges and court buildings, all at taxpayers' expense, in order to cope.

Basis of law

In the United Kingdom, the system of law used is the **common law**; this must be distinguished from the **civil law** which is operated on the continent of Europe and in many other countries throughout the world.

In both systems, the statutes of the country concerned are central to the legal system. In Britain, these statutes are known as Acts of Parliament, whereas in civil law countries they are known as the **codes**, for example the **civil code** or the **criminal code**.

Common law relies heavily on **precedents** which are the previous reported decisions of the higher courts. These decisions are binding on courts of the same level as that making the decision and all inferior courts and tribunals. Civil law does not rely on precedent in the same way.

In England, for example, the highest court is the House of Lords, below that is the Court of Appeal and below that the High Court. High Court decisions are binding on the High Court and below but not on the Court of Appeal and House of Lords, whereas House of Lords' decisions are binding on all courts and tribunals.

Thus the law of England and Wales (generally known as English law) and the law of Northern Ireland are subject to Acts of Parliament and the law of precedent, or previous higher court decisions.

The law of arbitration is no different. It is controlled and influenced by the current Arbitration Act but also by an enormous body of precedent.

CHAPTER 2

INTRODUCTION TO ARBITRATION LAW IN ENGLAND, WALES AND NORTHERN IRELAND

History of Arbitration Acts

The first recorded statute in England was the **Arbitration Act 1698**. The next major statute was the **Arbitration Act 1889**, which recodified the previous Act and brought in some further common law principles. There was an amendment through the **Arbitration Act 1934**, but it was not until the **Arbitration Act 1950** that all of the previous Acts were repealed and a new consolidated arbitration statute was enacted.

The Arbitration Act 1950 has been the cornerstone of arbitration law in England and Wales in the second half of the twentieth century. It has also been adapted, sometimes with very little change, into the arbitration laws of most Commonwealth countries.

Northern Ireland had its own statute, the **Arbitration Act (Northern Ireland) 1937**, which largely mirrored the English 1934 Act. The Arbitration Act 1950 did not apply to Northern Ireland.

In 1958 there was a United Nations conference on the recognition and enforcement of foreign arbitral awards. It was recognised that arbitration awards made in one country should be able to be enforced in any other country just as if the award had been made in that other country. A Convention was drawn up which became known as the New York Convention on the Recognition and Enforcement of Foreign Arbitral Awards 1958.

The United Kingdom eventually adopted that Convention through the **Arbitration Act 1975**.

By 1979 a specific problem had been identified in that foreign parties who had chosen arbitration in London were becoming very dissatisfied that too many of their arbitrations were ending up before the English courts to determine a question of law arising out of the reference. The court decisions were adding greatly to the body of precedent on English arbitration law, but foreign parties were of the view that they did not choose arbitration to end up before the English courts.

Parliament was persuaded to pass the **Arbitration Act 1979**, which severely limited the right to appeal an arbitrator's award and made it possible to contract to exclude an appeal to the court on a point of law.

Various other Acts of Parliament contained reference to arbitration, such as the Consumer Arbitration Agreements Act 1988. Other Acts of Parliament made small revisions to the existing Arbitration Acts; for example the Administration of Justice Act 1982 introduced a new Section into the Arbitration Act 1950 empowering the arbitrator to award simple interest.

The next significant event in the development of arbitration law was brought about by the United Nations Commission on International Trade Law (UNCITRAL) which met to consider standardisation of arbitration law throughout the world to assist world trade. In 1985 UNCITRAL published a Model Arbitration Law (UNCITRAL Model Law) which it recommended to United Nations member nations as a basis for arbitration law reform throughout the world.

In 1989 a powerful committee, under the chairmanship of Lord Mustill, recommended that the Arbitration Law of England should be fundamentally reformed but that England should not adopt the UNCITRAL Model Law as drafted.

The aim of the Committee was to produce an Arbitration Act that would bring together into a readily understandable document all the important principles of the English law of arbitration including important principles of common law contained in court precedent. The aim was to make the new Act clear of expression and to avoid technical or legal jargon. It was to apply to domestic UK arbitration as well as to international cases. Although the UNCITRAL Model Law was not to be enacted as it stood, the new Act was to follow the principles of the Model Law and have the same structure and language wherever possible.

The Arbitration Act 1996

From these beginnings the **Arbitration Act 1996** was born. With very minor exceptions, the Arbitration Act 1996 sweeps away all the previous legislation on arbitration in England, Wales and Northern Ireland. The law of arbitration in Northern Ireland is now therefore the same as the law of arbitration in England and Wales.

The Arbitration Act 1996 came into force on 31 January 1997, with the exception of Sections 85, 86 and 87 which have not been brought into force.[1]

In England, Wales and Northern Ireland all arbitrations commenced on or after 31 January 1997 are subject to the Arbitration Act 1996, notwithstanding that the arbitration agreement between the parties in their contract was entered into before that date.

In **Scotland** arbitration law has substantial differences. Scotland has adopted the UNCITRAL Model Law for international arbitration but at the time of going to print is in the process of considering a more fundamental revision of its domestic arbitration law.

The courts can only intervene in arbitration where the Arbitration Act 1996 specifically provides for such intervention. As well as the express provisions of the Arbitration Act, the courts and those applying to the courts are bound by rules of court, known as **Rules of the Supreme Court**, or affectionately as the "White Book", because of the colour of its cover. Order 73 of the White Book deals with arbitration. The Rules of the Supreme Court are published as part of **"The Supreme Court Practice"**[2] which is normally published every other year—that is 1995, 1997 etc. Order 73 was brought into line with the Arbitration Act 1996 through "The Rules of the Supreme Court (Amendment) 1996".[3]

THE UNDERLYING PRINCIPLES OF THE ARBITRATION ACT 1996[4]

There are three pillars on which the Arbitration Act 1996 is built; they are the general principles covered by **Section 1** of the Act, the general duty of the tribunal under **Section 33** and the general duty

---

1 See Appendix 2—Commencement Order.
2 The Supreme Court Practice 1997—Sweet & Maxwell.
3 S.I. 1996/3219.
4 The full text of the Arbitration Act 1996 is at Appendix 1.

of the parties under **Section 40**. It will be seen that each numbered paragraph of the Act is called a **"Section"**.

There is constant reference in the Act to "this Part"; this needs some explanation. The Act is divided into four parts: Part I contains Sections 1 to 84 and comprises the meat of the Act. Part II runs from Sections 85 to 98; it relates to consumer arbitration agreements, small claims arbitration in the county court, the appointment of judges as arbitrators and statutory arbitrations.

Part III deals exclusively with the recognition and enforcement of certain foreign awards; it runs from Sections 99 to 104.

Part IV deals with certain miscellaneous matters such as repeals to existing legislation and the rules for the Act coming into force.

Thus, for example, reference in Section 1 to "this Part" means Sections 1 to 84.

Section 1 sets out the principles which govern all arbitration under the Act:

1. The provisions of this Part are founded on the following principles, and shall be construed accordingly—
   (a) the object of arbitration is to obtain the fair resolution of disputes by an impartial tribunal without unnecessary delay or expense;
   (b) the parties should be free to agree how their disputes are resolved, subject only to such safeguards as are necessary in the public interest;
   (c) in matters governed by this Part the court should not intervene except as provided by this Part.

Everything that an arbitrator does under the Act must be measured against his general duties which are contained in **Section 33**:

33. (1) The tribunal shall—
    (a) act fairly and impartially as between the parties, giving each party a reasonable opportunity of putting his case and dealing with that of his opponent, and
    (b) adopt procedures suitable to the circumstances of the particular case, avoiding unnecessary delay or expense, so as to provide a fair means for the resolution of the matters falling to be determined.
    (2) The tribunal shall comply with that general duty in conducting the arbitral proceedings, in its decisions on matters of procedure and evidence and in the exercise of all other powers conferred on it.

The parties are required to co-operate with the arbitral tribunal and if they intend to challenge his jurisdiction to hear the dispute or if they intend to instigate any court intervention during the course of the proceedings they must do so speedily. These obligations are set out in **Section 40**:

40. (1) The parties shall do all things necessary for the proper and expeditious conduct of the arbitral proceedings.
   (2) This includes—
      (a) complying without delay with any determination of the tribunal as to procedural or evidential matters, or with any order or directions of the tribunal, and
      (b) where appropriate, taking without delay any necessary steps to obtain a decision of the court on a preliminary question of jurisdiction or law (see Sections 32 and 45).

The doctrine of party autonomy encapsulated in **Section 1 (b)** of the Act is brought into action in the Act by defining the various Sections of the Act as **mandatory** and **non-mandatory**. Thus the parties are free to contract out of or modify any of the non-mandatory Sections. For example Section 30 empowers the arbitral tribunal to rule on its own jurisdiction; that power may be excluded by agreement between the parties because Section 30 is non-mandatory.

Schedule 1 of the Act defines which Sections are mandatory; all others are non-mandatory.

There is nothing to stop parties giving arbitrators more power than the Act gives them, providing they do not cut across any of the mandatory provisions. Additional powers are often given by the parties adopting Arbitration Rules in their contract. For example, a charterparty in a shipping contract may require any arbitration to be conducted under the Rules of the London Maritime Arbitrators Association. Many international contracts provide for arbitration under the Rules of the International Chamber of Commerce in Paris.

CHAPTER 3

ARBITRATION AGREEMENTS

ORAL OR IN WRITING

Oral agreements

An arbitration agreement is an agreement to submit present or future disputes to arbitration; it may be oral, in writing or evidenced in writing. Oral arbitration agreements may be valid and binding but Part I of the Arbitration Act does not apply to such agreements. Oral arbitration agreements may still be given some effect as **Section 81 (1) (b)** of the Act preserves any rules of common law as to the effect of an oral arbitration agreement.

Written agreements

Part I of the Act only applies to written arbitration agreements. Prior to the 1996 Act there was often debate as to what constituted a written arbitration agreement. **Sections 5 and 6** of the Act define the following as written arbitration agreements:

• written signed agreement

• written unsigned agreement

• exchange of letters or other written communications

• reference in a written document to another document containing an arbitration agreement, such as a standard form of contract

• an unwritten agreement to a document containing an arbitration agreement, such as reference to a standard form of contract containing an arbitration clause

- any written record of an unwritten agreement whether the record was made by the parties or by a third party with the authority of the parties

- an unchallenged written submission in any legal or arbitral proceedings that an arbitration agreement exists

- anything described above as "written" may be recorded by any other means: this will include fax, telex or e-mail.

An example of an arbitration agreement:

In the event of any dispute or difference arising under, out of or in connection with this contract, such dispute or difference may be referred to arbitration by either party on written notice to the other. The arbitrator shall be appointed by consent or, if the parties cannot agree within 28 days of the giving of notice to concur in the appointment, to be appointed on application of either party by the President of the Chartered Institute of Arbitrators.

AGREEMENTS BEFORE OR AFTER DISPUTE ARISES

Most arbitration agreements are entered into before the dispute arises, normally as part of the principal contract between the parties. The parties sensibly assume that disputes might arise under the contract and if so that they should be resolved by arbitration. Most standard form contracts contain an arbitration agreement. For example in most package holiday contracts sold in Great Britain, the conditions will provide that in the event of any dispute, it will be resolved by arbitration.

Virtually all standard form contracts in the construction industry contain an arbitration agreement.

Agreements which provide for one party to pay the costs in any event

Frequently contracts are made between parties where they are not of equal bargaining power. In such cases the arbitration agreement may provide that in the event of an arbitration, the whole of the costs are to be met by the party in the weaker bargaining position. Any arbitration agreement that does provide for costs to be paid by one party in any event is only valid if it is entered into after the dispute has arisen; this is covered by **Section 60** of the Act.

Binding nature of arbitration agreements

If a contract does not contain an arbitration agreement, there is nothing to prevent the parties entering into a separate arbitration agreement before or after the dispute has arisen. Except for Statutory Arbitrations discussed in Chapter 13 below, no party can be forced into arbitration against his will. At some time both parties to the contract must have consented to arbitration. Once a party has entered into an arbitration agreement he cannot unilaterally opt out of that agreement and it may be enforced against him. The only exceptions to this are certain **"consumer arbitration agreements"** where the consumer may be able to avoid the arbitration agreement; this is discussed in detail in Chapter 13 below.

SEPARABILITY OF ARBITRATION AGREEMENTS

An arbitration agreement which forms part of a contract containing the substance of the agreement between the parties is separable from the remainder of the contract in law by virtue of **Section 7** of the Act. This means that if the primary contract does not come into force, is invalid for some legal reason or is brought to a premature end, then the arbitration agreement will survive and the parties may seek remedies under it notwithstanding that the primary contract is invalid, ineffective or is brought to a premature end.

STAY OF COURT PROCEEDINGS

When parties enter into an arbitration agreement, they are bound by it. However not infrequently a party to a contract which contains an arbitration clause will commence some kind of court action against the other party, for example for payment alleged to be due under the contract. What is the other party to do about it?

If a party to an arbitration agreement is in receipt of court proceedings against him, he has two choices:

- he can decide to defend the court proceedings, in which case he will not be able to insist the dispute is heard in arbitration, or

- he can merely acknowledge receipt of the court proceedings without taking any action whatever to contest the merits of the case made against him **and immediately after acknowledgement** he must make an application to the court in which those legal proceedings have been instituted for a stay of the court proceedings and for referral of the dispute to arbitration.

On receipt of an application for a stay of court proceedings and referral back to arbitration, the court will satisfy itself that:

- the defendant has taken no step to contest the merits of the case made against him in court proceedings, and

- the arbitration agreement is not null and void, inoperative or incapable of being performed.

If so satisfied the court will then stay the court proceedings and refer the dispute back to arbitration. Providing the court is satisfied on the above two conditions, it has no discretion and must stay the court proceedings. The stay procedure is contained in **Section 9** of the Act.

Domestic arbitration agreements

In the Arbitration Act 1996 as drafted, if none of the parties to the arbitration are foreign to the United Kingdom, the arbitration agreement is defined by **Section 85** as a **"domestic arbitration agreement"**. Under **Section 86** of the Act, as enacted but not brought into force, the court retains a discretion to stay court proceedings to arbitration if it considers there are other sufficient grounds for not requiring the parties to abide by the arbitration agreement. In other words, had these Sections been in force, the court would have been obliged to grant a stay under Section 9 in respect of an international arbitration, whereas for a domestic arbitration the court would have retained a discretion whether or not to grant a stay. However the Secretary of State has decided not to bring Sections 85 to 87 inclusive into force with the rest of the Act. Therefore the distinction between "domestic arbitration agreements" and other arbitration agreements is inapplicable and irrelevant. The result is that a stay of court proceedings will be mandatory in all cases providing the two conditions identified above have been satisfied.

ARBITRATION RULES

As mentioned in Chapter 2, the parties are free to agree any additions to or deductions from the powers of the arbitral tribunal given to it by the Arbitration Act 1996 providing the parties' agreement does not cut across those Sections of the Act which are mandatory as defined in **Section 4** and **Schedule 1**.

Further the parties may agree certain procedural matters which are not dealt with in the Act at all, for example the parties may agree a timetable for the exchange of written statements setting out their case and their answer to the case made by the other side. The parties could also agree that the practical administration of the arbitration should be carried out by some arbitral institution, such as the London Court of International Arbitration.

Many trade agreements use standard form contracts which often incorporate arbitration rules within the arbitration agreement. For example, in the construction industry many building contracts incorporate the use of the Construction Industry Model Arbitration Rules (CIMAR)[1]; similarly in civil engineering contracts, the arbitration rules of the Institution of Civil Engineers are incorporated. The Chartered Institute of Arbitrators has its own arbitration rules, as do many of the commodity trade associations (grain, coffee etc.). Shipping contracts often incorporate the use of standard arbitration rules. Even some consumer contracts are subject to standard arbitration rules, such as package holidays under the arbitration scheme of the Association of British Travel Agents (ABTA) run in conjunction with the Chartered Institute of Arbitrators.

This plethora of arbitration rules, of which only a few have been mentioned, is eloquent testimony to one of the basic principles of arbitration under the Arbitration Act 1996, namely that the parties are free to agree how their disputes are resolved subject to such

---

1 "CIMAR 1998" Rules—published by the Society of Construction Arbitrators—
February 1998.

safeguards as are necessary in the public interest—**Section 1 (b)**. This doctrine is known as **party autonomy**.

Ad hoc arbitration

There are however many arbitration agreements which are not subject to arbitration rules. In these cases the arbitration is conducted in accordance with the Arbitration Act, subject to the terms of the contract between the parties. This type of non-rules arbitration is generally known as **ad hoc arbitration**.

CHAPTER 4

APPOINTMENT

WHEN THE ARBITRATION COMMENCES

Subject to the right of the parties to agree when the arbitration proceedings are commenced, the default position under **Section 14** of the Arbitration Act 1996, where the parties are free to agree an arbitrator between them, is that the arbitration is deemed to have commenced on the date when one party writes to the other requiring it to agree to the appointment of an arbitrator in respect of the matter in dispute. Similar provisions apply where the arbitrator is named in the arbitration agreement or is to be appointed by a third party.

NUMBERS OF ARBITRATORS

Unless otherwise agreed the reference shall be to a sole arbitrator. If there is to be more than one arbitrator, there is usually an odd number, normally three. **Section 15** of the Act refers.

APPOINTMENT BY THE PARTIES

The procedure for appointing arbitrators is covered in **Section 16** of the Arbitration Act 1996.

Named in the arbitration agreement

There is nothing to prevent the parties naming the agreed arbitrator in their arbitration agreement. If a dispute arises that is referred to arbitration, he is merely requested by one of the parties to take up the reference.

Chosen after the dispute arises

Most arbitration agreements allow for the parties to try to agree their arbitrator when one writes to the other giving a notice of arbitration in connection with a dispute which has arisen. If there is one person agreeable to both parties and in whom they both have confidence as an arbitrator, then it is always best for that person to be appointed. Often informal contact between the parties' solicitors can result in agreement.

A common approach is for the party referring a dispute to arbitration to give the other party a list of three arbitrators, any one of whom would be acceptable to it. The danger is that the other party will come back with a list of three more names and each party will feel obliged to reject all the names proposed by the other. It can be said, perhaps cynically, that this method has the effect of excluding the best six arbitrators for the reference.

Various other methods can be tried. For example each party can simultaneously exchange a list of five arbitrators it would be happy to accept. If any names are common to both lists, each party will list those names in order of preference. The name with the highest joint preference is then appointed.

If an arbitrator is agreed between the parties, the parties' representatives will write to the arbitrator enquiring whether he is willing to accept appointment as arbitrator. Almost always the arbitrator, after considering if he has any conflict of interest and if he has the time to complete the reference without undue delay, will insist on both parties agreeing his scale of charges and terms of engagement as a precondition to appointment.

Regrettably the catalyst for disputes is often the breakdown of a personal relationship between individuals on each side. In such cases the parties are hardly able to agree the day of the week never mind the identity of an arbitrator to decide their dispute. Then the only alternative is for a third party to be asked to appoint or nominate the arbitrator.

APPOINTING BODIES

Some arbitration agreements specify that the arbitrator is to be appointed by an independent appointing body. In such cases, unless the parties agree to modify their arbitration agreement, the question of the parties attempting to agree an arbitrator or arbitrators does not arise. As soon as the notice of arbitration is given, the party requiring arbitration writes to the appointing body requesting an appointment.

A more common arbitration agreement will give the parties an opportunity to try to agree an arbitrator first, but if there is no agreement within a set period of time, typically 14 or 28 days, either party can request appointment from the appointing body named in the arbitration agreement.

In either case, the party requesting appointment must send brief details of the contract to the appointing body including a copy of the arbitration agreement and details of the nature of the dispute. A fee is payable by the applicant and usually a standard form has to be completed.

Typical procedure for appointment

The appointing body will write to the representatives of the other party for information purposes and will ask both parties if there are any potential arbitrators who should not be appointed because of conflict of interest. The appointing body, referred to in the Arbitration Act 1996 **Section 74** as an **arbitral institution**, must satisfy itself that it does indeed have power to appoint or nominate an arbitrator under the arbitration agreement.

Appointing bodies keep lists of approved arbitrators. Their procedures for appointment are different but similar principles apply. The procedures of the Royal Institution of Chartered Surveyors (RICS) in a dispute over rent review under a commercial lease will serve as an example.

The applicant will contact the RICS Arbitrations Department and ask for a form requesting appointment of an arbitrator. The applicant completes the form and encloses his appointment fee and a copy of the rent review clause in the lease containing the arbitration agreement. The RICS sends a copy of the application form to the nominated representative of the other party.

The RICS Arbitrations Department then enters details of the application into its computer including the geographical location of the property in respect of which the rent review is disputed and the size of the dispute. The computer is programmed to list a number of potential arbitrators who operate in that geographical area and are capable of handling a reference of that magnitude; the number of times each selected arbitrator has been appointed by the RICS in a set period is also displayed.

A potential arbitrator is selected, possibly after consultation with senior staff and even the President of the RICS who will actually make the appointment. The RICS then send a letter to the potential arbitrator asking if he or she is willing to have his or her name considered for appointment and to confirm that:

- the subject matter of the dispute falls within the sphere of his own normal professional practice and not merely that of his firm;

- he would be able to undertake the task with all reasonable expedition;

- after making inquiries within his organisation no possibility of conflict of interest exists;

- he meets any special contractual requirements of the arbitrator (for example, length of experience, area of geographical practice, etc.);

- he is not currently engaged as arbitrator or independent expert in another case where his duties and functions to the parties would conflict with his duties and functions to the parties in this case;

- he has and maintains adequate professional indemnity insurance cover;

- he knows of no other reason why he should not be appointed.

If all of the answers are satisfactory, the file with the recommendation for appointment goes to the President of the RICS or his nominated deputy. The appointment is in the discretion of the President who then signs a standard form appointing the arbitrator. The form of appointment is sent to the arbitrator with the papers which the RICS have received from the applicant and both parties are notified of the appointment.

RICS also send to the arbitrator a form to complete when the arbitration is completed. That is used for statistical purposes but also as a trigger for the RICS to write to the parties' representatives in order to monitor the performance of the arbitrator. If the arbitrator consistently performs badly he will not be appointed again.

Nomination or appointment

It is normal for an arbitrator when he receives an appointment from an appointing body to formally accept that appointment in writing. There is a slight distinction between nomination as arbitrator and appointment as arbitrator. **Nomination** is always subject to the potential arbitrator's acceptance; if he does not accept nomination he is not the arbitrator. **Appointment** often follows the potential arbitrator's earlier written confirmation that he is willing to accept appointment as arbitrator, such as in the RICS example quoted, when written acceptance of the eventual appointment may not be strictly necessary.

Conditional appointments

Some appointing bodies make conditional appointments, for example, subject to the arbitrator agreeing his fees and terms of engagement with both parties. Conditional appointments do not work well because one party can frustrate the appointment by refusing to satisfy the condition.

IMMUNITY OF ARBITRAL INSTITUTIONS

Section 74 of the Arbitration Act 1996 confers on arbitral institutions a limited immunity from legal action regarding their appointing functions. The effect will be that parties will not be able to allege negligence against the appointing body because, for example, the arbitrator appointed proves not to be competent. The only exception to this immunity is if the arbitral institution is proved to have acted in bad faith. Section 74 is mandatory so cannot be excluded by agreement.

Equally the arbitral institution will not be vicariously liable for the acts and omissions of the arbitrator it appoints.

The immunity granted is limited to the appointing function of the arbitral institution and should it carry out any other administrative functions relating to the arbitration then it will not enjoy immunity if it is negligent in carrying out those other administrative functions.

COURT APPOINTMENTS

If the parties are unable to agree an arbitrator and there is no contractual machinery for a third party appointment or that machinery has failed, either or both parties may ask the court to appoint an arbitrator.

The court is given power to appoint or to make directions as to the appointment of arbitrators by **Section 18** of the Arbitration Act 1996.

The court will respect any agreement of the parties as to particular qualities or qualifications that the arbitrator must possess. The court has four express powers regarding appointments:

- to give directions as to the making of an appointment;

- in cases where there is to be more than one arbitrator, to direct that the arbitral tribunal shall be constituted by such appointments as have been made;

- to revoke any appointments already made;

- to make any necessary appointments itself.

If the court appoints, it will make an order appointing the arbitrator, a copy of which will normally be sent to him by the parties. If the arbitrator has good reason, he can refuse to accept the appointment, in which case the court will be asked to reappoint.

ACCEPTANCE OF APPOINTMENT AND TERMS OF ENGAGEMENT

As stated above, an arbitrator will normally send a written acceptance of appointment. If he has the opportunity to agree his scale of charges and terms of engagement before accepting appointment, he will normally seize that opportunity and make his acceptance of appointment conditional on agreement to his terms. The opportunity to pre-agree charges and terms only arises when the appointment is by consent. When the arbitrator receives an appointment from an appointing body, he will normally accept appointment before inviting the parties' agreement to his scale of charges and terms of engagement.

A typical scale of charges and terms of engagement might be as follows:

In the matter of the Arbitration Act 1996
Appointment of . . . as arbitrator
Standard scale of charges and terms of engagement

1. This scale is effective from 1 January 1998 and relates to services provided up to and including 31 December 1998. The following rates will be augmented by . . . % on 1 January of 1999 and of each successive year.
2. Rates
   a. £XXX minimum fee in any event; if exceeded, to be set off against fees calculated as below.
   b. £YYY per day: for each day of hearing not exceeding six hours but otherwise regardless of its duration.
   c. £ZZZ per hour: for each hour:
      • of hearing beyond the sixth working hour of any day
      • actively engaged upon the duties of a reference other than at a hearing, including travelling and waiting time
      • actively engaged in preparation for a hearing
      • in conference
      • not otherwise defined by this scale and in which it is necessary by reason of the appointment to be away from my office at any time between the hours of 9:00am and 6:00pm.
   d. Disbursements: all travelling and other expenses and outgoings incurred by reason of the appointment, including the cost of obtaining such legal or other advice as in my absolute discretion I consider it desirable to take.
3. Once dates for a hearing have been fixed a fee shall be chargeable for each day set aside and not spent, calculated as a percentage of the daily rate stated above according to the period of receipt of notice of postponement or cancellation before the first day of the hearing, as follows:

more than six months	Nil
between 3 months and 6 months	20%
between 2 months and 3 months	40%
between 1 month and 2 months	70%
less than 1 month or during the hearing	100%

Should I be able to obtain additional work in order to gainfully employ time set aside for a hearing and not spent, then, at my sole discretion, the above cancellation charges may be reduced to the extent that the time set aside is able to be gainfully employed through such additional work.

4. Without in any way prejudicing the outcome of the reference in respect of the awarding of costs, each party shall provide equally for the due payment of my fees and expenses by making a cash deposit with me in a sum and on terms to be fixed by me, to be held in a separate identified deposit account, with interest accruing to the benefit of the parties; the money to be held in accordance with the latest regulations regarding the holding of client's money by members of (professional institution).

5. I reserve the right to submit accounts for fees and expenses on an interim basis and shall be entitled to payment of such accounts within 10 working days of presentation. Without in any way prejudicing the outcome of the reference in respect of the awarding of costs, each party shall bear and pay an equal proportion of any interim accounts for such fees and expenses.

6. Any award shall be taken up by one or other parties upon payment of my fees and expenses and in any event within 10 working days after issue of notice that the award has been made.

7. In the event of a settlement of the issues by agreement between the parties before an award is made the fees and expenses properly payable shall be paid by the party or parties responsible for so doing under the terms of the settlement within 10 working days after notification of the amount irrespective of whether an agreed award is required or made.

8. Any fees and expenses not paid within the time limits specified above shall be subject to the addition of simple interest at 3% above the current ... Bank Base Rate from the expiry of the time limit until payment.

9. All the above rates are subject to Value Added Tax, if applicable, at the appropriate rate.

Model terms of engagement

Certain arbitral institutions and other bodies representing the interests of arbitrators in a particular trade publish their own model terms of engagement and sometimes suggested scales of charges, for example model terms are published by the London Maritime Arbitrators Association (LMAA) and the Society of Construction Arbitrators. Many international arbitral institutions publish their own terms and scale of charges, which covers not only the remuneration of the arbitrators but also the charges of the institution for administering the arbitration; examples are the International Chamber of Commerce (ICC) and the London Court of International Arbitration (LCIA).

TERMINATION OF THE ARBITRATOR'S APPOINTMENT

The arbitrator's appointment usually only terminates on completion of his task as arbitrator, that is when he has made his final award and has dealt with the determination of the parties' recoverable costs, if appropriate.

There are circumstances, however, when the arbitrator's appointment may be terminated, or will come to an end earlier:

- on the arbitrator's death—Section 26 of the Act;

- if the arbitrator's authority is revoked by agreement between the parties—Section 23;

- if the arbitrator's appointment is revoked by the court under Section 18 of the Act (usually due to some irregularity in the appointment);

- if the arbitrator is removed by the court under Section 24 due to justifiable doubts as to his impartiality, his not possessing the qualifications specified by the arbitration agreement, physical or mental incapacity, his refusal or failure to properly conduct the proceedings or to use all reasonable dispatch in discharging his duties providing substantial injustice has been or will be caused to the party applying for his removal;

- if the arbitrator resigns—Section 25 of the Act.

LIABILITY FOR THE ARBITRATOR'S FEES

Each party is jointly and severally liable to pay to the arbitrator such reasonable fees and expenses as are appropriate in the circumstances (**Section 28 (1)** of the Act). This means that each party is liable individually and if one party should fail to pay and be incapable of paying, then the other party will be liable for the whole of the arbitrator's fees, irrespective of which party is ordered to bear those fees in the arbitrator's award. Section 28 is mandatory and cannot be excluded by consent.

If the parties have agreed the arbitrator's scale of charges and terms of engagement, then that contractual agreement will be enforced.

IMMUNITY OF THE ARBITRATOR

Unless the arbitrator acts in bad faith, he will not be liable for anything done or omitted in the discharge of his functions as arbitrator; this immunity also extends to employees of the arbitrator, for example, his secretary, who might mistakenly double book his diary.

Resignation exception

There is however one important exception to the immunity granted by **Section 29** of the Arbitration Act 1996 and that is if the arbitrator resigns.

If the arbitrator resigns he will immediately lose immunity from suit until he makes a successful application to the court under **Section 25 (3)** of the Act for relief from liability.

The potential exposure to legal action will certainly discourage arbitrators from resignation except in the most extreme circumstances. Even the possibility of action following resignation will mean that arbitrators will be wise to continue to hold professional indemnity insurance cover.

CHAPTER 5

THE ARBITRATOR

GENERAL DUTY OF THE ARBITRAL TRIBUNAL

Section 33 of the Arbitration Act 1996 is in the following terms:

33. (1) The tribunal shall—
    (a) act fairly and impartially as between the parties, giving each party a reasonable opportunity of putting his case and dealing with that of his opponent, and
    (b) adopt procedures suitable to the circumstances of the particular case, avoiding unnecessary delay or expense, so as to provide a fair means for the resolution of the matters falling to be determined.
    (2) The tribunal shall comply with that general duty in conducting the arbitral proceedings, in its decisions on matters of procedure and evidence and in the exercise of all other powers conferred on it.

It is generally said that an arbitrator is bound to apply the rules of natural justice, which in summary are:

• the arbitrator must be and be seen to be impartial and disinterested; and

• each party must be given a full and fair opportunity of putting its case and rebutting the case made against it.

The duties in Section 33 extend and slightly modify the rules of natural justice.

Instead of the arbitrator being required to give each party a **full opportunity** of putting its case and dealing with that of his opponent, the requirement under the Act is for each party to be given a **reasonable opportunity**. What is reasonable must be viewed in the context of the other requirements of the Act requiring the arbitrator to avoid unnecessary delay and expense and to adopt appropriate procedures for the dispute in question.

The arbitrator, as well as being impartial, disinterested and being required to give each party a reasonable opportunity to present its case and rebut the case of its opponent, must:

• adopt suitable procedures, and

• avoid unnecessary delay or expense.

All actions of the arbitrator throughout the reference must be viewed under the spotlight of Section 33 of the Act. If a proposed course of action does not comply with Section 33, it should be rejected.

SOLE ARBITRATOR

Unless the parties agree otherwise a sole arbitrator will be appointed. The majority of arbitrations in the United Kingdom are conducted by sole arbitrators, although there are exceptions in trades where the bulk of business is international, such as shipping, where the normal practice is to appoint tribunals of three arbitrators.

Section 15 (3) of the Arbitration Act 1996 states that "if there is no agreement as to the number of arbitrators, the tribunal shall consist of a sole arbitrator".

In the United States of America, for instance, three arbitrators are appointed to hear many arbitrations, whether domestic or international.

TRIBUNALS OF MORE THAN ONE ARBITRATOR

The parties are free to appoint as many arbitrators as they may agree, but if there is to be a multi-member tribunal, the number chosen will normally be odd, for example three, five or seven. This avoids the problem of the tribunal being equally divided on any issue. One of the arbitrators will be chosen as **chairman**.

Section 15 (2) of the Act, subject to the parties' contrary agreement, in effect implies a term into arbitration agreements that require the appointment of an even number of arbitrators, for the appointment of an additional arbitrator as chairman of the tribunal.

The Act sets out default rules for the appointment of arbitrators to tribunals of more than one member.

Three arbitrators or two arbitrators and an umpire

Some three-person tribunals consist of three arbitrators, one of whom will be chairman, whereas others consists of two arbitrators and an **umpire**. An umpire's function is different to an arbitrator. Although he attends the proceedings and is served with all of the documents served on the other arbitrators, he takes no part in the arbitration until the other two arbitrators disagree regarding a decision, order or award. In that case, the other two arbitrators immediately stand down and the umpire continues and completes the reference as if he was sole arbitrator.

JURISDICTION AND POWERS OF THE TRIBUNAL

An arbitrator only has **jurisdiction** if there is a valid arbitration agreement under which he is appointed and his appointment has been properly made. Further, he only has jurisdiction to decide those disputes referred to him which are so permitted by the arbitration agreement, subject to public policy restrictions.

Lack of jurisdiction

In summary, the reasons for lack of jurisdiction are:

• no valid arbitration agreement; or

• invalid appointment as arbitrator; or

• the arbitration agreement is not sufficiently widely worded to allow a matter in dispute to be referred to arbitration (for example an arbitration agreement may permit an arbitrator to decide if the quality of a consignment of coffee beans complies with an agreed sample, but may not permit him to set a new price if the consignment is better or worse than the sample); or

• the matters on which the arbitrator has been asked to decide have not been validly referred to arbitration; or

- the arbitrator has been asked to decide a matter which should not be decided in arbitration, but in the courts; for example, a criminal matter or custody of children.

Sources of jurisdiction

It can be said that jurisdiction defines the parameters or boundaries within which the arbitrator may operate.

An arbitrator derives his jurisdiction from the following sources:

- the arbitration agreement; and

- the notice or notices of arbitration

Powers

To be effective the arbitrator will need to exercise some or all of the **powers** that are available to him. Unless the arbitrator has jurisdiction, he has no powers.

Providing the arbitrator has jurisdiction, he has an extensive armoury of powers at his disposal. For example he may order the parties to disclose documents, or to appear before him on a certain date, or to provide security for costs.

Sources of powers

The arbitrator's powers are derived from a number of sources:

- the arbitration agreement

- any further ad hoc agreement of the parties

- agreed arbitration rules

- the Arbitration Act 1996

- common law—that is the precedent of previous reported decisions of the higher courts.

The Arbitration Act contains a number of default powers that the arbitrator will possess unless the parties agree to the contrary. There are also powers referred to in the Act that are only exercisable if the parties agree; the best example is the power to award provisional relief, usually a payment on account, subject to the final award.

This power, given by **Section 39,** cannot be used unless the parties agree. Such agreement may often be contained in standard arbitration rules which are incorporated into the arbitration agreement in standard form contracts.

EXAMPLES OF POWERS GIVEN TO ARBITRAL TRIBUNALS BY THE ARBITRATION ACT 1996

- to rule on its own jurisdiction (Section 30)

- to decide on procedural and evidential matters (Section 34 (2))

- to fix the time for compliance with its orders (Section 34 (3))

- by consent to order the consolidation of other arbitral proceedings (Section 35)

- to appoint experts, legal advisers or assessors (Section 37)

- to order a claimant to provide security for costs (Section 38 (3)—note that Section 82 (1) includes a counterclaimant in the definition of "claimant")

- to give directions relating to property (Section 38 (4))

- to administer oaths and affirmations and to direct examination on oath or affirmation (Section 38 (5))

- to direct preservation of evidence (Section 38 (6))

- by consent to order provisional relief (Section 39)

- to dismiss the claim for inordinate and inexcusable delay (Section 41 (3))

- to proceed in the absence of a party after failure to comply with orders after due notice (Section 41 (4))

- to make peremptory orders—that is an order which says words to the effect that "unless you do what is ordered by a set date there will be serious consequences" (Section 41 (5))

- to dismiss the claim if the claimant fails to comply with a peremptory order to provide security for costs (Section 41 (6))

- to enforce the consequences of non-compliance with peremptory orders (Section 41 (7))

- to make more than one award on different aspects of the matters in dispute (Section 47)

- to make a declaration (Section 48 (3))

- to order payment of money in any currency (Section 48 (4))

- to order a party to refrain from doing something, to order specific performance (honour actions required under a contract) or to order rectification of deeds or documents (Section 48 (5))

- to award simple or compound interest (Section 49)

- to withhold an award pending full payment of fees (Section 56)

- to correct an award to remove a clerical error or ambiguity or to make an additional award if not all matters presented have been dealt with (Section 57)

- to determine by award the recoverable costs of the arbitration (Section 63)

- to limit the recoverable costs of the arbitration (Section 65).

Until there have been more decided cases arising out of the Arbitration Act 1996, it is difficult to know what additional common law powers arbitrators will possess that are not described in the Act.

THE DIFFERENCE BETWEEN JURISDICTION AND POWERS

The popular analogy is the land owned by a farmer. The farmer's jurisdiction is defined by the boundaries of his land; he has no jurisdiction to work in fields beyond the boundaries of his own land. He may only work on his own land. The powers the farmer has to work within his jurisdiction are the tools he has at his disposal, tractor, plough, drill, harrow, muck-spreader, harvester etc. The farmer's powers are useless unless he is within his jurisdiction, that is within the land he owns.

An arbitrator can only work within the boundaries of his legal entitlement to arbitrate and on those matters which have been referred to his arbitration. He may employ all of the powers given to him by the sources described above to complete his task, but has no other powers at his disposal.

DETERMINATION OF AND CHALLENGE TO THE ARBITRATOR'S JURISDICTION

Arbitrator deciding his own jurisdiction

Unless the parties agree otherwise the arbitrator has power to decide and award on his jurisdiction; that is:

• whether there is a valid arbitration agreement

• whether he has been properly appointed

• what matters have been properly submitted to his arbitration.

These powers are contained in **Section 30** of the Arbitration Act 1996.

If the arbitrator considers at any time that there is a serious question as to his jurisdiction, he could ignore it and carry on but he would be wise to raise it with the parties and invite their submissions. Those submissions might be in writing or orally at a hearing or meeting called for the purpose.

It is more usual for points on jurisdiction to be taken by one of the parties, usually the respondent, at a fairly early stage in the reference. The sensible course is for the arbitrator to ask the party challenging his jurisdiction to put his challenge and his supporting submissions in writing within say seven days; the other party would be given a similar period to respond and finally the objecting party would have the right of reply. In a difficult case the arbitrator might perhaps call a hearing to hear evidence or oral submissions.

Awards on jurisdiction

He would then proceed to make his award on the challenge, deciding simply whether he had jurisdiction or not, and giving reasons for his decision.

An arbitrator, as an alternative to making an award on jurisdiction as described above, has the option, subject to the parties' agreement otherwise, to make his award on jurisdiction as part of the award on the merits of the substantive dispute.

Challenges to awards on jurisdiction

If a party considers the arbitrator lacks what is known as substantive jurisdiction, it must make objection as soon as it possibly can (**Section 31** of the Act). If it delays its challenge on jurisdiction it may lose the right to object later (**Section 73**).

Court deciding jurisdiction

If the parties have agreed that the arbitrator does not have power to determine his own jurisdiction, they may go to the court under **Section 32** for a determination.

Even if the arbitrator does have power under Section 30, the parties acting jointly or one party with the agreement of the arbitrator may go to court for the question of jurisdiction to be determined.

Any determination of jurisdiction by the arbitrator is appealable to the court, subject to conditions.

Challenges to arbitrator's awards on jurisdiction and determination by the court of preliminary points of jurisdiction are discussed in more detail in Chapter 9 below.

USE OF THE ARBITRATOR'S EXPERTISE

Awards reliant on arbitrator's expertise

Many arbitrators are chosen because of their specialist technical knowledge relating to the dispute in question. It is sometimes thought that the arbitrator with such knowledge is best placed to decide the dispute simply on the basis of his knowledge and experience. To reach that understandable conclusion is to fail to appreciate the nature of arbitration.

There are some disputes where it is the custom of the trade for an expert arbitrator to look at the matter in dispute and without the assistance of witnesses or lawyers to decide the case. Such disputes usually concern arguments over quality. For example an arbitrator may be asked to decide whether a consignment of coffee beans is of equal, lesser or greater quality than an approved sample. He will look at the sample, he will smell it and then do the same in various parts of the consignment. From his experience he will pronounce the result; he does not need another expert in coffee to assist him and is unlikely to need the ministrations of lawyers. This type of arbitration has become known as "look-sniff" for obvious reasons. It is the custom of the trade that the arbitrator is required to make his decision purely on the basis of his expertise.

Expertise only used to assist in understanding the evidence and the issues

There are many other arbitrations, of which construction, shipping and medicine are good examples, where the expertise of the arbitrator is required so that he can readily understand the often highly technical issues and evidence which he will hear. He will not decide on the basis of his own expert knowledge and experience but will use that expertise in helping to decide which of the various pieces of evidence adduced by the witnesses he prefers. The arbitrator will decide solely on the basis of the evidence he has heard and not on the basis of his own expertise.

If the arbitrator considers he has expert knowledge which might be relevant to his decision, he should put that knowledge to the witnesses and give them the opportunity to deal with it. An arbitrator who possessed such expert knowledge, but did not give the witnesses opportunity to deal with his opinions and proceeded to make his award on the basis of his own expertise, was removed by the court.[1]

The rule therefore is that unless there is a custom in the trade for an arbitrator to decide on the basis of his own expertise or the parties have consented to an arbitrator using his expertise alone to decide technical matters before him, the arbitrator must not use his own expertise, other than to assist in understanding the issues before him, and if he is minded to take note of his own specialist

---

1 *Fox* v. *P G Wellfair Ltd* (1981) 125 Sol Jo 413; [1981] 2 Lloyd's Rep 514; [1981] Com LR 140; (1981) 19 BLR 52.

knowledge he must first give the relevant witnesses opportunity to deal with his opinions.

REVOCATION OF ARBITRATOR'S AUTHORITY

Subject to agreement between the parties, the authority of the arbitrator cannot be revoked except:

• by the parties acting jointly; or

• by an arbitral institution vested with such powers by the parties; or

• by the court under Sections 18 or 24 of the Arbitration Act 1996.

This is covered by **Section 23** of the Act.

Unless the arbitrator is removed by the court under **Section 24**, he will still be entitled to his reasonable fees should the parties decide to revoke his authority.

REMOVAL OF AN ARBITRATOR BY THE COURT

Under **Section 24** of the Act any party may apply to the court to remove an arbitrator. There are five valid grounds of application:

• circumstances exist that give rise to justifiable doubts as to the arbitrator's impartiality; or

• he does not possess the qualifications required by the arbitration agreement; or

• he is physically or mentally incapable of conducting the proceedings or there are justifiable doubts as to his capacity to do so; or

• he has refused or failed properly to conduct the proceedings and as a result substantial injustice has been or will be caused to the applicant; or

• he has refused or failed properly to use all reasonable dispatch in conducting the proceedings or making an award and as a result substantial injustice has been or will be caused to the applicant.

Successful challenge for serious irregularity in award not sufficient for removal

Interestingly, if the arbitrator continues with the reference and makes an award and that award is successfully challenged for serious irregularity under **Section 68** of the Arbitration Act 1996, the court has no power to remove the arbitrator unless at least one of the five criteria set out in Section 24 of the Act is satisfied.

Continuing to act while proceedings pending

The arbitrator may continue with the proceedings and make an award while the court application is waiting to be heard, but he does so at some risk to himself because the court, if it removes him, will decide his entitlement to fees.

Entitlement to fees

If the arbitrator is removed, the court, as well as setting the fees (if any) to which the arbitrator is entitled, may order the arbitrator to repay any fees already received.

The arbitrator is entitled to appear and be heard by the court before it makes any order removing him.

RESIGNATION OF ARBITRATOR

An arbitrator is free to resign his office but should be very wary before doing so as it may have serious consequences for him. These are contained in **Section 25** of the Act.

If the arbitrator resigns he may reach agreement with the parties, either as a condition of his resignation or afterwards, as to his entitlement to fees and whether any liability will be incurred by him. If the arbitrator does not reach such agreement he has to make a personal application to the court, at his own expense, to grant him relief from liability incurred by him as a result of his resignation (normally the parties' wasted costs) and to make such order as the court thinks fit as to his entitlement, if any, to fees and expenses.

The court will only grant relief from liability if it is satisfied in all the circumstances that it was reasonable for the arbitrator to resign.

There are very few circumstances where it will be appropriate for the arbitrator to resign. Examples, by no means exhaustive, that come to mind are:

* serious illness or incapacity

* unexpected discovery of a conflict of interest that reasonable inquiry failed to detect

* unexpected removal overseas for family reasons.

ARBITRATOR'S PERSONAL ENTITLEMENT TO FEES AND EXPENSES

Effect of agreement to arbitrator's terms

As discussed in Chapter 4 above, the parties are jointly and severally liable for the arbitrator's reasonable fees and expenses. That is not to say that the arbitrator is necessarily entitled to recover the fees and expenses he requests. If the arbitrator obtains the agreement of both parties to his hourly or daily rate then such rates are sacrosanct and cannot be challenged on the grounds of unreasonableness. What can however be challenged is the number of hours the arbitrator has allocated and the amount of his expenses.

If the hourly rates or daily rates have not been agreed by both parties then they too may be challenged as being unreasonable. The arbitrator should be careful not to reach agreement with one party over his rates and terms of engagement and not reach the same agreement with the other party. In such cases the party that has agreed the fees should be released from its agreement to avoid a challenge of lack of impartiality.

Lien on award

The arbitrator is entitled by virtue of **Section 56** of the Arbitration Act 1996 to refuse to deliver his award except on payment of the full fees and expenses demanded by him; indeed this is standard practice.

Fees considered and adjusted by the court

Whether or not the full fees demanded have been paid, either party, usually the losing party, may apply to the court under **Section 28** of the Act for the arbitrator's fees to be considered and adjusted. The other party and the arbitrator must be sent a copy of the application. Although the Act, perhaps surprisingly, does not say so, the arbitrator will normally be entitled to appear and be heard on the application. The precise method the court will use to consider and adjust the arbitrator's fees is set out in Order 73 of the Rules of the Supreme Court ("White Book")[2]—Appendix 4.

The application to the court for the arbitrator's fees and expenses to be considered and adjusted may be made by any party. The applicant must state why it considers the arbitrator's fees and expenses to be unreasonable and what it considers would be reasonable. The application must be supported by an affidavit and copies of relevant documents. All applicants have to complete a special court form, known as Form No. 8A. Under Order 73 rule 10 (2), the arbitrator must be made a respondent to such an application and notice must be given to the arbitrator by serving on him the arbitration application and any affidavit in support.

If the arbitrator wishes to contest the application he must acknowledge service by completing a standard court acknowledgement of service form, known as Form No. 15A, within 14 days of service of the application. The arbitrator then has to serve an affidavit in support of the fees and expenses he has demanded before the expiration of 21 days after the expiry of the time limit for acknowledging service.

Eventually a hearing will take place in chambers[3] for the court to determine the arbitrator's entitlement to fees and expenses.

If the arbitrator has already been paid, the court may order repayment, but the applicant must show that it is reasonable in the circumstances for the court to so order. If the application is delayed, it may be unreasonable to order repayment as the arbitrator may well have already spent the fees.

---

2 Rules of the Supreme Court 1997—Order 73—published by Sweet and Maxwell (as amended by "The Rules of the Supreme Court (Amendment) 1996" S.I. 1996/3219).

3 Hearings and applications in chambers are not open to the public, press or court reporters.

CHAPTER 6

MULTI-MEMBER TRIBUNALS

APPOINTMENT

Section 16 of the Arbitration Act 1996 sets out the default procedure for appointment of arbitrators, although the parties are free to make what arrangement they consider appropriate.

If the arbitration agreement requires a tribunal of **two arbitrators**, each party shall appoint its own arbitrator within 14 days of service of a notice to do so. Under **Sections 15 (2) and 16 (5) (b)** of the Act the two arbitrators already appointed must then forthwith appoint a third arbitrator to be chairman. The reason a third arbitrator is appointed is that Section 15 (2) in effect implies a term into the arbitration agreement that an additional arbitrator shall be appointed as chairman to avoid the problems of decision-making if the two arbitrators are not in agreement.

If the tribunal is to consist of **three arbitrators**, the procedure is exactly as the last paragraph.

Finally if the agreement requires the appointment of **two arbitrators and an umpire**, each party shall appoint its own arbitrator within 14 days of service of a notice to do so. The two arbitrators do not have to appoint an umpire immediately but may do so at any time after their appointment and they must appoint him before the hearing or earlier if they cannot agree on any matter relating to the arbitration.

NUMBER OF ARBITRATORS

Subject to the right of the parties to agree otherwise, there will normally be an odd number of arbitrators. In multi-member tribunals it is usually three.

CHAIRMAN

The parties are free to agree the functions of the chairman in relation to the making of decisions, orders and awards, but in the absence of such agreement, all decisions, orders and awards shall be made unanimously or by the majority of all of the arbitrators including the chairman. If there is not unanimity nor a majority in respect of any decision, order or award, the view of the chairman shall prevail—**Section 20** of the Act.

If the parties agree that there should be no chairman, all decisions and the like are made by majority vote—**Section 22** of the Act.

UMPIRE

The functions of an umpire are completely different to that of chairman. Providing the other two arbitrators do not disagree, the umpire plays no role in the proceedings other than attendance at meetings or hearings and receiving copies of all documents sent to the other two arbitrators.

As soon as there is any disagreement between the other two arbitrators, they must give written notice of that fact to the parties and to the umpire and thereafter they take no further part in the proceedings. The umpire continues with the proceedings to the end as if he was sole arbitrator—**Section 21** of the Act.

HEARING

At the hearing all the arbitrators must be present at all times. The chairman keeps order and decides procedural matters after consultation with his colleagues. Usually any arbitrator can ask questions of clarification, after obtaining the chairman's approval.

AWARDS

In accordance with **Section 52 (3)** of the Act the award of a multi-member arbitral tribunal must be in writing as any other award and must be signed by all of the arbitrators, or in the case of dis-agreement, by all of those assenting to it. There is no provision for a minority award.

The date of the award is the date when it is signed by the last of the arbitrators—**Section 54 (2)**.

Normally there will be some discussion on the merits by all members of the tribunal and agreement will be reached as to who is to prepare the first draft of the award or parts of it; the chairman will normally take the leading role unless he finds he is in the minority. Drafts will be improved and circulated and then it should become clear whether agreement will be reached among all the arbitrators or not. If not, the majority in agreement will proceed to perfect drafts until they have an award on which they agree. It will then be printed and circulated for signature.

CHAPTER 7

THE PRELIMINARY MEETING

PURPOSE

The preliminary meeting is the first meeting the arbitrator will hold with the parties or their representatives. It will normally be held after the arbitrator's appointment is complete but before the parties start to exchange statements setting out the case against each other.

Its purpose is for the arbitrator to satisfy himself that he is properly appointed and to consider submissions from the parties as to the procedures required to be completed before he can make his award and the timetable for those procedures. The intention is for the arbitrator to issue an order for directions immediately following the preliminary meeting that will assist in the efficient and timely completion of the various tasks that need to be undertaken before the award can be made.

As a preliminary meeting is essentially procedural, it is usually only necessary for one representative of each party to attend. If solicitors or other lay representatives are instructed, then usually one solicitor or lay representative will attend with one person from the party that instructs him. The preliminary meeting is not a time for airing the disagreements between the parties other than to explain the subject matter of the dispute and it is certainly not an opportunity for evidence to be given or speeches to be made. Only in the most complex of cases, or where there is a large amount in dispute, will it be appropriate for counsel (a barrister) to attend on behalf of his client. Only rarely will it be necessary for expert witnesses to attend.

Although the arbitrator can try to persuade the parties not to bring large numbers of people to the preliminary meeting, he cannot prevent their attendance providing they are engaged by or employed by one of the parties. No representatives of third parties should be at the preliminary meeting. The only exception to this is when the arbitrator might request the approval of the parties to allow a pupil arbitrator to sit with him, to take no part, but for educational purposes only.

In some cases, for example arbitrations on documents only and many consumer arbitrations, it may be possible to dispense with the preliminary meeting altogether. However in any case where there might be a hearing, a preliminary meeting is usually invaluable.

FORMAT OF THE PRELIMINARY MEETING

Introductions

Both parties will have been sent an **agenda** by the arbitrator some days before the preliminary meeting. Preliminary meetings are normally held at the arbitrator's offices but can be held anywhere that is convenient. The arbitrator will chair the meeting and after introducing himself will ask the claimant's representative to introduce himself and anyone else he has brought with him; the respondent's representative will then do likewise. At this point the arbitrator might be aware that someone is at the preliminary meeting who is neither employed by nor acts for one of the parties but is there as an interested third party. In such a case the arbitrator should ask that person to leave the room.

Working through the agenda

The arbitrator will then work through the agenda item by item, asking both parties to address him on each issue. It is common at a preliminary meeting for there to be a large measure of agreement between the parties over procedural matters; it appears that neither party wishes to offend the arbitrator or appear unreasonable at this stage. Indeed sometimes the parties' representatives will have made contact after receipt of the agenda but before the preliminary meeting takes place and will have reached broad agreement on the timetable for the arbitration reference. It will be remembered that one of the general principles of arbitration as contained in Section

1 (b) of the Arbitration Act 1996 is that the parties should have autonomy to agree what they can. The arbitrator will be bound by such agreements.

If there is disagreement on any matter under consideration at the preliminary meeting, then the arbitrator must decide after hearing both sides. It is best for decisions of this nature to be given orally at the time rather than reserved for a later decision in writing, although of course all decisions and indeed all relevant agreements will be recorded in writing as an arbitrator's order for directions following the preliminary meeting.

Identifying the written arbitration agreement

One of the first items on a typical agenda for a preliminary meeting will be the demonstration by the parties that there is a **written arbitration agreement**. This is important because Sections 1 to 84 of the Arbitration Act 1996 only apply to written arbitration agreements. The definition of written arbitration agreements is dealt with in Chapter 3 above.

If there is any doubt whether a written arbitration agreement exists, the arbitrator will often invite the parties to enter into a simple written agreement to submit their disputes to his arbitration during or immediately following the preliminary meeting.

Any challenges to jurisdiction?

The next point of importance on the agenda is for the arbitrator to establish whether there are or are likely to be any **challenges to his jurisdiction**. If there are any matters of jurisdiction raised, almost always by the respondent, the arbitrator will not rule on them at the preliminary meeting. He must first establish that the parties have not removed his competence to rule on his own jurisdiction under **Section 30** of the Act.

If the arbitrator has power under Section 30, he will set a timetable for the exchange of written submissions on jurisdiction and then discover whether the parties are content for him to make an award on jurisdiction on the basis of written submissions alone or whether they require an oral hearing. Generally if one party requires an oral hearing, the arbitrator should agree. If there is to be a hearing on jurisdiction the arbitrator will usually set the date for that hearing at the preliminary meeting. Exceptionally the parties may agree or the arbitrator may decide to rule on jurisdiction as part of his award on the merits; this form of procedure is very unlikely to be adopted if a challenge to jurisdiction is raised at the preliminary meeting as it will be best for the jurisdiction issue to be resolved as soon as possible in order to save potentially wasted costs.

Any extension to or curtailment of default powers?

Another point of major importance is whether the parties have agreed to extend or curtail the powers given to the arbitrator by the Arbitration Act 1996. Agreements of this nature are rare once the dispute has arisen but it is very common for the parties to agree in their arbitration agreement that any arbitration will be subject to **arbitration rules**. Many standard form contracts incorporate arbitration rules which will usually extend and only rarely curtail the arbitrator's default powers under the Act.

Most of the other matters discussed at the preliminary meeting are of a procedural or timetabling nature.

ILLUSTRATIVE AGENDAS FOR PRELIMINARY MEETINGS

There is no standard preliminary meeting agenda, it will vary from case to case and from arbitrator to arbitrator. The only well-known attempt at producing such a standard agenda has been made by the United Nations in its **"UNCITRAL Notes on Organizing Arbitral Proceedings"**,[1] a copy of which is set out in Appendix 5. In an international context there is a great deal of merit in standardisation which breeds familiarity and confidence in the procedure, even if carried out in a country foreign to one or both parties.

A typical agenda for a preliminary meeting in England where both parties are British and the reference is to a sole arbitrator might be:

1 United Nations Commission on International Trade Law (UNCITRAL) Notes on Organizing Arbitral Proceedings—published by United Nations, Vienna 1996.

In the matter of the Arbitration Act 1996 and in the matter of an arbitration between

Party A   Claimant

and

Party B   Respondent

AGENDA FOR PRELIMINARY MEETING

To be held at the offices of the arbitrator at 10:00am on Friday 19 December 1997

1. Agreement of the arbitrator's Standard Scale of Charges and Terms of Engagement
2. To identify written arbitration agreement
3. To identify the nature of the matters in dispute in general terms
4. Whether arbitration to be governed by any institutional arbitration rules
5. Whether parties have entered into any other agreements affecting the arbitrator's powers under the non-mandatory Sections of the Arbitration Act 1996
6. Seat of the arbitration—is it agreed to be England?
7. Language of the arbitration—is it confirmed to be English?
8. Do any questions of jurisdiction arise?
    a. If so, is the tribunal to rule on the matter in an award as to jurisdiction or as part of an award on the merits?
    b. Timetable for exchange of submissions on jurisdiction
    c. Date for hearing on jurisdiction (if any)
    d. If an application is to be made to the court for a ruling on jurisdiction, should the proceedings continue meantime?
9. Whether any and if so what form of written statements of claim and defence are to be used, when they should be supplied and the extent to which such statements can later be amended
    a. Formal pleadings
    b. Full narrative statements of case annexing witness statements and principal relevant documents, listing all documents relied on, setting out arguments on points of law arising and a summary of evidence to be adduced
    c. Are requests for further and better particulars to be permitted?; if so, time for delivery and reply
    d. Scott Schedules—if so, protocol for exchange in electronic format
    e. Whether reply to defence to be allowed
10. Whether any and if so what documents or classes of documents should be disclosed between and produced by the parties and at what stage—if so, dates for exchange of lists and inspection
11. Whether any and if so what questions should be put to and answered by the respective parties and when and in what form this should be done
12. Do the strict rules of evidence apply?
13. Whether and to what extent the tribunal should itself take the initiative in ascertaining the facts and the law
14. Is there to be a hearing or is the matter to be decided on the basis of documents only?

     a. If written representations, what documents are to be provided and at what stage?

15. Whether and to what extent there should be oral or written evidence of fact:
     a. If written evidence, date for simultaneous exchange of statements of witnesses of fact
     b. Are rebuttal statements to be allowed?: if so date for exchange
     c. Witness statements to be treated as evidence in chief subject to right to ask limited further questions if the matters covered could not reasonably have been included in the witness statements

16. Expert witnesses:
     a. Tribunal appointed or party appointed
     b. If tribunal appointed, dates for joint instructions to experts
     c. If party appointed, number on each side; each party to advise the other of identity and disciplines
     d. If party appointed, experts of like discipline to meet on a without prejudice basis as often as necessary in order to attempt to narrow the differences between them; latest date for first meeting
     e. Date for delivery of expert reports; if party appointed to be exchanged simultaneously
     f. Joint signed statement of experts of like discipline setting out all matters agreed and not agreed to be served with reports
     g. Are brief supplementary reports in reply to be allowed?: date for simultaneous exchange

17. Pre-hearing review meeting; date, time and location—to be attended by advocate chosen for the hearing

18. Bundles of documents, restricted to those to be referred to at the hearing:
     a. Claimant to prepare draft bundles in chronological order with oldest documents at the top, at this stage unnumbered, and forward to respondent; date
     b. Respondent to interleave additional documents it requires to be added and return to claimant; date
     c. Claimant to number and copy bundles and deliver copies to the arbitrator and respondent; date
     d. Electronic storage and retrieval of documents; if so, protocol

19. The hearing:
     a. Duration, time and place; who is to arrange venue and facilities?
     b. Transcript of the hearing; electronic transcribing—transcript to be available, when?
     c. Restricting the length of the hearing—guillotine procedure, each party to be given half time available

20. Tribunal to appoint legal advisers and/or technical assessors

21. Are the parties to be represented at the hearing, if so, by whom?

22. Date for exchange of written opening statements:
     a. Full copies of all legal authorities to be provided

23. Are witnesses to be examined on oath or affirmation?:
     a. Solicitors/representatives to provide documents necessary for the

administration of oaths to witnesses not of the Christian or Jewish faiths

24. Closing submissions—oral or in writing?: if in writing dates for service
25. Have the parties agreed that the award shall be in any particular form?
26. Any agreement between the parties that the arbitrator may order provisional relief—Section 39 of the Arbitration Act 1996
27. Any points of law or issues that may be appropriate for a partial award—Section 47 of the Arbitration Act 1996
28. Confirmation that the substantive law applicable is English law
29. Do the parties choose **not** to have a reasoned award?
30. Any agreement to exclude powers of the court to determine points of law under Sections 45 and/or 69 of the Arbitration Act 1996
31. Any agreement that the arbitral proceedings shall be consolidated with other arbitral proceedings or that concurrent hearings shall be held; if so, on what terms
32. Security for the arbitrator's fees and expenses
33. Limiting the recoverable costs of whole or part of the arbitration (the legal or other costs of the parties) to a specified amount
34. Figures to be agreed as figures
35. Correspondence, plans and photographs to be agreed as such as far as possible
36. Communications with the arbitrator:
    a. Copies of all communications to the arbitrator to be sent to the other party and marked to that effect
    b. Telephone calls to the arbitrator's secretary only
37. Can arbitrator use his expert knowledge and experience?: any restrictions
38. Site inspection?: if so, when
39. Does the arbitrator have authority to record any agreements reached at the preliminary meeting on behalf of the parties?
40. Any other business

Typically the preliminary meeting may take one to one and a half hours if the full agenda is followed.

BRIEF COMMENTARY ON AGENDA ITEMS

1. *Agreement of the arbitrator's Standard Scale of Charges and Terms of Engagement*

Usually the arbitrator will have agreed his charges and terms of engagement with both parties before accepting appointment. If however he has been appointed by a third party, such as the president of a professional institution, then it may not have been possible to have reached such agreement. In such cases, before the preliminary meeting, the arbitrator will have sent a copy of his charges and terms of engagement to both parties and invited their agreement. Often parties will indicate their agreement at the preliminary meeting.

It may be thought inappropriate for the first item on the agenda to be the arbitrator's fees; it can of course be placed later. The reason it is sometimes placed first is that the arbitrator may not be prepared to carry on if his terms cannot be agreed, and by dealing with this issue first, costs can be saved if there is a problem with agreement.

2. To identify written arbitration agreement

This has been covered earlier in this chapter.

3. To identify the nature of the matters in dispute in general terms

The purpose of this item on the agenda is for the arbitrator to ensure, in cases where a technical arbitrator is required, that the nature of the dispute is within his professional knowledge and experience.

4. Whether arbitration to be governed by any institutional arbitration rules

This had been covered earlier in this chapter. The usual purpose of rules is to maximise the powers given to arbitrators and to set timetables for procedural steps in the arbitration in order to ensure rapid, efficient and cost-effective disposal of the dispute. Some rules provide for institutional administration of the arbitration, in which all of the early steps of the arbitration are carried out through the arbitral institution; the institution may also vet the award before it is delivered to the parties.

5. Whether parties have entered into any other agreements affecting the arbitrator's powers under the non-mandatory Sections of the Arbitration Act 1996

Many Sections of the Arbitration Act are non-mandatory; that is the parties are free to agree the relevant powers to be given to the arbitral tribunal, and it is only in the absence of such agreement that the default powers set out in the Act will apply. It would be tedious to set out every default non-mandatory power in the agenda for a preliminary meeting; it is best to let the parties tell the arbitrator if they have reached any agreements other than incorporation of any arbitration rules. There are over twenty Sections and Sub-Sections in the Act that set out default powers of the arbitral tribunal unless the parties agree otherwise.

6. Seat of the arbitration—is it agreed to be England?

Under Section 52 of the Arbitration Act 1996, the arbitrator, unless the parties agree otherwise, must state in his award the identity of the seat of the arbitration. The "seat of the arbitration" is defined in Section 3 of the Act as the juridical seat of the arbitration designated by the parties, designated by any arbitral institution with powers to do so, or designated by the arbitral tribunal if so authorised by the parties.

The concept is relevant primarily to international arbitrations. With very minor exceptions Sections 1 to 84 of the Arbitration Act only apply where the seat of the arbitration is in England, Wales or Northern Ireland. In cases where both parties and the subject matter of the arbitration are based within England, Wales or Northern Ireland, the Act clearly applies and the seat can be a town or country within those geographical limits, usually but not necessarily where the arbitration is held.

In international arbitrations the parties may agree that the seat of the arbitration is London even if neither party is British and the subject matter of the dispute has nothing to do with Britain. Such agreement will bring the arbitration under the Arbitration Act 1996.

7. Language of the arbitration—is it confirmed to be English?

Under Section 34 (2) (b) of the Arbitration Act 1996 it shall be for the arbitral tribunal to decide the language or languages to be used in the proceedings and whether translations of any relevant documents are to be supplied, always subject to the right of the parties to agree the language to be adopted.

8. Do any questions of jurisdiction arise?

a. *If so, is the tribunal to rule on the matter in an award as to jurisdiction or as part of an award on the merits?*

b. *Timetable for exchange of submissions on jurisdiction.*

c. *Date for hearing on jurisdiction (if any).*

d. *If an application is to be made to the court for a ruling on jurisdiction, should the proceedings continue meantime?*

This has been covered earlier in this chapter.

9. Whether any and if so what form of written statements of claim and defence are to be used, when they should be supplied and the extent to which such statements can later be amended?

a. *Formal pleadings*

Formal pleadings are Points of Claim, Points of Defence and Counterclaim (if any) and Points of Reply. They are the type of written statements required in court proceedings. They must state all of the facts relied on in support of the party's case and the remedies sought with as much particularity as will alert the other side to the case they have to meet. Pleadings do not state or summarise the evidence that will be called in support of the allegations, nor do they state points of law which will be relied on or argued. Pleadings are normally drafted by barristers and it has been cynically suggested that they often disguise rather than clarify the issues between the parties.

Pleadings do not identify documents nor are copies of principal documents annexed to them. Disclosure of documents is left for a process called discovery after pleadings have closed.

Lawyers are more familiar with pleadings than other forms of reducing the nature of the dispute to writing and often lawyers representing parties may agree to pleadings in arbitration because it is familiar territory.

b. Full narrative statements of case annexing witness statements and principal relevant documents, listing all documents relied on, setting out arguments on points of law arising and a summary of evidence to be adduced

Statements of case setting out the nature of the dispute in narrative form, rather like telling a story, are much more common in arbitration. Unlike pleadings they set out the summary of evidence to be called in support of each allegation and witness statements may be annexed. Relevant law is set out and argued; principal documents are annexed to the statements of case and each party will list all of the documents on which it intends to rely. The statements must be sufficiently full to enable the other party to fully understand the case it has to meet.

After receipt of the statement of case the respondent will serve a statement of defence together with a statement of counterclaim, if there is to be a counterclaim. This will be followed by the claimant's statement of defence to the counterclaim. As discussed below, each party may usually be permitted to serve a reply to the respective statements of defence.

c. Are requests for further and better particulars to be permitted?; if so, time for delivery and reply

In the case of pleadings, it may not be clear to the party in receipt of a particular pleading the precise case it has to meet. The usual reason is that rather vague allegations have been made. Unless further and better particulars are given it will not be possible for the party in receipt to seek confirmation from its own witnesses as to whether the allegation is true or not.

Frequently requests for further and better particulars are merely time-wasting exercises which can run up great expense. If statements of case are used including documents and a summary of evidence is included, the case being made out will usually be much clearer.

In an effort to comply with his duties under Section 33 of the Arbitration Act 1996, the arbitrator may restrict the right of parties to make indiscriminate requests for further and better particulars.

d. Scott Schedules—if so, protocol for exchange in electronic format

A Scott Schedule is so named after an Official Referee called Scott who devised it. An Official Referee is a special kind of judge who sits in the High Court to hear cases of a very technical nature (usually construction industry cases). A Scott Schedule is simply a type of document layout which is divided into a series of vertical columns as this illustration:

Identifier	Description of item	Claimant's contentions	Claimant's quantum	Respondent's contentions	Respondent's quantum	Arbitrator's quantum

This form of Schedule, which can be served as part of a pleading or statement of case, is particularly useful if there are a series of items of a similar nature in dispute. For example a house owner may be arbitrating against the builder for defects in construction. Each defect will be listed in turn, the particular clause of the specification that is alleged to have been breached together with the method of correcting it will be set out in the adjacent column, and the build up to and the total of the monetary claim made in respect of that item will be in the next column.

e. Whether reply to defence to be allowed

Each party will have had an opportunity to state its case through the statement of claim and statement of defence. The question then arises as to whether the claimant should be given an opportunity to serve a statement of reply to the defence. If new facts are alleged in the defence then it will normally be just to allow the claimant to reply to these allegations. In the case of counterclaims, all of the relevant facts usually come out in the statement of counterclaim and statement of defence to counterclaim, there is therefore usually no need for a reply to defence to counterclaim.

10. *Whether any and if so what documents or classes of documents should be disclosed between and produced by the parties and at what stage—if so, dates for exchange of lists and inspection*

The process of forced disclosure of documents is peculiar to the common law system as practised in Great Britain, USA and various former British colonies. In the civil law system there is no such requirement.

The process of forced disclosure of documents is called **discovery**. Each party has to prepare a list of all documents, which are or may become relevant, which are or have been in its custody, power or possession. The list is normally in three parts: the first part contains those documents in respect of which privilege is not claimed which are in that party's custody, power or possession; the second part is similar except that it comprises those documents which once were but no longer are in that party's custody, power or possession; the third part contains a list of those classes of documents in respect of which privilege is claimed, for example, legal advice.

The list must contain those documents which are harmful as well as helpful to that party's case. The other party can then inspect those non-privileged documents which have been listed; this is known as **inspection**.

Discovery is a very expensive process; civil law countries manage perfectly well without it. It does however have the advantage that each party may well believe that it ensures there are no hidden secrets, no smoking guns!

In civil law countries each party discloses only those documents it wishes to rely on. Research has shown that justice suffers little as a result.

Arbitrators are not bound to order traditional discovery; they can either adopt the civil law system or allow a limited form of discovery where each party has to make out a case to be allowed access to specific documents or classes of documents, and the arbitrator will decide whether that case is justified or not.

11. Whether any and if so what questions should be put to and answered by the respective parties and when and in what form this should be done

It is sometimes helpful that one or both parties should be permitted to put specific questions to the other which must be answered on oath. It can save large amounts of time in cross-examination if this process is conducted sensibly. The questions for answer are sometimes called **"interrogatories"**.

12. Do the strict rules of evidence apply?

The rules of evidence mainly concern admissibility of certain types of evidence, for example hearsay. The courts operate to very strict rules of evidence, particularly the criminal courts. In very formal arbitrations it may still be appropriate to adopt court-style rules of evidence, but for most arbitrations those rules will not be appropriate. The arbitrator will give appropriate weight to all the evidence he hears.

13. Whether and to what extent the tribunal should itself take the initiative in ascertaining the facts and the law

Unless the parties agree otherwise an arbitrator may act inquisitorially; that is instead of remaining relatively passive and considering only the evidence and legal argument presented to him, an arbitrator can take the initiative himself and make his own inquiries to attempt to ascertain the facts and the law.

This may take the form of the arbitrator asking questions of the witnesses at the hearing in an effort to establish the truth, or may go much further and involve detailed inquiries and research. Caution must be exercised as any inquisitorial process runs the danger of apparent or perceived bias. It will however be appropriate for an arbitrator with special technical skills to investigate and decide certain technical issues in conjunction with experts from each side.

Equally an arbitrator may think it appropriate to seek his own legal advice, providing such advice is disclosed to the parties and they have adequate opportunity to deal with it.

14. Is there to be a hearing or is the matter to be decided on the basis of documents only?

a. If written representations, what documents are to be provided and at what stage?

Many arbitrations are resolved without a hearing on the basis of documents alone. If there are no conflicts of fact or technical opinion, a hearing is rarely necessary.

15. Whether and to what extent there should be oral or written evidence of fact

a. If written evidence, date for simultaneous exchange of statements of witnesses of fact

b. Are rebuttal statements to be allowed?; if so date for exchange

c. Witness statements to be treated as evidence in chief subject to right to ask limited further questions if the matters covered could not reasonably have been included in the witness statements

If there is to be a hearing, it needs to be decided whether witnesses of fact will give oral testimony, unsupported by a written proof of evidence, or whether most if not all of the evidence which the party calling that witness wants to adduce can be reduced to writing. The modern practice is for arbitrators to require all witnesses of fact to produce signed witness statements which are exchanged. When the witness gives evidence, he will merely identify himself and state that his statement represents the evidence he wishes to give. He can then immediately be made available for cross-examination. The judicious use of written witness statements, sometimes called proofs of evidence, can save enormous amounts of time and money at the hearing.

16. Expert witnesses

a. Tribunal appointed or party appointed

Traditionally in common law jurisdictions each party has appointed its own expert witnesses. It is therefore not uncommon for there to be substantial disagreement between experts; this is not helpful. Arbitrators are not bound by traditional procedure and can adopt the system used in civil law jurisdictions, such as the continent of Europe, where the tribunal appoints one expert of each relevant discipline to inquire and report to it. Many parties still wish to retain the right to select their own experts. In this book the terms "expert" and "expert witness" are used interchangeably; sometimes a distinction is drawn by referring to tribunal-appointed experts as "experts" and to party-appointed experts as "expert witnesses".

b. If tribunal appointed, dates for joint instructions to experts

The arbitrator will rarely be sufficiently knowledgeable about the issues and background to the case to be able to prepare his own comprehensive instructions to an expert. It is therefore sensible to ask the parties to prepare joint instructions, or if that proves impossible, to ask the claimant to prepare draft instructions which are then sent to the respondent to be supplemented.

c. If party appointed, number on each side; each party to advise the other of identity and disciplines

Experts should be limited to one for each discipline. The arbitrator has the right and power to limit the number of experts.

d. If party appointed, experts of like discipline to meet on a without prejudice basis as often as necessary in order to attempt to narrow the differences between them; latest date for first meeting

It is standard modern practice for arbitrators and courts to order experts of like discipline to meet under the cloak of privilege to see if they can narrow the differences between them. If the expert witnesses really are experts in their field they ought to be able to agree most of their opinions. Partisan experts, who are merely there as advocates for their client's case, are of no help in arbitration.

There is a debate as to whether experts should meet before or after they have prepared their reports, at least in draft. The author is a strong advocate of without prejudice meetings of experts commencing as early as possible and certainly before reports are prepared. Once views are expressed in writing, it involves a certain amount of loss of face to change them, together with the risk of some loss of credibility.

e. Date for delivery of expert reports; if party appointed to be exchanged simultaneously

Expert reports will be exchanged sufficiently early to enable each side to absorb the contents of the report in good time prior to the hearing.

f. Joint signed statement of experts of like discipline setting out all matters agreed and not agreed to be served with reports

Many arbitrators will only allow experts to give evidence if they have first prepared and signed a joint report of experts of like discipline setting out all facts and opinions that they are able to agree and those they cannot agree. This assists in identifying the agenda for trial at the hearing.

g. Are brief supplementary reports in reply to be allowed?; date for simultaneous exchange

Sometimes it will be appropriate to give the experts opportunity to respond in writing to any opinions expressed in the reports of experts for the other parties. If this opportunity is given, the time period for it will be short, usually not more than 14 days after exchange of the original reports.

17. Pre-hearing review meeting; date, time and location— to be attended by advocate chosen for the hearing

In all medium and large cases, particularly those that will take several months to prepare, it is sensible for the arbitrator to hold a pre-hearing review. Any outstanding procedural issues between the parties will be aired and detailed arrangements can be made regarding the hearing and the run up to it. At this stage the outstanding issues between the parties will have been crystallised. For these reasons it is always best for the advocate who will represent each party at the hearing to be present at the pre-hearing review.

18. Bundles of documents, restricted to those to be referred to at the hearing

a. *Claimant to prepare draft bundles in chronological order with oldest documents at the top, at this stage unnumbered, and forward to respondent; date*

b. *Respondent to interleave additional documents it requires to be added and return to claimant; date*

c. *Claimant to number and copy bundles and deliver copies to the arbitrator and respondent; date*

d. *Electronic storage and retrieval of documents; if so, protocol*

Document handling and presentation at the hearing is crucial if the hearing is to run smoothly. Many firms of solicitors are so used to preparing document bundles for court that this head of agenda is superfluous. However so many arbitration hearings get off to a bad start because the bundles are not in order that arbitrators often wish to emphasise its importance by raising it as an item at the preliminary meeting.

19. The hearing

a. *Duration, time and place; who is to arrange venue and facilities?*

The hearing will be arranged where it is most convenient for most of the witnesses. Convenience of counsel should not be considered as paramount. In the absence of agreement, the claimant usually is responsible for arranging the venue.

b. *Transcript of the hearing; electronic transcribing—transcript to be available when?*

Arbitrators normally take notes of the evidence and submissions in longhand in a notebook. Unless the arbitrator is proficient in shorthand, the fact that the arbitrator is making notes will slow down the procedure. Court proceedings have historically been transcribed by stenographers or shorthand writers; they are also used in arbitration hearings. Typed or word-processed transcripts will be available about three days later unless the stenographers work in teams.

Modern technology has now permitted stenographer's ticker tape to be instantaneously translated into word-processed text which can be scrolled up computer monitors on the desk of the arbitrator and advocates.

Stenography, shorthand writing and electronic transcribing are expensive but in larger cases can so speed up proceedings, perhaps by 30 per cent or more, that the saving in hearing time more than compensates for the extra cost of the service.

c. *Restricting the length of the hearing—guillotine procedure, each party to be given half time available*

Unless some discipline is imposed, hearings can drift on for days longer than predicted because of over-long cross-examination or unnecessary examination-in-chief. If the arbitrator and advocates have only a certain number of days set aside, time may run out before the case is over; this means an adjournment, sometimes for weeks or even months until the advocates and arbitrator have diaries clear enough to arrange a further period of time for the reconvened hearing.

This problem can be avoided by ensuring that the hearing completes within the time allotted for it. Each party will be consulted as to their estimate for the length of the hearing. The hearing duration will be set and the number of working hours at the hearing will be calculated; that figure will then be divided into two and each party will be allocated half of the time so calculated to use as it wishes for examination-in-chief and re-examination of its own witnesses and cross-examination of the witnesses of the other side. Time in opening and closing submissions will also be booked against the party making them.

Time spent will be recorded each day and agreed with the parties. It will be up to each party to efficiently manage the presentation of its case so that it completes before the time expires. When time is exhausted, that party will not be permitted to adduce any more evidence or submissions or conduct any more cross-examination. That is why it is sometimes called a chess clock or guillotine procedure.

It has the main advantage that arbitrator and advocates can organise their diaries in confidence that the case will be over not later than the end of the period set aside and the parties can predict the likely costs with some degree of accuracy.

20. *Tribunal to appoint legal advisers and/or technical assessors*

If the arbitrator is not legally qualified and a particularly difficult or important point of law arises, it may be sensible for the arbitrator to appoint a legal adviser to sit through the legal submissions with him and to assist him in reaching a decision and drafting an award.

Likewise, if the arbitrator does not possess appropriate technical qualifications and experience and a particularly difficult technical point arises it may be sensible for him to appoint a technical assessor in the same way.

21. *Are the parties to be represented at the hearing, if so, by whom?*

The parties are free to be represented by whom they wish; they do not have to engage lawyers. If either party intends to instruct counsel it is normal for the other party to be informed so that it can decide whether or not to seek similar representation.

22. *Date for exchange of written opening statements*

a. Full copies of all legal authorities to be provided

Historically the claimant's advocate would open his client's case orally at the beginning of the hearing. The opening would usually take several hours and might take days; this procedure was wasteful of time and money. It is therefore now normal practice for the claimant's advocate (and the respondent's advocate if he wishes— particularly if there is a counterclaim) to prepare a written opening which is exchanged about a week prior to the hearing. The arbitrator can read the opening and any legal authorities which are relied on before the hearing starts. The opening may be in full or skeleton form.

The importance of providing full legal authorities is that sections of judgments read out of context can be misleading and the full authority will enable the arbitrator to understand the background to the decision.

23. Are witnesses to be examined on oath or affirmation?

a. *Solicitors/representatives to provide documents necessary for the administration of oaths to witnesses not of the Christian or Jewish faiths*

It is usual for witnesses to be examined on oath (or affirmation at the witnesses' choice). If the parties agree that they do not wish evidence to be given on oath, but subject only to a simple promise to tell the truth, that is quite acceptable. Arbitrators will carry copies of the Old and New Testaments and cards on which are printed the words of the standard oath and affirmation. If other documents or articles are required in order to administer oaths to witnesses of religious faiths other than Christianity or Judaism, then each party must be responsible for obtaining the necessary documents and articles and for bringing them to the hearing with a copy of the appropriate words.

An arbitrator who carries out international arbitration will also carry oath and affirmation cards for administering oaths to or taking affirmations from interpreters.

An arbitrator is empowered by Section 38 (5) of the Arbitration Act 1996 to administer oaths and take affirmations.

24. Closing submissions—oral or in writing?; if in writing dates for service

At the end of the evidence each party's advocate is entitled to make a closing submission. In the past, these submissions were made orally, a continuation of the court practice where the advocate needed to impress the jury. Oral closing submissions are now rare except in the smallest of cases and each party's advocate will sequentially prepare written closing submissions within a short period after the close of the hearing.

25. Have the parties agreed that the award shall be in any particular form?

If there is any agreement, the arbitrator should be told at an early stage.

26. *Any agreement between the parties that the arbitrator may order provisional relief—Section 39 of the Arbitration Act 1996*

Although an arbitrator has power to make more than one award, each award must be on different issues and be final in and of itself; this is covered by Section 47 of the Act. The Act does not give an arbitrator any default powers to order, for example, a payment on account, with the final decision left for a later award. However the parties may agree to clothe the arbitrator with just such powers under Section 39 of the Act. If the parties do so agree, one party may apply for provisional relief. In that case the arbitrator should order exchange of written submissions on that point alone and may call a short hearing to receive further oral submissions, before making his decision by order rather than award.

27. *Any points of law or issues that may be appropriate for a partial award—Section 47 of the Arbitration Act 1996*

It may be of assistance to the parties for the arbitrator to hear a preliminary point of law or a preliminary issue followed by a partial award limited to the preliminary matters put before him. Such a course of action can lead to early settlement of the dispute between the parties and therefore save the time and costs of a full hearing.

28. *Confirmation that the substantive law applicable is English law*

The contract may state which national substantive law is to apply. If it does not, the parties may agree or failing such agreement they may decide that the substantive law can be determined by the arbitral tribunal. In a case in England between English parties it would be very surprising if the substantive law was not English law, that is the law applicable to England and Wales.

29. *Do the parties choose not to have a reasoned award?*

Under Section 52 (4) of the Arbitration Act 1996 the award is required to contain the reasons for the award unless it is an agreed award (that is following a settlement) or the parties have agreed to dispense with reasons. Reasons are particularly important if there is to be an appeal from the award on a point of law.

30. Any agreement to exclude powers of the court to determine points of law under Sections 45 and/or 69 of the Arbitration Act 1996

Parties can agree to exclude the court's power to determine a preliminary point of law and/or to exclude their right to appeal an award on a point of law. If the parties agree to dispense with reasons for the award, they automatically exclude their right to appeal the award on a point of law.

31. Any agreement that the arbitral proceedings shall be consolidated with other arbitral proceedings or that concurrent hearings shall be held; if so, on what terms

The courts are able to cope effectively with multi-party proceedings, and to consolidate different actions between the same parties. It is possible to have a court action with many parties or to join in third parties. Because of the central importance of party autonomy, arbitration does not cope as well with multi-party cases. An arbitrator has no default power to join in third parties or to consolidate actions.

However under Section 35 of the Arbitration Act 1996, the parties are free to agree on consolidation with any other arbitral proceedings, provided all parties in both or all proceedings agree. It may also be agreed that concurrent hearings should be held.

This is sometimes appropriate in a case where there is a dispute between two parties which raises identical issues on identical facts to a dispute between one of those parties and a third party, such as a sub-contractor.

32. Security for the arbitrator's fees and expenses

The arbitrator will want to ensure that money is available to pay his fees and expenses at the conclusion of the arbitration; it is regrettably not unknown for both parties to become insolvent or to lose interest in the arbitration altogether. For this reason an arbitrator will normally wish to ask for his fees to be secured in some way, often by the payment of a cash sum to be held in a suitable deposit account to the arbitrator's order.

An arbitrator may obtain agreement of both parties to his scale of charges and terms of engagement which may provide for both parties to provide security for his fees and expenses. If so, he is entitled to ask each party to put up 50 per cent of the security. If, however, there is no such agreement the arbitrator will rely on his default powers under Section 38 (3) of the Arbitration Act 1996 (which of course can be removed or amended by agreement between the parties).

Under that Section the arbitrator can only require the claimant or counterclaimant to provide security for his fees and expenses, which are, of course, part of the costs of the arbitration under the definition contained in Section 59 (1) of the Act.

33. Limiting the recoverable costs of whole or part of the arbitration (the legal or other costs of the parties) to a specified amount

It is one of the stated objects of arbitration under Section 1 of the Arbitration Act 1996 that there should not be unnecessary delay or expense. The arbitrator is under a duty under Section 33 of the Act to adopt procedures which will avoid unnecessary delay and expense.

Regrettably it has become a regular feature of complex litigation and arbitration that the costs can be enormous; they can match or occasionally exceed the amount ultimately awarded. In such cases the parties end up fighting more about the costs than the issues themselves. It is standard practice for the loser to be ordered to pay the winner's reasonable costs.

An arbitrator cannot prevent a party spending as much in preparing its case as it wishes, but in the absence of contrary agreement between the parties, the arbitrator can set a cap or limit on the amount of costs that the winning party will be able to recover from the other. Such a cap on recoverable costs is a considerable disincentive to parties to spend costs they know they will not be able to recover even if they win.

If recoverable costs are to be capped, they must be capped early before the costs or a considerable proportion of them, have been spent. The costs cap limit is also subject to review. Before capping recoverable costs the arbitrator will consider representations from each party as to their current estimates of costs of pursuing and defending the claim and pursuing and defending the counterclaim. The arbitrator will normally make separate orders in respect of claim and counterclaim.

34. *Figures to be agreed as figures*

It is usually non-controversial that the parties should be required to agree figures as figures as far as possible to avoid wasted time at the hearing. For example one party may say—"I do not agree the principle, but if the principle is held to be correct, I agree the figures as claimed".

35. *Correspondence, plans and photographs to be agreed as such as far as possible*

Likewise it is helpful to agree that items of correspondence were exchanged between the parties and that plans and photographs are true representations of what they show.

36. *Communications with the arbitrator*

a. *Copies of all communications to the arbitrator to be sent to the other party and marked to that effect*

b. *Telephone calls to the arbitrator's secretary only*

This is routine administration to ensure that the arbitrator does not have any communication with either party without the other knowing about it immediately or being present.

37. *Can arbitrator use his expert knowledge and experience?; any restrictions*

One of the great advantages of arbitration is that the arbitral tribunal is often expert in relevant technical matters. Nevertheless, subject to the right for the tribunal to take the initiative in ascertaining the facts and the law, the award must be made on the basis of the evidence adduced, not the expert knowledge and experience of the tribunal. To do otherwise would be likely to breach the mandatory requirement for the arbitrator to act fairly and impartially (Section 33 (1) (a) of the Arbitration Act 1996).

For this reason the arbitrator will normally seek the parties' express agreement that he may use his own technical knowledge and experience, often subject to the obligation to put his views to the relevant witnesses if he intends to be influenced by them.

38. Site inspection?; if so, when

To be able to understand the evidence better, it may be sensible for the arbitrator to visit the location of the subject matter of the dispute, usually just before or just after the hearing.

39. Does the arbitrator have authority to record any agreements reached at the preliminary meeting on behalf of the parties?

If the parties have reached agreement at the preliminary meeting on matters which, had they considered the matter, may have formed part of their arbitration agreement, the parties may agree that the arbitrator's order for directions confirming those agreements amounts to part of the written arbitration agreement as defined by Section 5 of the Arbitration Act 1996.

40. Any other business

ILLUSTRATIVE ORDER FOR DIRECTIONS FOLLOWING A PRELIMINARY MEETING

In the matter of the Arbitration Act 1996 and in the matter of an arbitration between

Party A   **Claimant**

and

Party B   **Respondent**

Arbitrator's order for directions No. 1

Having carefully considered the oral submissions of Ms A solicitor for the claimant and Mr B representative for the respondent at a preliminary meeting held at my offices at 10:00am on Friday 19 December 1997, **I ORDER AND DIRECT**

1. Both parties indicated that my Standard Scale of Charges and Terms of Engagement are agreed.
2. The arbitration will not be governed by any institutional arbitration rules.
3. Other than recorded in this order for directions the parties indicated that they have not entered into any other agreements affecting my

powers under the non-mandatory Sections of the Arbitration Act 1996.
4. The seat of the arbitration is to be England.
5. The language of the arbitration is to be English.
6. The respondent indicated that my jurisdiction to arbitrate on the matters of dispute identified by the claimant is challenged on the grounds that some or all of those matters have not been submitted to arbitration in accordance with the arbitration agreement. I will rule on the matter in an award on jurisdiction after considering written submissions only. The parties are to serve written submissions as to their case on jurisdiction to the following timetable:
   a. Respondent's submissions to be served not later than 9 January 1998;
   b. Claimant's submissions to be served not later than 14 days from service of the respondent's submissions;
   c. Respondent's reply to be served not later than 7 days from service of the claimant's submissions.
7. The parties are to set out their cases in writing by serving fully particularised narrative statements of case annexing witness statements and principal relevant documents, listing all documents relied on, setting out arguments on points of law arising and a summary of the evidence to be adduced; to the following timetable:
   a. Claimant's statement of case not later than 30 January 1998
   b. Respondent's statement of defence and statement of counterclaim not later than 28 days from service of the claimant's statement of case
   c. Claimant's statement of reply and defence to counterclaim not later than 28 days from service of the statements of defence and counterclaim
   d. The parties have leave to serve a Scott Schedule. It shall be exchanged in electronic format on floppy disk in Microsoft Excel spreadsheet format.
8. If either party considers that there are documents or classes of documents in the possession, custody or power of the other party and which have not been disclosed or listed in the statements of case and which are important to its case or defence, it shall make application to me for an order for disclosure setting out the grounds for the application.
9. The strict rules of evidence do not apply.
10. Each party shall simultaneously exchange proofs of evidence of all witnesses of fact not later than 30 April 1998. Proofs of evidence shall stand as evidence-in-chief subject to the right to ask limited further questions if the matters covered could not reasonably have been included in the proofs of evidence.
11. There will be one expert witness appointed by me to carry out inquiries and to serve a report in connection with ... The claimant shall serve on the respondent its detailed instructions to the expert not later than 15 May 1998. The respondent shall serve on the claimant its supplemental instructions to the expert not later than 31 May 1998 and serve two copies of the combined instructions on me by the same date.

12. Not later than 15 May 1998 both parties shall inform me whom they have agreed as expert, or in the absence of agreement, each party shall by the same date advise me of the names of three persons whom they consider would be suitable for appointment as expert.

13. A copy of the expert report will be delivered to both parties not later than 31 July 1998.

14. There will be a pre-hearing review meeting at my offices on 26 August 1998 at 10:00am to be attended by the advocates chosen by each party for the hearing.

15. The claimant shall prepare draft bundles of documents to be referred to at the hearing in chronological order with oldest documents at the top, at this stage unnumbered, and forward them to the respondent not later than 1 September 1998. The respondent is to interleave additional documents it requires to be added and return the bundles to the claimant not later than 8 September 1998. The claimant to number and copy the bundles and deliver copies to me and to the respondent not later than 15 September 1998.

16. There will be a hearing in this arbitration to be held at the Kings Hotel, Queensford, for 3 weeks from 5 to 22 October 1998 inclusive sitting Monday to Thursday each week. The claimant is to make the necessary arrangements including retiring rooms for the parties and for me, and is initially to bear the costs which will be part of the costs of the arbitration.

17. The claimant is to arrange for an electronic transcription service with hard copies of each day's proceedings to be available by 6:00pm each evening. The claimant is initially to bear the costs which will be part of the costs of the arbitration.

18. The hearing will be subject to a time guillotine to ensure that it is completed within the three weeks set aside. Each party will be allocated 28 hours, representing an estimate of 50% of the time available during the 12 days set aside for the hearing, to use as they wish to complete their case. No more time will be allowed, unless there are exceptional reasons for me to so allow. The time to count against each party will include opening and closing submissions during the hearing itself, examination-in-chief (if any) and re-examination of that party's witnesses and cross-examination of the other party's witnesses. Time will be recorded to the nearest minute and the cumulative total time used by each party will be recorded to the nearest minute and the cumulative total time used by each party will be agreed at the end of each day's hearing. Time taken by me in questions of clarification during testimony will count against the party examining at that time. Time taken in questions asked by me at the close of a witness's testimony will not count against either party.

19. Statements of witnesses of fact will not be deemed to be proved merely if not challenged in cross-examination by the other party. Neither party shall be under any absolute duty to put all of the relevant parts of its case to each witness of the other party.

20. The claimant indicated that it will be represented at the hearing by counsel.
21. Written opening statements shall be exchanged not later than 28 September 1998. If any legal authorities are relied on, full copies of the law report or text book extract shall be provided.
22. Witnesses are to be examined on oath or affirmation. Solicitors/ representatives are to provide documents necessary for the administration of oaths to witnesses not of the Christian or Jewish faiths.
23. Closing submissions shall be in writing after the close of the hearing. Dates for submission to be decided at the close of the hearing.
24. It is confirmed that the substantive law applicable to this arbitration is English law.
25. The claimant shall deposit the sum of £10,000.00 (ten thousand pounds) with me not later than 20 January 1998, to be held in a new interest-bearing account in my name at National Barcland Bank as security for my fees and expenses. The account will identify the names of both parties and will be held in accordance with the Royal Institution of Chartered Surveyors Regulations for the holding of Client's money. Interest will accrue to the benefit of the claimant.
26. The recoverable costs of each party in respect of the claim (but not the counterclaim) shall be limited to £75,000.00 (seventy-five thousand pounds) excluding Value Added Tax. The recoverable costs of each party in respect of the counterclaim (but not the claim) shall be limited to £20,000.00 (twenty thousand pounds) excluding Value Added Tax.
27. Figures are to be agreed as figures and correspondence, plans and photographs are to be agreed as such as far as possible.
28. It is agreed that I can use my expert knowledge and experience in assisting in the determination of any of the disputes in this arbitration.
29. There will be a site inspection on 2 October 1998. Each party will be entitled to designate one person only to accompany me; I will also invite the expert witness to be present. I shall not take any oral evidence during the site inspection.
30. It is confirmed that I have authority to record agreements reached at the preliminary meeting on behalf of the parties in the terms of this order.
31. Liberty to either party to apply to amend any of these directions.
32. Costs in the arbitration.
33. All directions are by consent except those in paragraphs 6, 7(b), 11, 18 and 26.

19 December 1997

Signed

Arbitrator

Distribution:
Claimant's solicitors
Respondent's representatives

CHAPTER 8

PREPARATION FOR THE HEARING

The period between the preliminary meeting and the hearing is often referred to as the **interlocutory** stage of the arbitration. It is often the most difficult part of the arbitration for the arbitrator who has to balance a series of competing interests:

• the wish of the parties to take as much time as they need to prepare their case including making such revisions to their case as they consider necessary

• the objections of the other party who thinks that its opponent is only interested in wasting time and delaying the day of reckoning when the award is published

• the overriding duty of the tribunal to act fairly and impartially between the parties, giving each a reasonable opportunity of putting his case and dealing with that of his opponent

• the additional overriding duty of the tribunal to adopt suitable procedures and to avoid unnecessary delay or expense, so as to provide a fair means of resolving the dispute.

GENERAL DUTY OF THE PARTIES

Section 40 of the Arbitration Act 1996 sets out the mandatory duty of each of the parties:

40. (1) The parties shall do all things necessary for the proper and expeditious conduct of the arbitral proceedings.
    (2) This includes:
        (a) complying without delay with any determination of the tri-

bunal as to procedural or evidential matters, or with any order or directions of the tribunal, and

(b) where appropriate, taking without delay any necessary steps to obtain a decision of the court on a preliminary question of jurisdiction or law (see sections 32 and 45).

PLEADINGS OR STATEMENTS OF CASE

Pleadings and statements of case and the differences between them are discussed in Chapter 7 above under item 9 of the agenda for the preliminary meeting. Generally pleadings are appropriate where the dispute is essentially legal in nature, and therefore appeal is likely, or it is of such magnitude that counsel and probably leading counsel (Queen's Counsel) will be employed on each side. The Rules of the Supreme Court (White Book) lay down precise rules of pleading with which barristers will be very familiar.

If, however, the case is essentially technical so that the employment of lawyers, and particularly counsel, is unlikely to be necessary, or the amount in dispute is relatively modest, or one or both parties is based in a country where formal common law pleadings are likely to be totally strange, then it will usually be appropriate to order statements of case.

The advantages of pleadings are that they are:

• readily understood by lawyers familiar with court procedure

• subject to precise Rules of Court and therefore their effect and application is more certain

• concise and easily read

• limited to facts relied on, contain no opinions.

The disadvantages of pleadings are that:

• they often disguise rather than explain the true case, particularly so in respect of weak cases

• they often give rise to extensive requests for further and better particulars

• the documents which are relied on are not identified

• they are not easily understood by laymen

- they do not summarise the evidence to be adduced

- they do not state a summary of the legal submissions to be made on relevant points of law

- they are not easily understood by foreign parties from civil law backgrounds.

Advantages of statements of case are that:

- they state the case being put forward in a narrative form, rather like telling a story

- they summarise the evidence to be adduced

- they summarise the legal arguments which will be made

- copies of the key documents are attached and all the documents to be relied on are listed

- they are familiar to parties from civil law backgrounds

- they can easily be produced by non-lawyers

- they are readily understood by laymen.

Disadvantages of statements of case are that:

- the narrative can be rambling; the real issues can be difficult if not impossible to identify

- they can give an opportunity for pejorative and offensive statements to be made which can inflame the dispute

- they have to be served before the proofs of evidence of witnesses have been finalised; the evidence eventually given may therefore differ from the summary of evidence contained in the statements

- there is no effective machinery to deal with under-particularised cases

- they often produce vast amounts of paper, most of which will be copied again before the hearing

- they lack precision

- there are no Rules of Court to rely on when difficulties arise.

Reducing the issues to writing

Whether pleadings or statements of case are ordered, the parties, by each serving a statement in defence or reply to the last statement of the other party, will identify the issues and differences between the parties. There is a standard procedure by which this objective is accomplished.

The claimant will state all the facts and matters he relies on, including the identity of the contract out of which the arbitration arises, the arbitration clause itself, the substance of the dispute including all the alleged facts in support of its contentions and the remedy or remedies sought.

In respect of each allegation made, the respondent must indicate whether the allegation is **admitted, not admitted** or **denied**.

If the respondent agrees with a particular statement made, including its context and any twist which may be put on the words, he will indicate that the allegation is **admitted**. Admissions are helpful because they mean that there is a degree of common ground between the parties and no time will have to be wasted at the hearing in proving allegations which are admitted.

If the respondent indicates that an allegation is **not admitted**, this means that the respondent does not assert the contrary but puts the claimant to strict proof. In other words, the respondent is saying, "I do not deny it, but you must prove it". This response can occur when the allegation contains an element of truth but the words have been spun or twisted so that the meaning is not exactly as the respondent would express it. At the hearing, the claimant must prove all allegations that are not admitted.

If the respondent completely disagrees with an allegation, it will be **denied**. This means that the allegation is put into issue and must be proved by the claimant at the hearing. However it goes farther than this, in that the respondent positively asserts the contrary to the allegation made. It is usual for the respondent to plead his version of events so that the claimant is fully aware of the respondent's position. The respondent is not, however, under any obligation to plead a positive case; he can merely deny the case made against him in so many words and put the claimant to strict proof at the hearing.

Where the respondent makes any positive allegations of fact in the defence, the claimant is given an opportunity in the points of reply or statement of reply to admit, not admit, or deny the allegations.

Equally, where the respondent makes a counterclaim, the claimant has an opportunity to serve a defence in exactly the same way and if necessary the respondent has a right of reply.

It can therefore be seen that the pleadings or statements of case form the **agenda for trial**. Neither party is entitled to ask the tribunal to make any findings of fact that are not pleaded and any evidence which goes outside the pleaded case is irrelevant and therefore inadmissible.

APPLICATIONS TO EXTEND TIME FOR SERVICE OR FOR LEAVE TO AMEND

Extending time for service

At the preliminary meeting the arbitrator will have decided to order pleadings or statements of case and will have given effect to his decision by issuing an Order for Directions giving a strict timetable for compliance, including dates for service of pleadings/statements of case. Not uncommonly the parties will find that they need more time and will try to obtain the agreement of the other party to an extension of time. Whether agreement is obtained or not, the party who wants more time will then write to the arbitrator to request an extension of time. More often than not, the other party will object to the extension of time in any event and the arbitrator must therefore decide whether or not to grant an extension and if so the length of it.

The rule, in all matters which require a decision, is for the arbitrator not to make up his mind until he has considered submissions from both parties. Submissions will usually be in writing, unless exceptionally an **interlocutory meeting** is required for oral submissions.

Under Section 34 (3) of the Arbitration Act 1996 it is for the tribunal to extend time for compliance with its orders if it thinks fit.

The usual practice is for one relatively short extension to be given on application unless there are compelling reasons not to do so. Further requests for extensions will come under much closer scrutiny, the arbitrator at all times balancing fairness with avoiding unnecessary delay or expense.

For extensions of time, or indeed any interlocutory matter, the arbitrator will issue another order for directions, known as an **interlocutory order**, in this case modifying the dates previously set. At the end of each interlocutory order the arbitrator will deal with costs and will normally give leave for either party to apply to him in the future to modify the order. As the other party is unlikely to suffer any financial prejudice by an extension of time for the service of a pleading or statement of case, the normal order for costs will be that **costs are in the arbitration**. This means that whichever party obtains an order for costs in its favour at the end of the arbitration will also recover the costs of the application for extension and subsequent order for directions.

Leave to amend

Part way through the interlocutory stage, or even at the hearing itself, one party may realise that the evidence that will be adduced will not support part of the case it has pleaded without modification or that the evidence would support another cause of action that has not been pleaded at all. In such cases the party concerned would make an immediate application to the arbitrator for **leave to amend** its case, with a copy to the other party. The application must be accompanied by a draft of the amendment proposed to be made, with any redundant text struck out and new text underlined for identification.

As before the arbitrator will consider representations from both parties. He will look to see whether the proposed amendments are fully particularised so that there could be no possibility of a request for further and better particulars being made. The arbitrator will also consider the prejudice that would be caused to the other party if he allowed the amendments. He will also have in mind whether the date for the hearing would be prejudiced if the amendment was allowed.

Generally amendments to pleadings or statements of case will be allowed if it is possible for the arbitrator to adequately compensate the other party for the prejudice it will suffer by a costs order against the party wishing to amend.

Reasons which might justify an arbitrator refusing an amendment are:

• draft amendment inadequately particularised

• if allowed, the hearing would have to be postponed, the amendment being a new cause of action which could be commenced under a new arbitration notice and be heard at a later date

• the proposed amendment is a new cause of action which is statute barred, that is, it has been brought too late under the Limitation Acts (the Limitation Acts apply to arbitral proceedings as they do to legal proceedings—see **Section 13** of the Arbitration Act 1996)

• the hearing would have to be postponed and the prejudice to the other party is too great for costs to be an adequate compensation because it would be a long time before the matter could be relisted for hearing, witnesses might have died or their memories become too faint.

If the proposed amendment is allowed it would be on the following terms:

• the costs of, thrown away and consequential on the amendment, should be paid in any event by the party being given permission to amend.

This decision will be communicated to the parties by the arbitrator in an order for directions. The order will also deal with all of the consequential amendments to his previous orders. Again there will usually be "**liberty to apply**".

REQUESTS FOR FURTHER AND BETTER PARTICULARS

The purpose of a pleading and a statement of case is to fully alert the other party to the case it has to meet so that it has full opportunity to bring evidence to rebut all of the allegations which it denies. It is therefore necessary for each party to have a full understanding of the other's case; that is not to say, in the case of pleadings, that a party is entitled to know the evidence the other party will adduce in order to prepare its defence, but it is entitled to know **all of the facts and matters relied on**.

An example will best illustrate the point. The claimant may plead "It was orally agreed between the parties that the consignment of wheat was acceptable notwithstanding its moisture content". Such a statement does not fully alert the respondent to the case it has to meet. It might therefore request further and better particulars, as follows:

"In respect of paragraph XX, of 'It was orally agreed between the parties that the consignment of wheat was acceptable notwithstanding its moisture content', please state:

1. The means of communication of the agreement, whether face to face, by telephone or some other means and if so, what
2. If face to face, between whom the oral agreement was made, giving the identity of each person present and whom they represented
3. If by telephone or some other means, the like particulars as paragraph 2 above
4. The date, time and precise place of the agreement
5. The precise words used by each of the persons present, or if not possible, the gist of the words used
6. Whether the oral agreement was evidenced by any document or by any other means; if so identify the document or other means and supply a copy
7. By the words 'was acceptable', state precisely to whom it was acceptable
8. State the precise moisture content that 'was acceptable'."

On receipt of this request the claimant must supply answers in writing within a time set by the arbitrator. Requests for and answers to requests for further and better particulars should not delay the timetable for pleadings.

In respect of statements of case, if they do not fully alert the other side to the case being made against them, it will usually be possible to request clarifications in a similar way.

DISCOVERY AND INSPECTION

One of the historic central planks of the common law system of justice has been the principle that each party can have no secrets from the other; everything, whether helpful or unhelpful to each party's case, is brought into the open. The only exception is that documents which attract **legal professional privilege** or **litigation privilege** need not be disclosed, for example legal advice or the advice of experts in connection with the arbitration or details of documents evidencing genuine attempts to compromise the dispute or documents which have come into existence as a result of the proceedings.

Discovery

The process of discovery has two elements; **discovery** and **inspection**. Discovery is the making of lists of documents. Each party has to list all the documents, which are or might be relevant to the dispute, which are or have been in its **custody, power or possession**. The list is in three parts, the first part being those documents which it still has in its custody, power or possession and in respect of which it does not claim privilege; the second part is a list of those documents which it once had but no longer has in its custody, power or possession and in respect of which it does not claim privilege, and the third part is those documents in respect of which it claims privilege.

Privilege

All legal advice and communications from and with lawyers will attract privilege save in exceptional circumstances. Unlike litigation parties in arbitration are often represented by non-lawyers. The question as to whether communications with non-lawyers administering arbitration on behalf of one of the parties attracts the same legal professional privilege as for lawyers, is difficult to answer. It is generally true that only Parliament can extend the scope of legal professional privilege; although Parliament has expressly stated that parties to an arbitration can be represented by non-lawyers (**Section 36—Arbitration Act 1996**), it has not yet extended privilege to non-lawyers in arbitration despite strong representations to do so. Justice demands that legal professional privilege should be extended to any person representing a party in arbitration; perhaps this question will be resolved by a test case or a change in the law.

Privilege will also extend to certain other documents not sent to or produced by lawyers, for example experts or consultants. The test for privilege in these cases is whether the documents came into existence for the sole or primary purpose of the arbitration, whether after commencement or when proceedings were in direct contemplation.

The third category of privilege that will be considered here consists of those documents which came into existence in connection with a genuine attempt to compromise the dispute; a compromise is where one or both parties indicate that to settle they may not insist on what they maintain are their full legal rights. Documents produced in the course of settlement negotiations are usually marked "**without prejudice**". These words do not in themselves clothe a document with privilege, unless the document is the first or a subsequent communication in an attempt to settle. The fact that a document is not marked "without prejudice" does not prevent it being privileged.

Confidential documents do not usually attract privilege. Of course such documents remain confidential within the arbitration and cannot be disclosed or copied outside of the reference.

The privileged documents in the third part of the list on discovery will be identified by class, not individually; for example—"instructions to and advice from counsel".

Inspection

Once each party has disclosed its list to the other, the non-privileged documents can be inspected, usually on appointment, and copies requested.

Disputes over discovery

There are frequently disputes between the parties that inadequate discovery has been given; for example it is maintained that documents exist that have not been disclosed. Occasionally there will be a debate as to whether certain classes of documents are relevant or not, and finally there are debates as to whether certain documents correctly attract privilege. The arbitrator will have to resolve these disputes. As always the principle is to hear both sides before any decisions are made; often the decision will be able to be made on the basis of written representations only but if necessary, or if specifically requested by one of the parties, it may be necessary to convene an interlocutory meeting to hear oral submissions.

If one party maintains documents do or should exist and the other says it cannot find them or they do not exist, the party asserting the non-availability of the documents is usually asked to confirm its position in respect of the documents by affidavit.

Controlling discovery

As can be seen, discovery and inspection can be a long and very expensive process and of questionable value in the administration of justice. As stated earlier in this book, those countries with civil law systems manage without discovery; each party puts forward the documents it relies on and no more. If the other side has documents which are believed to be specifically important, a case can be made out to the arbitral tribunal for an order for disclosure.

This civil law system of document disclosure is gaining acceptance in the United Kingdom. A sensible compromise is for each party to disclose all of the documents it relies on and after they have been considered, each party may make a request for what is known as **specific discovery**. Each party will list the documents or classes of documents which it believes are in the possession, custody or power of the other party and which it maintains are directly relevant to the issues in the arbitration. Specific discovery will not be ordered unless the arbitrator is persuaded that it really is necessary in the interests of justice for the documents to be disclosed. The arbitrator's powers in respect of controlling discovery are set out in **Section 34 (2) (d) of the Arbitration Act 1996**.

THE ROLE OF THE EXPERT WITNESS

Limiting the number of experts

Arbitration is generally about technical matters; it is therefore a characteristic of arbitration that expert evidence plays a very important part. Historically each party engaged its own expert in each and every discipline that was relevant to the dispute. Thus each party might have three or four **expert witnesses**. If there were more than two parties, the numbers of experts could be significant. For many years it has been the practice to limit each party to one expert of each discipline. For example, in a medical matter only one orthopaedic surgeon would be allowed to give evidence for each party, although it might be appropriate for each party to also call an anaesthetist. Although both are specialisms of medicine, it would be unreasonable to expect an orthopaedic specialist to be an expert on anaesthetics, although he was no doubt trained in it at medical school.

The expert is only allowed in arbitration with the leave of the arbitrator; each party has to seek leave for the number of experts they wish to call and they have to make out a case for each discipline. The order for directions following the preliminary meeting will have limited the number of experts and set conditions on them giving evidence.

Without prejudice meetings and joint reports of matters agreed and not agreed

The conditions are that experts of like discipline should meet as often as necessary, certainly after pleadings are complete and usually after witness statements have been exchanged, in order to discuss the issues and their various opinions under the cloak of privilege. Nothing that is said in those meetings can ever be disclosed to the tribunal. The aim is to attempt to narrow the differences and to reach consensus on as many matters as possible. Once agreement is reached between the experts, that agreement is reduced to writing and disclosed; it then loses its privilege. Most arbitrators also require the experts of like discipline to identify where they disagree and to summarise their different opinions. The object is to save time at the hearing and to identify an agenda for trial of the expert matters in issue.

Primary duty of expert is to the tribunal

All experts have an overriding and primary duty to the tribunal to explain technical issues to the arbitrator so that he can understand the matter and reach a conclusion. Although experts are instructed and paid by one of the parties, they must not be partisan and only put forward opinions favourable to their client. There is always a strong temptation for an expert to put his client's case in a favourable light; if he genuinely believes it, then fine; all too many experts merely act as a mouthpiece for their clients; they can become emotionally attached to the case, which is never helpful. An expert ought to give the same opinions and the same evidence irrespective of which party has instructed him and is paying his fee.

Tribunal appointed experts

In the civil law system, it is common for the tribunal to appoint its own expert to investigate and report. The tribunal expert is paid by the tribunal and therefore owes no allegiance to either party. His opinions and evidence are therefore much more likely to be independent. The disadvantage of the tribunal-appointed expert is that at the time the expert needs to be instructed the arbitrator does not have sufficient knowledge to be able to prepare the expert's instructions.

This disadvantage can be overcome if each party in turn is invited to prepare instructions for the tribunal expert. The expert may wish to consult each party either individually or together and providing he is totally open about all that he does, says and is told, and copies any documents he receives to the other party, then his independence will be retained.

Eventually the expert will prepare a report which will be circulated to each party and to the arbitrator. Each party will be given an opportunity to cross-examine the expert at the hearing.

Experts and assessors

This concept of **tribunal appointed expert** has been introduced into the Arbitration Act 1996 through **Section 37**, which expressly empowers the tribunal to appoint experts or **assessors** and for them to attend the hearing. The difference between an expert and an assessor is that the expert himself prepares a report and gives evidence whereas the assessor sits with the arbitrator at the hearing while expert evidence is being given and is there as an adviser to the arbitrator to assist him in understanding the evidence and assessing its worth.

Party appointed experts

If there are no tribunal experts, each party will appoint its own. If possible after the without prejudice meetings have taken place, each expert will produce and simultaneously exchange his report with that of his fellow expert for the other party. Further without prejudice meetings might take place and if necessary each expert might produce a brief supplemental report to deal with opinions raised in the other expert's report but not dealt with in his own.

Either at the same time as reports are exchanged, or subsequently, the experts of like discipline will draw up a statement of what opinions and facts are agreed and what are not agreed between them.

WITNESSES OF FACT

Witnesses of fact are those persons who will give evidence at the hearing from their own personal knowledge of what they did, said, saw, smelled, heard or touched. In other words they will be able to give evidence of facts, not opinions. It is on the basis of this evidence that many of the pleaded allegations will be proved or disproved.

In years gone by each potential witness of fact would agree a written statement of the evidence he would give at the hearing; this was known as a proof of evidence. The proof was not disclosed to the other side or the arbitrator, but would be available only to the advocate instructed by the party calling the witness. As a result the witness was asked questions at the beginning of the evidence which would hopefully provoke the witness to state orally in the hearing what he had approved in his proof of evidence. This was a time-wasting process and therefore since the 1980s a process developed whereby the witness produced a written statement of the evidence he wished to give; that statement was given to the other party and to the arbitrator. All the witness needed to do at the hearing was to confirm that the witness statement contained the evidence he or she wished to give, they could then be handed over immediately for cross-examination, thus saving a considerable amount of time.

Therefore arbitrators normally order witness statements of witnesses of fact to be exchanged soon after all of the documents have been disclosed and copied.

SECURITY FOR COSTS

There are two types of security for costs which need to be considered, security for the arbitrator's fees and expenses and security for the parties' costs.

Security for the arbitrator's fees and expenses

This is discussed in Chapter 7 under item 32 of the preliminary meeting agenda.

Security for the parties' costs

Who can be asked to provide security?

The arbitrator is given express power by **Section 38 (3)** read in conjunction with **Section 82 (1)** of the Arbitration Act 1996 to order a claimant or counterclaimant to provide security for the costs of the arbitration. The purpose of this power is to protect a respondent or counterrespondent in the circumstances where it may be wholly successful in its defence of the claim or counterclaim and yet the claimant or counterclaimant will be unable to pay the costs of the party which has been successful in its defence.

The principle is that a claimant or counterclaimant takes the risk that a respondent may not be able to pay its costs if it is successful in its claim; it must weigh that risk when it decides to commence the arbitration. The position of a respondent is, however, different. The respondent did not choose to start the arbitration and it is entitled to be sure, if it is successful in its defence, and subject to certain safeguards, that its costs will be met.

Principles to be adopted

Very often an arbitrator will be asked by a respondent to order security for costs against a claimant. An arbitrator is not bound to follow the same procedure and apply the same tests as the court in similar circumstances; the arbitrator must act fairly and justly.

However in the opinion of the author, an arbitrator will be very wise to be guided by the same tests that the court would apply.

Security for costs is only normally given against limited companies; individuals and partnerships are usually exempt, but an arbitrator would appear to have power to order security against an individual. In respect of a company it must be proved that the claimant would not, not merely might not, be able to pay the respondent's costs of the defence if the respondent was successful in its defence. To defeat a claim for security a claimant might wish to establish that it would not have been in this financial position if it were not for the acts of the respondent complained of in this arbitration.

Problems for arbitrators in hearing applications for security for costs

The claimant might also wish to establish that the respondent is not genuine in suggesting it might be wholly successful in defending the action, because it has already made an open or without prejudice offer to settle, indicating, at least under the cover of privilege, that it accepts some liability. The last argument can present almost insurmountable difficulties for an arbitrator. Unlike the court, where the judge hearing the application for security for costs is not the same judge who hears the substantive action, the arbitrator will hear both applications for security and the case itself. If he becomes aware of the amount of offers to settle he might consider that his ability to decide the issues fairly has been compromised.

This issue was considered by the Government's Departmental Advisory Committee during the passage of the Arbitration Act

1996 through Parliament and it was suggested that this would not cause arbitrators any difficulty. Arbitrators have to develop the ability to put things out of their minds and this is a particularly important area. If an arbitrator, or for that matter the parties, considers he will or may be prejudiced by hearing of any without prejudice offers, he should suggest to the parties that another arbitrator hears and decides on the application for security for costs. This can only be done by consent, but it avoids the problems outlined above, be they real or perceived.

The maximum amount of security ordered will be the amount of the recoverable costs of the defence, excluding the costs of any counterclaim. Security will normally be given in respect of the anticipated costs to be incurred up to the first day of the hearing. Even if the arbitrator is persuaded that the estimate of anticipated costs is accurate, he is entitled to order security for any lesser amount he considers appropriate. It is possible for further applications for security for costs to be made, but only in respect of subsequent periods. Orders for security for costs are only amended if there has been a material change in circumstances justifying a departure from the terms of the previous order.

INTERLOCUTORY MEETINGS AND ORDERS

Sometimes issues which arise between the parties between the preliminary meeting and the hearing cannot be resolved through correspondence. In such cases the arbitrator will call an **interlocutory meeting** or **interlocutory hearing**. There are occasions when one of the parties will request such a meeting; generally the arbitrator will accede to such request.

Decisions and reasons

The arbitrator will produce an agenda for the meeting and give both parties adequate notice. He will hear both sides on each issue before making a decision. An interlocutory decision is not an award, even a partial award. The arbitrator is therefore under no obligation to give reasons for his decisions and should certainly not do so in writing. It is however helpful to the parties if the arbitrator makes decisions during the interlocutory meeting which he communicates to the parties orally. The author's practice is to give the briefest of oral reasons with the decision.

The exception to the rule that reasons should not be given is when the purpose of the interlocutory meeting is for it to be a hearing on jurisdiction. In this case, the arbitrator should reserve his decision and communicate it to the parties through a reasoned award, not an interlocutory order for directions. Great care must be taken to distinguish between an interlocutory meeting and a hearing on jurisdiction.

Orders for directions

With the exception of jurisdiction hearings, the decisions reached at an interlocutory meeting, as for any interlocutory decisions that are made, are communicated formally to the parties through an order for directions. Unlike an award, the parties can always apply for an order for directions to be changed.

Typical interlocutory issues

There are many matters which might come before an arbitrator at an interlocutory meeting. They will include:

• Extension of time for pleadings or statements of case

• Request for leave to amend pleadings or statements

• Request for additional experts

• Request for additional time to comply with previous orders

• Disputes over discovery

• Request to postpone hearing or for a longer hearing

• Security for costs.

An order for directions following an interlocutory meeting might be as follows:
In the matter of the Arbitration Act 1996 and in the matter
of an arbitration between

Party A   **Claimant**

and

Party B   **Respondent**

Arbitrator's order for directions No. 2

Having carefully considered the oral submissions of Ms A solicitor for the claimant and Mr B representative for the respondent at an interlocutory meeting held at my offices at 11:00am on Friday 10 July 1998, **I HEREBY ORDER AND DIRECT**

1. The claimant is given leave to amend its statement of case in the terms of the draft sent to me on 16 June 1998; the amended version to be served not later than 15 July 1998. The respondent may serve an amended statement of defence within 21 days of service of the amended statement of case; any amended statement of reply shall be served within 7 days thereafter. All costs of, consequential on and thrown away as a result of the amendments shall be borne and paid by the claimant in any event.
2. Not later than 31 July 1998 the claimant is to provide security for the respondent's costs of defending the claim in the sum of £20,000.00 to be provided by means of suitable bank guarantee in terms to be agreed between the parties and in the event of failure to agree to be determined by me.
3. Liberty to either party to apply.
4. Costs to be borne and paid by the claimant in any event.

10 July 1998

Signed

Arbitrator
Distribution:
Claimant's solicitors
Respondent's representatives

PRE-HEARING REVIEW

This is special kind of interlocutory meeting, usually held a few weeks before the hearing is due to commence. By this time pleadings or statements of case will have been exchanged, documents will have been disclosed, witness statements will have been exchanged and expert reports will either be to hand or will be exchanged imminently. It is usual for the advocates who will represent the parties at the hearing to be present at the pre-hearing review. This meeting will go through every outstanding item to be completed before the hearing and if necessary the arbitrator will issue orders to ensure all outstanding matters are dealt with speedily.

All of the practical details for the hearing will be discussed and agreement reached or orders given. In particular the arbitrator will be keen to ensure that the parties will be able to complete the presentation of their respective cases within the time set aside and that the bundles of documents will be in order.

In Chapter 7 on the preliminary meeting above, the agenda and the subsequent order for directions assumed that all matters would be dealt with at the preliminary meeting, with the pre-hearing review being used to ensure and confirm that all procedural steps were completed and in hand. In larger cases it may be appropriate to cut short the preliminary meeting after dealing with witnesses of fact and experts and leave all remaining items to be dealt with at a pre-hearing review or other interlocutory meeting.

COMPLIANCE WITH ORDERS FOR DIRECTIONS

There are occasions when orders for directions are not complied with. Usually the other party will complain but in any event it is beneficial for arbitrators to keep a diary which records the dates by which the various matters have to be dealt with. If a party realises it will not be able to comply with an order by the set date, it should always apply for an extension of time before the time for compliance has expired. Arbitrators will usually allow one short extension on proper application, but if there has been previous non-compliance or there is very little time available for an extension whilst keeping the hearing dates intact, the arbitrator will issue what is known as a **peremptory order** and the order for directions is prominently marked as such. A peremptory order means there will be no further extension for compliance and in the event of further non-compliance the arbitrator may do any of the following:

- direct that the party in default shall not be entitled to rely upon any allegation or material which was the subject of the order;

- draw such adverse inferences from the act of non-compliance as the circumstances justify;

- proceed to an award on the basis of such materials as have been properly provided to him;

- make such order as he thinks fit as to the payment of costs of the arbitration incurred in consequence of the non-compliance.

If the peremptory order is in connection with the provision by a claimant or counterclaimant of security for costs, the arbitrator may make an award dismissing the claim or counterclaim if the order is not complied with.

Some arbitrators prefer to issue a **final order** after the first act of non-compliance and then in the event of still further non-compliance they will issue a peremptory order. A final order simply means that in the event of non-compliance the next order will be a peremptory order with possible draconian consequences. A peremptory order is sometimes known as an **unless order**, because the order is usually prefaced with the word "unless" and sets out the consequences for non-compliance.

An arbitrator is not obliged to set out the consequences of non-compliance in a peremptory order, but can do so if he wishes.

The arbitrator's powers in connection with non-compliance with orders is set out in **Section 41 (5) to (7)** of the Arbitration Act 1996.

Under **Section 42** of the Act, the arbitrator, one of the parties with the arbitrator's permission, or either party if the arbitration agreement prescribes that the court's powers under Section 42 are available, may ask the court to enforce a peremptory order. This Section will only be used where the arbitrator does not have any effective sanctions at his disposal. This will usually be where the arbitration agreement has removed all or some of the arbitrator's powers under Section 41 (6) and 41 (7).

LIMITING THE RECOVERABLE COSTS OF THE PARTIES

This has been discussed in Chapter 7 under item 33 of the pre-liminary meeting agenda. Although the costs limit may well be set at the preliminary meeting, there will often be requests by the parties for the costs cap to be lifted in the light of ensuing events. As before the arbitrator should consider representations from both parties and if he is so persuaded he can lift the limit. If the limit is to be lifted, it must still represent a reasonable target for the future and not be used oppressively.

CHOICE OF REPRESENTATION AT THE HEARING

The parties can be represented at the hearing by anyone of their choice; there are no restrictions on rights of audience as in the courts. Parties can and often do choose to be represented by lawyers and in many cases are represented by barristers who are professional advocates. Barristers are sometimes known as **counsel**. An advocate who is not a barrister or solicitor is known as a **lay advocate**.

Some lay advocates are excellent, but like any other calling, the person who is trained as an advocate will often be the most effective. The barrister's skill is not merely in the law but knowing which questions to ask and not ask and how to ask them. Advocates are habitually polite to arbitrators and hearings and interlocutory procedures are conducted in a friendly and professional way, totally unlike the television picture of court drama.

A party can choose to represent himself and a company can be represented by a director or employee. The arbitrator will be prepared to assist unrepresented parties on matters of procedure only, but not on matters of substance.

BUNDLE FOR THE HEARING

This item was discussed briefly in Chapter 7 under item 18 of the agenda for the preliminary meeting.

Getting bundles of documents in order before the hearing is one of the most important factors to ensure a good start to the hearing and an efficient use of hearing time.

The bundle, a euphemism for what can be 100 or more lever arch files in a large case, should only contain those documents which will or may be referred to at the hearing and no more. It may be conveniently divided into correspondence, diaries, drawings, photographs and the like, but irrespective of the source of individual documents each document should be in date order within its class with the oldest document at the top so the bundle reads like a book.

Each volume and each page in the bundle should be individually and uniquely numbered before it is copied so that if any document is removed from a file, it can be replaced in the correct place. Where a letter or document has more than one page, each page should be separately numbered.

At least four copies of the bundle need to be prepared; one each for the advocates, one for the arbitrator and one for the witness who is giving evidence at the time.

Sometimes the arbitrator may request a copy of the bundle to be delivered to him during the week prior to the hearing so that he can do some pre-reading.

PRELIMINARY ISSUES OR POINTS OF LAW

This is briefly discussed in Chapter 7 under item 27 of the preliminary meeting agenda. If issues or points of law can be identified that if decided would probably lead to a settlement of the dispute or a substantial part of it, then it may be attractive to the parties to ask the arbitrator to make a partial award on those matters. If the arbitrator accedes to such request he will ask for pleadings on those issues alone, if they have not already been exchanged, and for witness statements and expert reports to be limited to those issues alone. A bundle of documents for the preliminary issues will also be assembled.

The arbitrator will hold a mini-hearing on the preliminary issues or points of law if it is not possible to deal with them through written submissions. After the mini-hearing, the arbitrator will proceed to make a partial award on the matters before him, leaving the remaining issues for a further partial award or his final award.

The benefits of preliminary issues or preliminary points of law are often illusory. Sometimes, whatever decision is reached, the case will continue and the time taken in dealing with the preliminary points could have been better spent in progressing the main action to a hearing. Therefore it is essential to decide whether the determination of a preliminary issue or point of law is a short cut to the conclusion of the dispute or a time wasting exercise.

INSPECTION OF SUBJECT MATTER OF DISPUTE

Such inspection is not always necessary or practicable. For example, in a shipping arbitration, only rarely will it be possible for the arbitrators to visit the vessel in question; it may well be at the far side of the world or in mid-ocean. There are other disputes, particularly those concerning quality, where inspection is vital. If there is urgency the arbitrator should inspect at the first opportunity, possibly even before the preliminary meeting. Other cases, of which non-quality disputes in construction are a good example, may not demand a visit as essential but the arbitrator may well be able to understand the evidence better if he visits the site before the start of the hearing.

Inspections are not an extension of the hearing where oral evidence will be given. The rule on inspections is that what the arbitrator sees, smells or touches is real evidence but what he hears people say is not evidence.

CHAPTER 9

COURT ASSISTANCE AND INTERVENTION

One of the central planks of the philosophy of the Arbitration Act 1996 is that the court should not intervene except as expressly provided in the Act—see **Section 1 (c).**

The court's role in appointing and removing arbitrators has been dealt with in Chapter 4. In Chapter 5, the court's role in the determination of the arbitrator's personal entitlement to fees and expenses has been considered.

This chapter discusses the other roles of the court both in assistance and intervention, except enforcement of awards which is dealt with in Chapter 11.

WHICH COURT?

Section 105 of the Arbitration Act 1996 says that "the court", where referred to throughout the Act, means the High Court or a county court. However the Lord Chancellor is given power to make an order allocating proceedings under the Arbitration Act to the High Court or to county courts and to specify which proceedings may be commenced or taken only in the High Court or in a county court.

By **"The High Court and County Courts (Allocation of Arbitration Proceedings) Order 1996"**[1] the Lord Chancellor has exercised his powers under Section 105 of the Act.

The general rule is that proceedings under the Arbitration Act 1996 shall be commenced and taken in the High Court.

1 See Appendix 3.

The exceptions are:

• cases where the financial substance of the case does not exceed £200,000 or the case does not raise questions of general importance to persons who are not parties to the arbitration, where the case may be commenced and taken in the Central London County Court Business List;

• applications to stay legal proceedings in favour of arbitration **(Section 9 of the Act)** shall be taken in the court in which the legal proceedings are pending;

• proceedings to enforce an award may be taken in any county court.

ENFORCEMENT OF PEREMPTORY ORDERS OF TRIBUNAL

This has been discussed in Chapter 8 above. Generally the arbitrator will have sufficient powers at his disposal to deal effectively with a party's failure to comply with a peremptory order; those powers are set out in **Section 41 (7)** of the Arbitration Act 1996. There will however be circumstances where the assistance of the court is required. Examples will be failure by a party to comply with a peremptory order concerning preservation or control of property, taking of samples or permitting experiments or preservation of evidence.

The court will only act if it is satisfied that the applicant has exhausted any available arbitral process in respect of failure to comply with the order, that the person to whom the arbitrator's order was directed really has failed to comply within the time stated or, if no time is given, within a reasonable time.

SECURING THE ATTENDANCE OF WITNESSES

A witness cannot be compelled by the arbitrator to attend before him to give oral testimony or to produce documents or other evidence. The court, however, may order such attendance by means of issuing subpoenas. This is dealt with in **Section 43** of the Arbitration Act 1996.

There are two common forms of subpoena, a *subpoena ad testificandum* which requires the recipient to attend to give oral testimony; a *subpoena duces tecum* which obliges the recipient to attend before the arbitrator and to bring certain identified documents or classes of documents with him. If a witness is required to be brought up from prison or custody, the type of subpoena required is a *subpoena habeas corpus ad testificandum*.

The court will not issue a subpoena unless all parties agree or with the agreement of the arbitrator. The procedure for obtaining subpoenas is only available if the witness is in the United Kingdom and the arbitral proceedings are being conducted in England, Wales or Northern Ireland.

The procedure for applying for and the issuing of subpoenas by the court is exactly the same as for legal proceedings in court[2].

GENERAL COURT POWERS EXERCISABLE IN SUPPORT OF ARBITRAL PROCEEDINGS

The purpose of **Section 44** of the Arbitration Act 1996 is for the court to be able to act in respect of certain limited matters where the arbitrator has no power or is unable for the time being to act effectively. Any orders of the court under this Section can be ordered to cease to have effect by the arbitrator at any time in the future. In other words it can be seen that this is not a prop for the timid arbitrator but important assistance where he has no effective power.

The matters in which the court can intervene are as follows:

a. the taking of evidence of witnesses;
b. the preservation of evidence;
c. making orders relating to property which is the subject of proceedings or as to which any question arises in the proceedings—
   i. for the inspection, photographing, preservation, custody or detection of the property, or
   ii. ordering that samples be taken from, or any observation made of or experiment conducted upon, the property;
   and for that purpose authorising any person to enter any premises in the possession or control of a party to the arbitration;

2 Rules of the Supreme Court—Order 38, Rules 14 to 19.

d. the sale of any goods the subject of the proceedings;
e. the granting of an interim injunction or the appointment of a receiver.

Urgent applications may be made by one party acting alone, that is *ex parte*, on affidavit; for example to preserve property or in seeking an injunction. All non-urgent applications must be made with the permission of the arbitrator or the agreement in writing of the other parties.

DETERMINATION OF PRELIMINARY POINT OF LAW

All applications to the court to determine a preliminary point of law under **Section 45** of the Arbitration Act 1996 must satisfy certain criteria. In all cases the following must be satisfied:

- the court must be satisfied that the question of law substantially affects the rights of one or more of the parties.

In addition one of two further criteria must be satisfied:

- the application is made with the agreement of all the other parties to the arbitration; or

- the application is made with the permission of the arbitrator and the court is satisfied that the determination of the question of law is likely to produce substantial savings in costs and that the application was made without delay.

How these criteria will be interpreted will have to await case law on the Arbitration Act 1996.

Unless the parties otherwise agree, the arbitrator can continue the arbitral proceedings and make an award while an application to the court for the determination of the point of law is pending. It is hard to imagine how substantial savings in costs will be produced if the arbitrator completes the hearing and makes an award before the court has determined the point of law, but it may be appropriate for a partial award to be made on discrete issues.

DETERMINING A PRELIMINARY POINT OF JURISDICTION

In Chapter 5 the arbitrator's power to determine his own jurisdiction has been discussed. The arbitrator only has those powers unless the parties agree otherwise.

If the arbitrator's power to determine his own jurisdiction is taken away from him by agreement of the parties (**Section 30**), then questions of jurisdiction can only be determined by the court under **Section 32**. Before considering an application to determine a preliminary point of jurisdiction, the court will satisfy itself that:

- the application is made with the agreement of all the other parties to the proceedings—**Section 32 (2) (a)**; or

- the application is made with the permission of the arbitrator and the court is satisfied that the determination of the question of jurisdiction is likely to produce substantial savings in costs, that the application was made without delay and that there is good reason why the matter should be decided by the court—**Section 32 (2) (b)**; the grounds for the application must be stated—**Section 32 (3)**.

Even if the arbitrator does have power to determine his own jurisdiction:

- the parties may agree in writing to refer the matter for the decision of the court, in which case the court must hear it—**Section 32 (2) (a)**;

- one party can apply for the matter of jurisdiction to be determined by the court and the arbitrator can give his permission for the application. In that case, the court must be satisfied that the determination of the question of jurisdiction is likely to produce substantial savings in costs, that the application was made without delay and that there is good reason why the matter should be decided by the court—**Section 32 (2) (b)**; as above, the grounds for the application must be stated—**Section 32 (3)**.

No appeal lies from the court's determination of jurisdiction unless the court gives leave—**Section 32 final paragraph**.

CHALLENGING THE AWARD FOR ALLEGED LACK OF SUBSTANTIVE JURISDICTION

Under **Section 67** of the Arbitration Act 1996, an award can be challenged by any of the parties to the arbitration on the grounds that the tribunal lacked substantive jurisdiction, either generally or in connection with one or more specific matters covered in the award.

In other words it might be possible that the arbitral tribunal makes a decision on a series of issues, one of which was not referred to arbitration. In such a case, the award might be challenged on the grounds of lack of jurisdiction, but only in respect of that part of the award which went outside the terms of reference to arbitration. The same considerations apply where the arbitral tribunal makes a decision on a matter not covered in the pleadings or statements of case; again the award can be challenged on the grounds of lack of jurisdiction, but only in respect of that part of the award in which decisions were made on matters not pleaded.

There are two distinct types of challenge to jurisdiction that can be made:

- challenge to an award as to jurisdiction made under powers given to the arbitrator under **Section 31 (4) (a)**—see Chapter 5;

- challenge to an award on the merits by seeking a court order that the award is of no effect, in whole or in part, because the arbitrator lacked substantive jurisdiction.

Challenge to an award as to jurisdiction

This is an appeal from an award as to jurisdiction made by the arbitrator under Section 31. It must be distinguished from the court's own power to determine jurisdiction under Section 32 which power can only apply if:

- the parties have divested the arbitrator of his powers to determine his own jurisdiction; or

- the parties have agreed, despite the arbitrator's general powers to determine his own jurisdiction, that the court should determine a particular point of jurisdiction; or

- the arbitrator has consented to one party's application to the court to determine jurisdiction and the court is satisfied that it should hear the issue.

It will be remembered that an arbitrator's award on substantive jurisdiction can be made in a specific award as to jurisdiction or as part of an award on the merits. This section deals only with the first category of awards—specific awards as to jurisdiction.

There are formidable hurdles to overcome before an award as to jurisdiction can be successfully challenged in court—see **Sections 70 (2) and (3)** of the Act:

1. any arbitral appeal process must have been exhausted; and
2. the appeal must be brought within 28 days of the award or 28 days of notification of the result of any arbitral appeal process, whichever is later; and
3. any possibility of the arbitrator correcting the award under **Section 57** to remove a clerical mistake or error arising from an accidental slip or omission, or to clarify or remove any ambiguity, has been exhausted.

If a party fails to take any of these steps within the time limits specified it will lose its right to object later to the arbitrator's substantive jurisdiction on any ground which was the subject of the award as to jurisdiction—see **Section 73 (2)**.

If the hurdles are overcome, the court has three options when considering the challenge to an award as to jurisdiction:

- confirm the award;

- vary the award;

- set aside the award in whole or in part.

If there is a challenge to an award on jurisdiction, the arbitrator may continue the proceedings and make a further award while the application to the court is pending—see **Section 67 (2)**.

Challenge to an award on the merits on the grounds that the arbitrator lacked substantive jurisdiction

As with an appeal to an award as to jurisdiction, the same hurdles set by **Sections 70 (2) and (3)** of the Arbitration Act 1996 have to be overcome but with the addition of one new major hurdle:

- the objecting party must show that at the time he took part or continued to take part in the proceedings, he did not know and could not with reasonable diligence have discovered the grounds for now maintaining that the arbitrator lacks substantive jurisdiction—**Section 73 (1)**.

If the objecting party either fails to take the steps set out in Section 70 (2) and (3) or fails to satisfy the court on this last hurdle, it may not raise that objection later before the arbitrator or the court and will lose the right to object on grounds of lack of jurisdiction.

If the hurdles are overcome, the court has only one option when considering a challenge to an award on the merits on the grounds that the tribunal lacks substantive jurisdiction:

- it can declare the award to be of no effect, in whole or in part—see **Section 67 (1) (b)**.

CHALLENGING THE AWARD FOR SERIOUS IRREGULARITY

Under **Section 68** of the Arbitration Act 1996 any party may, on notice to the other parties and the arbitral tribunal, apply to the court challenging an award on the ground of serious irregularity, affecting the arbitrator, the proceedings or the award.

Serious irregularity is defined as one or more of the following, **providing the court considers that substantial injustice has been caused or will be caused to the applicant:**

- failure by the arbitrator to act fairly and impartially as between the parties, giving each party a reasonable opportunity of putting his case and dealing with that of his opponent;

- failure by the arbitrator to adopt procedures suitable to the circumstances of the particular case, avoiding unnecessary delay or expense, so as to provide a fair means for the resolution of the matters falling to be determined;

- the arbitrator exceeding his powers, except by exceeding his substantive jurisdiction;

- failure by the arbitrator to conduct the proceedings in accordance with the procedure agreed by the parties;

- failure by the arbitrator to deal in his award with all of the issues put to him;

- any arbitral or other institution or person vested by the parties with powers in relation to the proceedings or the award, exceeding its powers;

- uncertainty or ambiguity as to the effect of the award;

- the award being obtained by fraud;

- the award or the way it was procured being contrary to public policy;

- failure by the arbitrator to comply with the requirements as to the form of the award, either the form agreed by the parties or that set out in **Section 52** of the Act (that is award not in writing or not signed by the arbitrator, award not containing reasons, award not stating the seat of the arbitration, or award not stating the date it was made);

- any irregularity in the conduct of the proceedings or in the award **which is admitted** by the arbitrator or by any arbitral or other institution or person vested by the parties with powers in relation to the proceedings or the award.

On the face of it, this is a surprisingly wide and comprehensive list. Undoubtedly there will be many opportunities for serious irregularity to be alleged and it may be thought that this **Section 68** is an ideal vehicle for a disgruntled party, who does not like the outcome of an award, to attempt to frustrate the arbitral process. However, as with most Sections providing for court intervention, there are hurdles to overcome before a successful challenge can be mounted. These are, where applicable:

- the applicant must establish to the satisfaction of the court that the particular serious irregularity complained of has caused it or will cause it substantial injustice;

- there is no arbitral process of appeal or review or that process has been exhausted;

- the applicant has not applied or has not successfully applied to the arbitrator to correct the award under **Section 57** to remove a clerical mistake or error arising from an accidental slip or omission, or to clarify or remove any ambiguity;

- the applicant has not applied or has not successfully applied to the arbitrator to make an additional award under **Section 57** to cover claims which were presented to the arbitrator but not dealt with in his award;

- the appeal must be brought within 28 days of the award or 28 days of notification of the result of any arbitral appeal process, whichever is later;

- the objecting party must show that at the time he took part or continued to take part in the proceedings, he did not know and could not with reasonable diligence have discovered the grounds for now maintaining that:

  - the proceedings have been improperly conducted; and/or

  - there has been a failure to comply with the arbitration agreement; and/or

  - the arbitrator failed to act fairly and impartially as between the parties, giving each party a reasonable opportunity of putting his case and dealing with that of his opponent; and/or

  - the arbitrator failed to adopt procedures suitable to the circumstances of the particular case, avoiding unnecessary delay or expense, so as to provide a fair means for the resolution of the matters failing to be determined; and/or

  - there has been any other irregularity affecting the arbitrator or the proceedings.

If serious irregularity is or should have been apparent to the objecting party during the course of the proceedings and that party failed to make the relevant objection to the tribunal or the court at the time, that party will lose its right to object—see **Section 73 (1)**.

Providing the restrictions set out above have been satisfied, the court will decide whether or not there has been serious irregularity. If the court is satisfied, it has three options. It can:

- remit the award to the arbitrator, in whole or in part, for reconsideration;

- set the award aside, in whole or in part, but it shall only do so if it is satisfied that it would be inappropriate to remit the matters in question to the arbitrator for reconsideration;

- declare the award to be of no effect, in whole or in part, but it shall only do so if it is satisfied that it would be inappropriate to remit the matters in question to the arbitrator for reconsideration.

APPEALING AN AWARD ON A POINT OF LAW

Arbitration is meant to be a process that results in a final and binding award by the arbitrator. It is therefore surprising to some that there should be a provision for appeals to the court on points of law. It is however important that arbitration awards are, wherever possible, in accordance with the general law. It is also true that certain standard form contracts provide for all disputes under them to be referred to arbitration. Those standard form contracts may give rise to questions of legal interpretation which various arbitrators have to grapple with. Arbitration is a private process and therefore one arbitrator does not have the benefit of knowing how another arbitrator dealt with an identical problem of legal interpretation.

For these reasons, amongst others, it is helpful for the court to give guidance to parties and arbitrators by making decisions on such questions of legal interpretation and for those decisions to be in the public domain by being reported.

Appeals from arbitrators' awards on points of law under **Section 69** of the Arbitration Act 1996 are therefore allowed subject to the following restrictions:

- any agreement between the parties to dispense with reasons for the arbitrator's award amounts to an agreement to exclude the court's jurisdiction to hear an appeal on a point of law;

- an appeal can only be brought by agreement with all of the parties to the proceedings or with the leave of the court;

- there is no arbitral process of appeal or review or that process has been exhausted;

- the applicant has not applied or has not successfully applied to the arbitrator to correct the award under **Section 57** to remove a clerical mistake or error arising from an accidental slip or omission, or to clarify or remove any ambiguity;

- the applicant has not applied or has not successfully applied to the arbitrator to make an additional award under **Section 57** to cover claims which were presented to the arbitrator but not dealt with in his award;

- the appeal must be brought within 28 days of the award or 28 days of notification of the result of any arbitral appeal process, whichever is later;

- before giving leave to appeal the court must be satisfied that the determination of the question of law will substantially affect the rights of one or more of the parties;

- before giving leave to appeal the court must be satisfied that the question of law before the court is one which the arbitrator was asked to determine;

- before giving leave to appeal the court must be satisfied that, taking into account the findings of fact in the award (which, of course, are unappealable), the decision of the arbitrator on the question of law is obviously wrong or the question is one of general public importance and the decision of the arbitrator is at least open to serious doubt;

- before giving leave to appeal the court must be satisfied that despite the parties' agreement to resolve their disputes by arbitration, it is just and proper in all the circumstances for the court to determine the question of law.

The effect of these restrictions is to discourage appeals unless they are necessary to correct a substantial injustice or the question of law is one of general public importance.

No appeal can be heard unless the court is first persuaded to give leave to appeal.

If the court decides to hear the appeal, it has four options:

• to confirm the award;

• to vary the award at its discretion;

• to remit the award to the arbitrator, in whole or in part, for reconsideration in the light of the court's determination;

• set the award aside, in whole or in part, but it shall only do so if it is satisfied that it would be inappropriate to remit the matters in question to the arbitrator for reconsideration.

GENERAL POINTS ON CHALLENGES TO AWARDS

If, when considering any appeal from or challenge to an arbitrator's award, the court is of the view that the award does not contain the arbitrator's **reasons,** or contains insufficient reasons, the court may order the arbitrator to state its reasons in sufficient detail for the purpose of the challenge or appeal—see **Section 70 (4)** of the Arbitration Act 1996.

The court may ask a party challenging or appealing from an award to provide security for costs for the application or appeal. Although the wording of the court's power to order security for costs in these circumstances (**Section 70 (6)**) is identical to the provisions in **Section 38 (3)** where the arbitrator is given power to order security for costs, in the opinion of the author the court will be bound to exercise its powers strictly in accordance with the Rules of the Supreme Court Order 23. There is no statutory requirement for an arbitrator to exercise his powers to order security for costs in the same way as prescribed for courts.

The court may also order that any money ordered to be paid in the arbitrator's award shall be paid into court as a condition precedent to the court hearing the application or appeal, and if the party fails to pay the money into court, the court may dismiss the application or appeal—see **Section 70 (7)** of the Act.

Section 71 (3) of the Act provides that if an award is remitted to the arbitrator for reconsideration, he must make a fresh award in respect of the matters remitted within three months of the date of the order for remission.

POSITION WHERE A PERSON ELECTS TO TAKE NO PART IN THE ARBITRATION PROCEEDINGS

Occasionally a person may receive a notice of arbitration, but may consider that there is no valid arbitration agreement, that the arbitral tribunal is improperly constituted, or that the matters in question have not properly been referred to arbitration.

Such a person, who is alleged to be a party to arbitral proceedings but elects to take no part in such proceedings, has his rights preserved to challenge an award for either lack of jurisdiction or for serious irregularity just as if he was an active party to the arbitration—see **Section** 72 of the Act. If a person elects to take no part in the proceedings, he will not lose his right to object under **Section** 73 if he failed to take the objection timeously.

CHAPTER 10

THE HEARING

TIME AND PLACE

Unlike court proceedings, an arbitration hearing can take place anywhere that is most convenient; perhaps on board ship, in a timber yard, in an office or hotel room.

Length of hearing

The hearing should take place as soon as convenient after all the interlocutory stages have been completed. The period of time set aside for the hearing should be determined with care, as, for all except the largest cases, it will be most convenient to complete the hearing in one sitting rather than going part-heard for several weeks or months. The arbitrator will consult the parties about the anticipated length of the hearing at the preliminary meeting and it will be finalised no later than the pre-hearing review.

The possibility of imposing a guillotine procedure to ensure completion of the hearing within the time set aside is discussed above in Chapter 7 under item 19(c) of the preliminary meeting agenda.

Sitting days

In long cases most arbitrators prefer to sit four-day weeks from Monday to Thursday. This leaves Friday free for all the participants to catch up on their other work and for the arbitrator to hold interlocutory or preliminary meetings on other arbitrations.

Multiple booking

The hearing must be held to the convenience of the arbitrator or arbitrators, who are often very busy people with diaries booked up months if not years ahead. For this reason many busy arbitrators may double or treble book hearings ahead on the premise that the majority of cases settle before the hearing and it is likely that time will be found for the hearing in the event. The parties are told when the hearing is booked, whether it is on a first fix, second fix or third fix basis.

Convenience of parties, witnesses and counsel

The time of the hearing must also be convenient to the parties and in particular the witnesses who will need to give evidence. The other participants with busy diaries are counsel; it is rarely appropriate to arrange a hearing for the convenience of counsel; other barristers will always be available to take over the case at short notice. Where a case goes part-heard, that is the hearing has to be adjourned for weeks or months and then re-convened, it is more important to try to accommodate the diaries of the counsel who have been involved in the earlier hearing, but primarily it is the convenience of the parties that is of paramount importance, and if counsel has to be replaced, even on a part-heard hearing, relatively little difficulty is encountered in practice.

Sitting hours

Actual sitting hours at an arbitration hearing rarely exceed five and a half per day; this is not because the arbitrator is lazy, but the intense concentration needed for the arbitrator, counsel and witnesses means that it is not productive to sit long days. The hearing will normally commence at 10:00am and conclude at 4:30pm with a break of one hour for lunch. It may be possible to programme in short coffee and tea breaks mid-morning and mid-afternoon.

A full day of arbitration hearing is exhausting and it must also be remembered that counsel will certainly need to work into the evening to prepare for the next day. The arbitrator may also need to work into the evening making notes on the evidence for use in his award.

Location

Arbitration hearings will often take place in hotels, conference facilities or specialist arbitration suites which are available in London and other centres. The main hearing room needs to be sufficiently large to easily accommodate all of the participants and all of their documents.

Layout of the hearing room

The tables in the hearing room are arranged in a U-shape with the arbitrator at the bottom of the U and one party along each of the legs. It does not matter which party sits along which leg, but some arbitrators prefer to have the claimant on their right hand and the respondent on their left. There is a table for the witness between the legs of the U facing the arbitrator.

Although this is an ideal configuration, some rooms are of such a shape that this layout is impossible or impracticable. Another layout that is used with success mirrors the layout in a court room. The arbitrator sits at the head of the room and the parties sit in rows in classroom style facing him with one party on the left side of the room and the other on the right side. Counsel sit in the front row of desks nearest to the arbitrator with solicitors and witnesses in the rows behind. The witness sits at a table between the arbitrator and counsel but at the side of the room at right angles to the arbitrator and counsel.

The most common error made in organising rooms for arbitration is that a room with insufficient space is booked. A large airy room, preferably with daylight, is ideal. There are nearly always large numbers of documents and therefore storage space for those documents is essential as is sufficient room on the desks for several files to be open at once.

Retiring rooms

In addition to the main hearing room, each party will have a retiring room where it can consult privately. The arbitrator will also be given a private room for use during adjournments or meal breaks. It is essential that the arbitrator does not allow himself to get into a position where he is alone with only one of the parties. Even though nothing untoward may have occurred, the perception to the party who was not present may be different. As an arbitrator gains in experience and as the parties and their representatives gain confidence in his absolute impartiality, the arbitrator may become more relaxed about meeting the parties during the course of the hearing over coffee, for example, and discussing matters of general interest unconnected with the case. However, the safe option is to avoid contact with one party in the absence of the other.

Pupils

Being a sole arbitrator at a hearing is a lonely task; it is therefore beneficial for an arbitrator to have one or more pupil arbitrators with him during the hearing. Under the Chartered Institute of Arbitrators' education scheme, every new candidate for the panels of arbitrators has to undergo a period of pupillage with an experienced arbitrator; the only exception is in countries where pupil masters are not readily available. The pupil is only able to be present with the express permission of both parties. He will take no part whatever in proceedings and must undertake to keep all he sees and hears strictly confidential. He will see and hear what goes on and will take notes and complete an award, either in whole or part as if he was the arbitrator. Pupils gain enormous benefit from their pupil masters at hearings in that they are able to discuss various procedural or other issues with the arbitrator who is hearing the case. There is also a hidden benefit for the arbitrator in that it reduces loneliness.

RECORDING THE EVIDENCE

Notebooks

The traditional method of recording evidence and submissions is by the arbitrator making notes in longhand in a book. Purpose-made evidence books can be obtained from legal stationers which are very useful to that end. The difficulty with that approach is that if the arbitrator is taking a comprehensive note, the evidence can only proceed as fast as the arbitrator can write. Unless the arbitrator is proficient in shorthand, the evidence will proceed rather slowly.

How often does one hear counsel exhorting a witness to watch the arbitrator's pen and not to say any more until he sees the arbitrator has stopped writing?

Stenographers and tape recorders

Old and modern technology has assisted immeasurably in the efficiency of recording evidence. This started with stenographers, who are court reporters who sit in the hearing with silent finger-operated machines that produce punched paper tape that can be read back and converted into text, usually within two or three days but faster if a team of stenographers are used. Stenographers are regularly used in arbitration today. The next development was the tape recorder which would allow the recording to be played back or to be transcribed into text. The only problem with tape recorders, especially those operated by amateurs, is that occasionally they do not record properly and there is nothing worse than for an arbitrator who has taken few notes and who is relying wholly on a tape recording, to find that the tapes are blank.

Electronic recording systems

In recent years a system has been developed where stenographer's paper tape can be simultaneously read by a machine and converted into word-processed text. This text is then edited by an operator and the corrected text is available immediately to the arbitrator and to counsel by scrolling it up computer monitors on their desks. The arbitrator can then mark text that is important and review it either overnight or when he comes to do his award. The existence of word-processed text also allows the arbitrator to operate devices such as word search to quickly locate relevant pieces of evidence. With this method a complete printed transcript of the day's evidence plus a comprehensive index will be available within two hours of the close of the hearing. The arbitrator can therefore make very limited notes as he can be confident he will have a full transcript within hours.

This method of recording evidence is expensive, but it has been estimated that savings of about 30 per cent of time can be made, which if translated into a 30 per cent reduction in the length of the hearing, will be cheaper overall.

DUTY OF THE ARBITRATOR

Listening to the evidence

The duty of the arbitrator at the hearing is to listen carefully and courteously to the submissions and evidence which will be given and to ensure that an adequate record is kept. Both parties must be treated alike. If the arbitrator does not understand a point which is being made, he should seek clarification. His primary role is to listen, not to intervene.

If the arbitrator is aware of any personal contact with any person who gives evidence or is referred to in evidence, he should declare it. In many ways the function of the arbitrator is to act like a referee in a football match; he observes, ensures the rules are honoured and obeyed, blows the whistle if necessary, but otherwise takes no part in the game.

Controlling the proceedings

Professional advocates are usually impeccably behaved, but it has been known for emotions and tempers to rise; the arbitrator must keep strict but courteous control. Witnesses will often be nervous and tense and initially not perform at their best; the arbitrator must do all he can to make them feel comfortable and relaxed. An occasional shaft of humour can often diffuse a difficult situation. A smile to counsel or the witness can often help.

The arbitrator must be confident and appear confident without being arrogant. He is the master of procedure. If a decision needs to be made, it should be made quickly, confidently and fairly. If the arbitrator realises he has made a mistake, he should immediately correct it.

Stopping counsel

If counsel is taking a long time to explain a point that is obvious to the arbitrator, he should gently explain to counsel that he understands; the difficulty will often be that counsel does not! If counsel is making submissions with which the arbitrator agrees, the arbitrator may stop counsel to save time, but the danger is that the other counsel's arguments may be so convincing that the arbitrator will doubt his initial conclusion, in which case he will have to allow the first counsel to complete his submissions. The arbitrator should never stop counsel when he disagrees with the submissions.

PROCEDURE AT THE HEARING—ADVERSARIAL APPROACH

The following is a typical order of procedure using the adversarial system; the inquisitorial system is summarised later:

- The arbitrator opens the hearing, introduces himself, runs through any housekeeping matters such as the times for drink and meal breaks and his hours of sitting. He may also confirm the details of the parties, the arbitration agreement, his appointment and any important interlocutory matters. If there are any pupils present, the arbitrator will introduce them and confirm the basis of their attendance.

- The claimant's counsel introduces himself, his opponent and all those present in the room. He then proceeds to open the claimant's case. Normally the opening will be in writing and will have been exchanged and served on the arbitrator a few days before the hearing commences. Almost certainly the arbitrator will have read the opening before the hearing starts. The purpose of the opening is to identify the issues between the parties, what the pleadings say about those issues and in summary what the evidence will be on both sides. The claimant's counsel will then go on to explain the key elements of the claimant's case and how he intends to prove it. There may be some limited reference to documents. At the same time the claimant's counsel will open his defence to the counterclaim, explaining the issues and the claimant's position on them. Where the opening is in writing, counsel will normally skim through his written submissions and highlight the important points. There may be some limited submissions on law in the opening but most legal submissions will be left for closing statements.

- The claimant's counsel will then call his first witness. It is usual to call witnesses of fact before expert witnesses. The witness moves into the witness's chair. In front of him on the table will

be a New Testament and possibly an Old Testament or Jewish holy book; there will also be two printed cards. On one card will be printed the words of the standard oath and on the other the words of the standard affirmation. The words are as follows:
The oath is:

I swear by Almighty God that the evidence I shall give touching the matters in difference in this reference shall be the truth, the whole truth, and nothing but the truth

and the affirmation:

I solemnly, sincerely, and truly affirm and declare that the evidence I shall give touching the matters in difference in this reference shall be the truth, the whole truth, and nothing but the truth

The witness will take the oath or affirmation as he wishes. Solicitors will have made arrangements for documents, objects and forms of words to be available for witnesses of other faiths. If a witness objects, he should be required to affirm.

Assuming the witness has prepared a witness statement, the claimant's counsel will first ask the witness to confirm his name and address and his involvement with the subject matter of this reference. This is the start of what is known as **examination-in-chief**. In examination-in-chief, leading questions (questions that suggest the answer) can only be asked on non-controversial subjects. The witness will be asked whether he produced a witness statement, he will be asked to identify it and his signature on the last page. He will be asked if he wishes to make any additions, deletions or alterations to his statement and if not to confirm that its contents are the truth, the whole truth, and nothing but the truth.

- The witness is then cross-examined by the respondent's counsel. **Cross-examination** has two primary purposes; the first is to test the evidence given by the witness in his witness statement by reference to documents or other evidence and the second purpose is to put the relevant parts of the respondent's own evidence to the witness. A third purpose might be to test and challenge the credibility of the witness. Leading questions can be asked in cross-examination; in fact there are virtually no restrictions as to the questions that can be asked. Effective cross-examination demands a great deal of skill; sometimes it is like watching a spider gradually enticing a fly into its web before entangling it so that escape is impossible.

- At the end of cross-examination the witness can be re-examined by his own counsel.

  Re-examination is strictly controlled. It is limited to questions raised in cross-examination and no leading questions can be asked. Its primary purpose is to try to repair the damage done to the evidence in cross-examination.

- The arbitrator is then invited to ask the witness any questions. Depending on the nature of the questions, it might be appropriate to allow each counsel to ask supplementary questions on the issues raised by the arbitrator, but normally the arbitrator's questions will be restricted to clarification only. The evidence of that witness is then concluded and he leaves the witness table.

- The second and subsequent witnesses are called and an identical procedure is followed. The procedure for expert witnesses is the same except that the expert will have a report instead of a witness statement. Witnesses of fact are usually not permitted to check their papers except for the documents they are being shown at the time; expert witnesses are allowed to look at their own notes when giving evidence. The exception for witnesses of fact is where the witness made notes at the time of the event, in which case he can ask to look at them.

- When all of the claimant's witnesses have been called, the claimant's counsel closes his case and it is now the respondent's turn.

- If he wishes, the respondent's counsel can open his case in the same way as the claimant. Often it is not necessary, as by this time the nature of the case has become clear.

- The respondent's counsel calls his first witness who goes through examination-in-chief, cross-examination and re-examination in exactly the same way. The same procedure is followed for all other witnesses including expert witnesses.

- The respondent's counsel then has an opportunity to make closing submissions or sum up his case. Closing submissions are often done in writing after the hearing is over; this saves considerable cost at the hearing and enables the submissions to be carefully cross-referenced to the evidence. Usually the respondent will submit his closing submissions within seven days of the close of the hearing and the claimant will follow seven days later. Closing submissions must not only summarise the evidence but also explain the law including citing any relevant legal authorities (reported past cases of the higher courts). Full copies of each law report cited must be given to the arbitrator. If there are to be oral closing submissions, the respondent's counsel will go first and the claimant's counsel will have the last word.

- Finally the arbitrator closes the hearing, thanks the advocates for their assistance, announces that his award is reserved and usually gives some approximation of when it will be available.

This procedure can be varied where appropriate. There are cases where it is sensible to hear all of the factual evidence first and then to hear the expert evidence. Often experts of like discipline give evidence one after the other, rather than the claimant completing his case before any of the respondent's witnesses are called. The reason is that it will be sensible for the opposing expert to be present during the testimony of an expert of his discipline and by dealing with all evidence of that discipline together, costs are saved.

In arbitration it is usually acceptable for witnesses who have not yet given evidence to be present during the testimony of earlier witnesses. The only exception is where credibility may be in question.

PROCEDURE AT THE HEARING—INQUISITORIAL APPROACH

Under **Section 34 (2) (g)** of the Arbitration Act 1996 it is for the tribunal to decide whether and to what extent it should itself take the initiative in ascertaining the facts and the law. This means that the arbitrator can act inquisitorially if he considers it appropriate. A typical inquisitorial procedure at the hearing would be as follows:

- After the arbitrator has opened the hearing, he will call the claimant's first witness. Witnesses will have prepared statements in writing and the advocates will have agreed with the arbitrator when witnesses should be available. The witness will take the oath or affirmation in the normal way and the arbitrator will ask him to confirm his name and address and to confirm that the content of his witness statement is true and is the evidence he wishes to give. The arbitrator will then ask the witness such questions as he considers appropriate. The aim of the questions is a search for the truth; the arbitrator may ask leading questions.

- When the arbitrator has completed his questions, first the respondent's advocate and then the claimant's advocate can ask such further questions as they consider appropriate. The claimant's counsel cannot ask leading questions. The arbitrator may then ask further questions arising from the line of questioning adopted by either advocate. That will conclude the evidence of the witness. The author's experience is that when conducting inquisitorial hearings, the arbitrator may ask about 70 per cent of the questions put to each witness. The degree of preparation required by the arbitrator is infinitely greater for inquisitorial hearings than for adversarial; all in all, it is much harder work.

- Other witnesses will follow the same procedure, first the claimant's witnesses and then the respondent's.

- Finally the respondent's counsel will present his closing submissions including submissions on law, either orally or in writing as for the adversarial approach, and the claimant's counsel will follow with his closing submissions.

Although the inquisitorial system has the advantage that the evidence is generally confined to a search for the truth, in the author's experience the adversarial system has the advantage that it entails a much more comprehensive and thorough examination of the available evidence. Cross-examination is an excellent procedure to test the quality of evidence providing the ability of the advocates is well matched.

TECHNICAL AND LEGAL ASSISTANCE FOR THE ARBITRATOR

Under **Section 37** of the Arbitration Act 1996, the arbitrator can not only appoint but also request the attendance at the hearing of experts, technical assessors or legal advisers to assist him in understanding evidence or submissions and to advise him in connection with such evidence or submissions.

The arbitrator is obliged to give each party a reasonable opportunity to comment on any information, opinion or advice so offered before he acts on it.

For example if the arbitrator is a lawyer, he might find it very helpful to have the assistance of a technical assessor during expert evidence that was very technical in nature; equally a non-lawyer arbitrator might gain significant benefit from the assistance of a legal adviser sitting with him during complex legal argument.

Whatever assistance an arbitrator receives, the decisions he reaches must be his alone and not those of the adviser or assessor who has been assisting him.

An assessor or legal adviser will not sit throughout the hearing but only during those times when their expertise is required. There is of course no obligation on an arbitrator to avail himself of the opportunity of engaging legal or expert assistance. The use of legal advisers or technical assessors is the exception rather than the rule.

The fees and expenses of those assisting the arbitrator in this way are expenses of the arbitrator as far as the Arbitration Act is concerned.

BURDEN AND STANDARD OF PROOF

The party making an assertion has the burden of proof. It is not for a party to say the other side has not disproved what he says; each party must prove its own case and all of the facts and opinions on which it relies to establish that case.

In criminal cases, facts have to be proved beyond all reasonable doubt. That standard does not apply in arbitration. The standard of proof in arbitration as for all civil cases in court is the standard of **balance of probabilities**. In other words if conflicting evidence is weighed in the scale, the scale must tip down, however slightly, in favour of the party making the assertion if he wishes to prove his case. It is sometimes said that to prove a matter on a balance of probabilities means that it must be 51 per cent proved; this is rather simplistic but the facts must be established to be more probable than not, in order to be proved.

SECRET EVIDENCE

Witnesses who prepare witness statements but do not give evidence at the hearing

The arbitrator has to make up his mind on the basis of the evidence adduced at the hearing. If a party serves a witness statement but that witness does not give evidence at the hearing, the contents of the witness statement should be ignored.

Arbitrator's own opinions and expertise

Equally the arbitrator's own opinions are usually irrelevant; he must make his decision on the basis of the evidence given at the hearing alone. However if the arbitrator does have particular knowledge which he believes he may find it hard to ignore, he should put his opinions to the relevant witness and ask him to deal with them.

If the arbitrator makes a decision on the basis of his own opinions, he has, in effect, given evidence to himself. This is secret evidence which has not been brought into the open so that both parties can not have been given an opportunity to deal with it. It is likely to be held to be a serious irregularity for an arbitrator to act in this way and it is likely an award would be successfully challenged.

HEARINGS EX PARTE

Occasionally one party will choose to take no part in the hearing, or will have been so in breach of peremptory orders that the arbitrator will be entitled to proceed to an award on the basis of such materials as have properly been provided to him.

In such cases the party that is present will not be entitled to an award in the amount claimed merely because the other party is not present.

If one party fails to appear at a hearing of which proper notice has been given, the arbitrator should ask the party that is present to make inquiries of the other party to see if it has been unexpectedly delayed or there has been some confusion in the dates. If no satisfactory response is received, the arbitrator should adjourn the hearing and immediately issue a peremptory order that the hearing will take place on a date and time stated and if the absent party does not attend the hearing will continue in its absence, in other words *ex parte*.

Despite the party's non-attendance, the arbitrator should continue to copy all notices to it and give it the opportunity to be present if it so wishes.

The *ex parte* hearing will continue as if the other party was present. Assuming the claimant is present, the claimant's witnesses will be called in turn, prove their witness statements, and the arbitrator will ask any questions of clarification. There will obviously be no cross-examination in the absence of the respondent. The arbitrator must take particular care not to adopt the role of cross-examiner.

When all the witnesses have been called, the claimant will present his closing submissions and the arbitrator will go away to prepare his award in the normal way.

CHAPTER 11

THE AWARD

The arbitrator has power to make more than one award and make awards at different times on different aspects of the matters to be determined. Each award is complete in itself; it is a final decision on the matters to which it relates.

CHOICE OF LAW

The case must be decided in accordance with the law chosen by the parties as applicable to the substance of the dispute, or in accordance with such other considerations as are agreed by the parties or, if the parties agree, by the arbitral tribunal. Conflict of laws is not a subject for a text book at introductory level and in general will not cause difficulty as the law of the contract will be clear.

The Arbitration Act 1996 does not demand that the dispute must be decided in accordance with the laws of England and Wales or Northern Ireland. The Arbitration Act 1996 is relevant because the law of the arbitration is that of England and Wales or Northern Ireland. The law of the arbitration must be distinguished from the law of the contract. Unless otherwise agreed the award must be in accordance with the law of the contract.

Thus, for example, it would be possible to conduct an arbitration in London using the Arbitration Act 1996, but the contract might be subject to the law of South Korea. Unless otherwise agreed the decision in the award therefore has to be in accordance with the law of South Korea despite that the procedural law of the arbitration is English.

PROVISIONAL ORDERS, PARTIAL AWARDS AND FINAL AWARDS

Provisional orders

Subject to the parties' express agreement the arbitrator can be given power to make **provisional orders** in respect of any relief which he would have power to grant in a final award. This is detailed in **Section 39** of the Arbitration Act 1996. The side note to Section 39 is confusing in that it refers to "Power to make provisional awards". The text of the Act does not empower arbitrators to make provisional awards, but to make **orders for provisional relief** in respect of any matter that could be covered in a final award.

There is a distinct difference between an order and an award. An award is final on the matters it addresses, whereas an order can be changed at a later date. The power in Section 39, which is not a default power, is only available if the parties expressly agree.

If the arbitrator is so persuaded, he can, for example, order money to be paid, property to be disposed of, or order an interim payment on account of costs. Such orders are provisional and subject to the arbitrator's final decision in his final award which must take account of any provisional order under this Section.

Partial awards

Partial awards are, as their name suggests, final awards on one or more but not all of the matters in dispute. There can be any number of partial awards. A partial award cannot be reviewed later; it is not a provisional award. In any partial award the arbitrator must specify the issues that are being dealt with and will be wise to identify those issues that are reserved to a further partial award or his final award. Partial awards, sometimes called **interim awards**, are permitted by **Section 47** of the Arbitration Act 1996.

Examples of partial awards are awards on liability but not quantum and costs, or awards on liability and quantum but not costs. A partial award will also be appropriate on a preliminary issue or preliminary point of law.

Final awards

A **final award** is the last or final award an arbitrator will make on the substantive issues before him for decision. It will deal with all remaining issues before him. It must deal with interest and costs. Final awards cannot be reviewed at a later date.

REMEDIES AVAILABLE IN AN AWARD

The following remedies are available to an arbitrator under **Section 48** of the Arbitration Act 1996:

- to make a declaration as to any matter

- to order payment of money in any currency

- to order a party to do or to refrain from doing anything in the same way as the court

- to order specific performance (except contracts relating to land) in the same way as the court—for example to deliver a consignment of timber, or to rectify defects

- to order rectification, setting aside or cancelling a deed or other document in the same way as the court.

Other remedies can be given to the arbitrator by consent.

INTEREST

Under **Section 49** of the Arbitration Act 1996, the arbitrator has a very wide discretion as to the award of interest. He can award **simple or compound interest** from such dates and at such rates as he considers meets the justice of the case. In respect of compound interest the arbitrator can compound the interest at such rests as he considers appropriate. However such wide powers must always be exercised judicially, that is in the way a judge would correctly exercise those powers if they were available to him.

Rate of interest

The rate of interest chosen should, as far as possible seek to compensate the injured party for being stood out of the money awarded during the period of interest awarded. It will be appropriate generally to award commercial rates of interest at perhaps 1 per cent or 2 per cent above relevant bank base rates. The arbitrator may need to make his own inquiries as to the base rate changes during the relevant period.

From what date?

Equally interest should not be awarded from a date prior to when money was properly due. No interest should be awarded on general damages, that is money awarded for disappointment, pain and suffering or the like; the award should reflect current levels of compensation. Interest should also not be awarded on sums in respect of which expenditure has not yet been incurred, for example where estimates have been provided for the cost of repairs; the award should reflect the current estimate of the cost of repairs without interest. There can be no assumption that interest rates reflect the rate of inflation.

Interest can be awarded on the whole or any part of the sum awarded in respect of any period up to the date of the award. If money was claimed originally in the arbitration but part has been paid prior to the award, the arbitrator can award interest in respect of any period up to the date of payment.

Simple or compound?

The decision as to whether to award simple or compound interest must be assessed afresh in each case. As interest is essentially compensatory in nature, it will be appropriate to award compound interest if the injured party has had to borrow money as a result of the matters complained of in the arbitration and has incurred compound interest in respect of those borrowings. The rests for compounding will reflect the rests imposed by the lender of the money borrowed. Banks will impose monthly or quarterly rests depending on the amount of the borrowings and the status of the borrower. Evidence will normally be required as to whether money has been borrowed, the amount of borrowing at any time, the rates of interest incurred and the compounding rests applied.

If the arbitrator finds that the cost of the injured party being stood out of the money it is awarded is the interest it would have earned on deposit, then the interest rate awarded can reflect that. The important factor is that interest must not be used in any punitive way, either for or against the injured party.

After the date of the award

As well as pre-award interest the arbitrator has power to award simple or compound interest from the date of the award (or any later date) to the date of payment at such rates and with such rests as the arbitrator considers meets the justice of the case. He can also award interest on costs.

Amounts paid late but before arbitration commenced

The only interest an arbitrator cannot award is in respect of money due, paid late but before the commencement of arbitral proceedings. If money was due, was paid late, but was paid before arbitration proceedings were commenced, the arbitrator has no power to award interest on the late payment except if there is a claim for **special damages**. Special damages are those damages which do not flow in the ordinary course of things but which are or ought to have been in the contemplation of the parties as a consequence of a breach of contract. To learn more about special damages, reference should be made to a text book on the law of contract.

COSTS

Liability for costs

In his final award, if not before, the arbitrator must deal with the liability of the parties for the costs of the arbitration including his own costs. It is unlikely that the arbitrator will determine the amount of the costs that are to be paid either for his own fees and expenses or for the parties' costs in his award as to the substantive issues. The arbitrator will determine who bears the costs and in what proportion.

Under **Section 61** of the Arbitration Act 1996 it is stated that the principle in arbitration, as with court cases, is that costs follow the event. This means that in principle the winner will be awarded his costs.

A party does not have to be awarded all it claims to be entitled to an award of costs; equally it does not have to succeed on each issue before the arbitrator.

For example, if the claimant obtains an award in its favour, then following the principle of "costs follow the event" and providing there are no other relevant factors, the award would state that "the respondent shall bear and pay the recoverable costs of the arbitration".

Costs on claim and counterclaim are dealt with separately providing the counterclaim really is a cause of action in itself and is not merely a set-off to the claim. The analogy given is of a sword and shield. If the counterclaim is merely a shield to ward off the claim then the costs of claim and counterclaim will be dealt with together; if the counterclaim is a sword which could have been started as a claim in its own right, then the costs will be dealt with separately. Except in the case of a pure set-off, the net result between the awards on claim and counterclaim is irrelevant.

Costs are dealt with in more detail below.

FORM, CONTENT, STYLE AND EFFECT OF AN AWARD

Form

An award has certain statutory requirements as to form:

• it must be in writing

• it must be signed by all the arbitrators or, in the event of disagreement, by all the arbitrators assenting to the award

• it must contain reasons except if it is an agreed award (award following settlement) or the parties have agreed to dispense with reasons

- the seat of the arbitration must be stated
- it must be dated.

Content

If the award is not to be challenged for serious irregularity it must also have certain characteristics as to content:

- all of the issues before the arbitrator must be dealt with
- it must be certain as to its effect
- it must not be ambiguous as to its effect
- it must comply with any agreed requirements as to form

and the following conditions must also be satisfied:

- it must not be obtained by fraud
- it must not be contrary to public policy
- the way the award was procured must not be contrary to public policy
- it should not be the subject of admission of irregularity by the arbitrator.

Effect

The effect of an award is to bring to an end the arbitrator's competence and authority to deal further with any of the issues decided in that award. In respect of these matters the arbitrator becomes what is known as *functus officio*.

The award is final and binding on the parties and on any persons claiming through or under them (**Section 58** of the Arbitration Act 1996). The award can only be challenged if the contract provides for a scheme of arbitral appeal or some other step is taken under the Act to challenge the award.

An award is also an instrument that can be used to enforce the decision against the losing party.

Style

In terms of style, an award will commence with identifying the statute under which it is made and any arbitration rules which apply. The parties will then be named fully and accurately and the precise matters out of which the arbitration reference arises will be identified. The award will state whether it is a partial award, and if so it should be identified by sequential number (for example, Partial Award No. 2), or whether it is the final award.

The award will then detail the contract out of which the arbitration arises including its date and any special characteristics. The law of the contract must be identified (for example, English law). The arbitration agreement, either within the contract or in a separate document, will be quoted in detail. The precise circumstances and details of the arbitrator's appointment will then be set out, followed by a summary of the meetings held and any important interlocutory procedures that have been dealt with including challenges to jurisdiction.

All earlier awards arising out of the same matter will be identified. If the award is partial, the precise matters dealt with in the award must be identified and all items to be dealt with in later awards should be summarised.

If there has been a hearing, that should be stated including the dates on which the hearing took place and who represented the parties.

Up to this point, what have been written are the **recitals** to the award.

The award will then deal with the matters in dispute, issue by issue. There is no right or wrong way to write an award, but it must be clear what the issue is that is being addressed, the key points of evidence in connection with it, clear findings of fact on matters in contention with a brief explanation or reasons for the decision, which might simply be that "I prefer the evidence of Mrs A to that of Mr B". If there is any relevant law that needs to be decided, the arbitrator should cite the authorities and any specific passages that are being relied on and come to a clear and concise decision.

Issues should be addressed in a logical way so that the award can be read as a well-reasoned and logical argument and conclusion. Care must be taken to make findings on all points in issue. Difficulties can arise where because of certain findings that have been made, other issues become irrelevant and decisions on them are not necessary. In such cases it may be appropriate at the end of the award to list those issues and the arbitrator's findings on them with very brief reasons. This may help the parties to decide whether or not to appeal.

Legal precedent

Particular skill is needed when dealing with legal authorities, which are usually decided cases that one or other of the advocates considers to impact favourably on his client's case or unfavourably on the case of the other party. The arbitrator must firstly ensure that he is given a full copy of the judgment, not just an extract. Many law reports provide a commentary which is a dispassionate précis of the important matters of principle decided by the court. Possible conflicts with other judgments will also be highlighted.

If the arbitrator is persuaded that the authority has not been superseded by any later decision of a higher court, he must decide whether it impacts directly, indirectly or not at all on the matters he has to decide. If the court judgment is not on all fours with the case being considered by the arbitrator and the facts are sufficiently different to call into question the applicability of the judgment, the arbitrator is entitled not to follow the precedent by a process known as **distinguishing the authority**.

If the arbitrator is minded to distinguish an authority, he must set out detailed findings of fact and cogently and fully explain why he has not followed the authority.

Conclusion of award

After all of the issues have been dealt with the conclusions in terms of any money award should be summarised and totalled. Interest must then be dealt with. Finally if this is an award which deals with costs there must be a clear decision as to who is to bear and pay what proportion of the costs of the arbitration. The costs of the arbitrator and any arbitral institution involved must not be forgotten.

Finally the decision is summarised and an order made, which if it concerns a money award must state who pays whom, how much and when. The award must also make it clear whether interest runs on the amount awarded after the date of the award and if so from when, at what rate, on what amount and whether interest is simple or compound, and if compound, the identity of the rests.

The arbitrator must also make provision for reimbursement of any fees and expenses paid to him to release the lien on the award by a party who is not responsible under the award to meet the full amount of the arbitrator's fees and expenses.

In conclusion the award should state the matters on which it is final and the matters on which decision is reserved for later awards.

The seat of the arbitration must be stated, the award must be dated and signed. It is often preferable to have the arbitrator's signature witnessed but this is not an absolute requirement.

NOTIFICATION THAT AWARD IS AVAILABLE AND READY FOR COLLECTION: LIEN

The arbitrator is obliged to notify the parties of his award by serving copies of it on them without delay after the award is made. An award is made when it is signed by the arbitrator, or if more than one, by the last of them. However the arbitrator is allowed to retain the award until the fees and expenses he demands have been paid either to him or into court.

Section 56 of the Act sets out the right of lien on the award.

The normal practice is for the arbitrator to write to both or all parties and notify them that the award is made and is available for collection on payment of his fees and expenses in the sum of £X. The party that thinks it has won will normally happily pay. As soon as funds have cleared, the arbitrator sends a copy of his award to each party.

If the party ordered to pay the arbitrator's fees and expenses in the award wishes to challenge the amount of the arbitrator's fees and expenses it may do so under **Section 28** of the Arbitration Act 1996 notwithstanding that the arbitrator has already received the full amount of the fees and expenses demanded by him. The court can order the arbitrator to repay such amount as it considers excessive after considering submissions from the challenging party and the arbitrator.

If, however, neither party is prepared to pay the sum demanded by the arbitrator for release of his award, either party may apply to the court under **Section 56(2)** of the Act which may order that the fees demanded shall be paid into court, and upon such payment into court, the arbitrator shall release the award to both parties. The court will determine the amount of fees and expenses to which it considers the arbitrator is entitled, pay that amount to him and return the balance to the applicant.

In either case, the court is bound to honour any agreement between the arbitrator and the parties as to the amount of his fees and expenses.

In circumstances where neither party takes up the award and no application is made to the court for the award to be released on payment into court of the amount demanded by the arbitrator, the arbitrator's only option to obtain his fees, in the absence of adequate or any security, is to sue the parties jointly and severally.

SETTLEMENT: AGREED AWARDS

More often than not arbitrations settle before a hearing is held or completed. In such cases the parties will advise the arbitrator of the settlement. The arbitrator should immediately terminate the substantive proceedings and if requested by the parties should record the settlement in the form of an agreed award which should expressly state that it is an award of the arbitrator.

There is no compulsion on the parties to record their agreement in the form of an agreed award and there will be cases where for commercially sensitive reasons the terms of settlement are kept strictly confidential. However there are advantages in having an agreed award in that it can be enforced just as any other award. Any court which is assessing (or taxing) the recoverable costs of the parties following a settlement will require to see an agreed award before any recoverable costs are assessed.

Settlement is covered under **Section 51** of the Act.

SEAT OF THE ARBITRATION

As stated above, all awards under the Arbitration Act 1996 must state the seat of the arbitration. The concept of the seat or place of arbitration is important in international arbitrations. It decides which procedural law should apply to the administration of the arbitration and the enforcement of the award. Part I (that is, the first 84 Sections) of the Arbitration Act 1996 only applies to those arbitrations whose seat is in England, Wales or Northern Ireland.

The seat is defined in **Section 3** of the Act as the juridical seat of the arbitration designated either by the parties, an arbitral institution or the tribunal if it is given express power to do so. The seat may be where the hearing is held, but not necessarily. Sometimes hearings are held in more than one country and the awards may be signed in yet further countries or even on aeroplanes flying between them. To avoid confusion as to what law is to be the procedural law of the arbitration, a seat is designated wherever different parts of the arbitration are conducted.

It will be sufficient for the parties to designate the seat of the arbitration as London; equally it could be England, Wales or Northern Ireland or any town or city within those three countries.

An arbitrator should not himself determine the seat of the arbitration in his award unless he is given or obtains the express permission of all parties to do so.

CORRECTION OF THE AWARD OR MAKING AN ADDITIONAL AWARD

Notwithstanding that an award is final as to the matters it addresses, the arbitrator does have limited power to make corrections to an award either of his own volition or on the application of one or more party. The power is only open for a limited time; if the arbitrator is minded to correct the award on his own volition, he has **28 days** from the date of the award to do so. If either of the parties makes an application for a correction, that application must be made within **28 days** of the date of the award and the correction shall be made within **28 days** thereafter.

Corrections are limited to the following:

• removal of a clerical mistake

• removal of an error arising from an accidental slip

• removal of an error arising from an accidental omission

• clarification of an ambiguity

• removal of an ambiguity.

In all cases, no corrections shall be made without first affording the other parties a reasonable opportunity to make representations to the arbitrator. In practice the arbitrator would write to the parties stating that he proposed to make a correction in terms set out and would invite written submissions within a period of time that would allow him to comply with the absolute time limit to make the correction.

It should be stressed that the arbitrator is not being given an opportunity to have second thoughts, merely to correct an obvious error or to clarify or remove an ambiguity. The arbitrator should not make any charge for corrections.

The corrections will form part of the award to which they relate.

Section 57 of the Arbitration Act 1996, as well as allowing limited corrections, permits an additional award in very limited circumstances. It allows an arbitrator on his own initiative or on the application of a party, within **56 days** of the date of the original award, to make an additional award to deal with any claims which were made in the arbitration but not dealt with in the award; this includes claims for interest or costs.

This appears to allow an arbitrator to deal with matters he accidentally overlooked in his award without the need to go to the expense and trouble of asking the court to remit the award to him for reconsideration.

It is interesting to note that under **Section 68 (2) (d)** of the Act, it is, or may be, a serious irregularity for the arbitrator to fail to deal with all the issues that were put to him. In the author's view it may be necessary for a party challenging an award on this ground to show good reason why it did not ask the arbitrator to make an additional award under **Section 57** before taking action to attack the award as any substantial injustice caused to the applicant might have been avoided if the arbitrator had been asked to make an additional award.

ENFORCEMENT OF AN AWARD

If arbitration awards could not be enforced, the whole system of arbitration would collapse. Indeed arbitration awards can be enforced in many countries in the world, providing those countries are signatories either to the **Geneva Convention** on the Execution of Foreign Arbitral Awards, signed by the United Kingdom in 1927, or the **New York Convention** of 1958 on the Recognition and Enforcement of Foreign Arbitral Awards.

In England, Wales and Northern Ireland there are two methods of enforcing arbitral awards:

- action on the award

- under **Section 66** of the Arbitration Act 1996; or for foreign **New York Convention** awards, under **Section 101 (2)**.[1]

Action on the award

It is an **implied term** in any arbitration agreement that the parties promise to perform any valid award. If an award is not honoured, the aggrieved party can sue for breach of the implied term by an action on the award. It is likely that often there will be no defence to such an action and it will often be possible on the basis of affidavit evidence with a copy of the award to obtain **summary judgment** from the court fairly speedily.

Under Section 66 of the Act

Under this Section, an award may, providing **leave of the court** is obtained, be enforced as if it was a judgment of the court to the same effect. Where leave is given, **judgment may be entered in the terms of the award.**

When an award will not be enforced

The only statutory reason why judgment will not be entered is if it can be shown that the arbitrator lacked substantive jurisdiction and that the right to challenge jurisdiction has not been lost through failure of the challenging party to take the point earlier. There will however be other reasons why an award may not be enforced; these will include cases where the award is obviously defective in form or

---

1 New York Convention awards are defined in Section 100 of the Arbitration Act 1996.

content or where there may be some question of fraud or collusion. It is unlikely that an award will be enforced while there is an outstanding challenge to it in court, although the court may wish to secure the amount awarded pending the outcome of the challenge.

Procedure for enforcement

Proceedings to enforce an award under **Section 66** can be taken in the High Court or any county court.[2] The procedure is set out in Order 73 rule 31 of the Rules of the Supreme Court, currently contained in the Rules of the Supreme Court (Amendment) 1996[3] Briefly the procedure is as follows:

• the applicant has to apply for leave to enforce the award in the same manner as a judgment; the application can be made to the **High Court**, either at the **Royal Courts of Justice** in London or to any **district registry** or to **any county court**

• the application for leave can be made *ex parte*, that is without service on the party or parties against whom the award is sought to be enforced (the respondent)

• if an *ex parte* application is made the court may order the application to be served on such parties to the arbitration as it may specify

• the applicant has to complete a special court form—form 8A, known as an **Arbitration application**

• the applicant has to serve an affidavit which must state the name and the usual or last known place of residence or business of the applicant and of the person against whom it is sought to enforce the award respectively, stating, as the case may require, either that the award has not been complied with or the extent to which it has not been complied with at the date of the application

• the affidavit must be accompanied by the arbitration agreement and the original award or, in either case, a copy thereof

• where the applicant applies to enforce an **agreed award** within

2 The High Court and County Courts (Allocation of Arbitration Proceedings) Order 1996 (S.I. 1996/3215)—Section 4. See Appendix 3.
3 See Appendix 4.

the meaning of **Section 51 (2)** of the Arbitration Act 1996, the application must state that the award is an agreed award and any order made by the court must also contain a statement to such effect

• there is no requirement for the other party or parties to acknowledge service or to serve affidavits in rebuttal at this stage

• a court order giving leave must be drawn up by or on behalf of the applicant

• the court will consider the application, usually without a hearing; the judge will satisfy himself that all the documents are in order and seal the court order

• the applicant must serve the sealed court order on the party against whom he wishes to enforce the award by delivering a copy to him personally or by sending a copy to him at his usual or last known place of residence or business or in such other manner as the court may direct

• within 14 days after service of the order, the respondent may apply to set aside the order and the award shall not be enforced until after the expiration of that period or, if the respondent applies within that period to set aside the order, until after the application is finally disposed of: the applicant is obliged to point out the rights of the respondent to seek to set aside the order and the award when he serves the court order on him

• if no application is made to set aside the court order and award within the stated 14 days, or if an application is made but is unsuccessful, the court will enforce the award exactly as a judgment of the court.

Under Section 101 (2) of the Act

International arbitrations and the problems of enforcement of foreign arbitral awards are outside the scope of this book. The procedure for enforcement of New York Convention awards in England, Wales and Northern Ireland is very similar to that described above under **Section 66**. The essential differences are set out in the Arbitration Act 1996 in **Sections 101 to 104** inclusive.

EXAMPLE OF AN AWARD

Because of the limitation of space, the example is of an actual simple arbitration arising from a package holiday contract under one of the arbitration schemes administered by the Chartered Institute of Arbitrators. The arbitration was dealt with on documents only, that is without a hearing. Names have obviously been changed.

In the matter of the Arbitration Act 1996 and in the matter of an arbitration under the Rules of the Arbitration Scheme for the Association of British Travel Agents
(19.. Edition)
between

Party A	**Claimant**
and	
Party B	**Respondent**

Arbitrator's Final Award

1. On or about 21 May 1997 the Claimant entered into a contract with the Respondent whereby for the sum of £682.00 the Respondent would provide a 14 night self-catering package holiday at the Tranquil Studios, Silencia, Corfu. The party was two people, the Claimant and his wife.
2. The Claimant and his wife flew from London Gatwick to Corfu and return. The holiday price included transfers from the overseas airport to the Studios and return, the use of a studio and also the services of the Respondent's representative in resort. The holiday was featured in the Respondent's Wonderful Greek Islands brochure for Summer 1997.
3. The cost of the holiday was £341.00 per person making £682.00 in all.
4. The date of departure from England was the evening of 8 June 1997, returning in the early hours of the morning on 23 June 1997.
5. During the holiday certain events occurred which have resulted in a dispute arising between the parties.
6. Such dispute has not been amicably settled and has been referred to arbitration in accordance with the Chartered Institute of Arbitrators Scheme for the Association of British Travel Agents.
7. The parties to the arbitration have agreed that the arbitrator will make his award with reference solely to the documents submitted by the parties for transmission to the arbitrator.
8. On 12 January 1998 a Vice-President of the Chartered Institute of Arbitrators appointed me, Piers Brocklesparrow, FCIArb and of the Chartered Institute of Arbitrators' Register of Arbitrators, to act as arbitrator in the reference. I received the letter of appointment on 15

January 1998 and accepted the appointment in writing on the same day.

9. Under Rule 7(vii) of the Scheme referred to in Paragraph 6 above, and under Section 52(4) of the Arbitration Act 1996, I am required, unless the parties otherwise agree, to set out the reasons in my award.

History

10. The facts in this case are relatively straightforward and not materially in dispute. The Claimant and his wife had booked this particular holiday in this resort for two primary reasons, they knew Silencia was a quiet resort and they were attracted by the Respondent's brochure description of the Studios as being in a quiet area on the edge of town and in a tranquil setting. This is just what they were looking for, namely a quiet and restful holiday.

11. All went well initially, indeed the first week seems to have passed without incident or complaint.

12. On 15 June 1997, two young men, also on holiday with the Respondent, arrived at the Studios and were allocated an adjacent studio. The evidence of the Claimant, which is not contradicted, is that at some time before midnight extremely loud music could be heard coming from the studio allocated to the young men; the music continued at that volume until 04.00 or 05.00 the next morning.

13. Complaints were made to the Respondent's representative and the young men were spoken to. The next night exactly the same thing happened and again on the third night for similar times on each occasion and always at what the Claimant describes as an intolerably loud volume. The evidence of the Claimant is that neither he nor his wife slept at all. He complained each morning even though it involved a long walk to the Respondent's representative's office. On each occasion the young men were spoken to.

14. After the third noisy night, the Respondent's representative confiscated the audio equipment that was being used to amplify the music. I am told that the following night was characterised by equally loud singing from the same studio and that again sleep was impossible.

15. The fifth night was reasonably quiet.

16. On the sixth night there was a great deal of noise and the sound of vomiting which against prevented much sleep.

17. During the next day the audio equipment was returned by the Respondent's representative and the noise of very loud music was heard again during a considerable portion of the next and indeed last night, during which the Claimant tells me he had little or no sleep.

18. Complaints were made daily to the Respondent's representative but without success. The Claimant's evidence is that he had booked excursions but was so tired during the day that any benefit and enjoyment was entirely spoiled.

19. The Claimant tells me that any benefit be enjoyed from the first week was totally erased by the events of the second week and by the end of the holiday he was exhausted and in need of another holiday.

20. In particular the Claimant draws my attention to the Respondent's brochure. In the conditions under a heading of "Your commitment to us" the Claimant relies on paragraph 6 which states "*We reserve the right to decline to accept or retain any person as a client if their conduct is disruptive and affecting the enjoyment of other holidaymakers, and we shall be under no liability for any extra costs incurred by such a person as a result of our doing so.*" The Claimant also refers to the section in the brochure dealing with caring for the environment, where under a heading of "Respect the rights of others" it states "*We all enjoy some peace and quiet on holiday. Loud noise can be annoying, so please think of your fellow guests.*"

21. The Claimant states that in the exceptional circumstances of such excessive noise in a location that was advertised as being tranquil, the Respondent was under a duty to exercise its contractual right under paragraph 6 of the Conditions which I have quoted above to decline to retain the young men as clients after their failure to respond to initial requests for quiet at night, in the interests of the other guests. The Claimant's case is that the Respondent's failure to exercise its contractual right to effectively put an end to the noise, led to his holiday being completely spoiled and of no benefit to him or his wife whatever.

22. The Respondent, while not denying the facts, denies liability on the basis that the nuisance was completely outside its control and was not due to any failing on its part. They point out that they actioned every complaint that was made, but that the young men did not respond to the entreaties made. The Respondent also points out that accommodation owners sometimes strictly enforce the removal of nuisances, but did not do so in this case. The Respondent alleges that there has been no breach of contract and therefore no compensation should be awarded.

23. The Claimant claims a full refund of the price paid for the holiday, £682.00, although he alleges that his true loss is far greater if insurance, airport parking, excursions, the waste of a holiday and stress are taken into account.

Findings and Reasons

24. Although I have only summarised parts of the evidence above, I have read all of the submissions of both parties very carefully and have taken all the evidence into account in reaching my decision.

25. I am persuaded by the evidence of the Claimant that because of the excessive and unreasonable noise during six of the last seven nights in resort, the holiday was completely ruined and of no benefit to the Claimant or his wife at all. Indeed I find on the evidence that they both were more in need of a holiday when they returned than when they went. However a ruined holiday in and of itself is not sufficient to establish entitlement to compensation.

26. In my judgment, this is a case that primarily turns on the application of the relevant law. I hold that this contract is subject to the Package

Travel, Package Holidays and Package Tours Regulations 1992.

27. I hold that under Regulation 15(1) the Respondent is liable for the failure to provide the quiet and tranquil holiday promised. I hold that this Regulation applies a strict liability on the Respondent subject only to the defences available in Regulation 15(2).

28. Regulation 15(2) provides that in the event of failure to perform the contract or improper performance of it, the tour operator, the Respondent in this case, can avoid liability if it can prove that (b)— and I quote the relevant sub-section—"the failure is attributable to a third party unconnected with the provision of the services contracted for, and is unforeseeable or unavoidable".

29. The Claimant having persuaded me that there was a failure to provide the tranquil holiday promised, I hold that the burden of proof now switches to the Respondent to establish that the potential defence in Regulation 15(2) should bite.

30. I hold that the Respondent must firstly prove that the failure to perform was attributable to an unconnected third party and secondly that the particular nature of the failure to perform was either unforeseeable or unavoidable.

31. On the basis of the evidence I find that the failure to provide the quiet and tranquil surroundings was attributable to the young men who played loud music into the night. I hold that the said young men were parties unconnected with the provision of the services contracted for and therefore the Respondent succeeds in the first leg of the matters it must prove to gain protection from the possible defences in Regulation 15(2).

32. I am not persuaded from the evidence that the disturbance caused by the young men playing loud music was unforeseeable. Indeed the Respondent sought fit to provide contractual powers to remove any holidaymakers causing such a nuisance in its standard conditions in the brochure. Further the section in the brochure from which I quoted earlier dealing with "Respecting the rights of others" reinforces the foreseeability of just such an event.

33. I also find that the Respondent fails on the unavoidability test. It was in the Respondent's power and control to allocate young people to accommodation and in resorts suitable for them. It is admitted that the young men were allocated to the Studios on a Square Deal package where the tour operator allocates accommodation to the arriving holidaymakers at the overseas airport. The Respondent should have known better than to allocate two young men to accommodation advertised as being quiet and tranquil.

34. Further I find that the Respondent could and indeed should have exercised the powers given to it by conditions to "decline to retain" the young men at the Studios after the first warning was not heeded. Had the Respondent properly exercised those powers the disturbance would have been restricted to two or maximum three nights. I therefore hold that the failure to provide the quiet and tranquil holiday promised was not unavoidable.

35. Therefore I hold that the Respondent has failed to prove either alternative of the second leg of the proof required to succeed with a defence under Regulation 15(2) and is therefore liable to the Claimant for compensation under Regulation 15(1) as I have found above.

36. On the basis of my finding of a total failure of consideration due to the holiday being of no benefit whatever to the Claimant and his wife, I hold that the Claimant is entitled to recover the full cost of the holiday, £682.00, and I so award.

37. Had the Claimant made a claim for incidental costs, mental distress damages or for interest, I would have so awarded in addition, but hold that under the rules of this arbitration scheme I am restricted to award not more than the sum claimed.

38. In exercising the discretion in Rule 12 of the Arbitration Scheme regarding the awarding of costs, I have a duty to act judicially. The normal rule under Section 61(2) of the Arbitration Act 1996 is that costs follow the event. As the Claimant has succeeded in his claim, he is entitled to his costs. Under the rules of this arbitration scheme I am restricted to ordering one party to pay the other a sum equivalent to the registration fee paid by the Claimant for this arbitration. I therefore award that the Respondent should refund to the Claimant his registration fee.

    NOW I, Piers Brocklesparrow, having carefully considered all of the submissions of the parties as set out in the documents provided to me, **HEREBY AWARD AND DIRECT as follows:**

39. The Respondent shall pay to the Claimant within 21 days of the date this award is delivered to the parties the sum of **£682.00** (six hundred and eighty two pounds only) as damages.

40. The Respondent shall further pay to the Claimant within 21 days of the date this award is delivered to the parties the sum of **£50.00** (fifty pounds only) being the registration fee paid by the Claimant in this reference.

41. The seat of the arbitration is London.

2 February 1998

Signed . . . .

Piers Brocklesparrow—Arbitrator

Witnessed by . . . .

Occupation . . . .

CHAPTER 12

COSTS OF THE ARBITRATION

Costs of the arbitration are defined in **Section 59** of the Arbitration Act 1996 as comprising:

- the arbitrators' fees and expenses,

- the fees and expenses of any arbitral institution concerned, and

- the legal or other costs of the parties.

Principles in awarding costs

There are certain general principles that govern the question of costs. If there is any agreement between the parties that one party is to pay the whole or part of the costs of the arbitration in any event, such agreement is invalid and unenforceable unless entered into after the dispute has arisen—reference **Section 60** of the Act.

The next principle is that the arbitrator has a very wide discretion as to the award of costs between the parties but he must act judicially and unless agreed otherwise, must follow the rule that **costs follow the event** unless there are circumstances to warrant a departure from that principle. The meaning of "costs follow the event" has been explained in the last chapter, but in general terms means that the winner gets his costs.

The principles that should guide an arbitrator in awarding costs are summarised below:

- the costs of the arbitration are within the arbitrator's **discretion**, and he may direct by and to whom and in what manner those costs or any part of them shall be paid

- he is obliged to exercise his discretion in relation to costs using the same principles that a judge should adopt; that is **judicially**

- **costs should follow the event,** except where it appears to the arbitrator that in the circumstances of the case, some other order should be made

- the general rule that costs should follow the event does not cease to apply simply because the successful party raises issues or makes allegations on which he fails

- where the successful party raises issues or makes allegations on which he fails and where that has caused a significant increase in the length or cost of the proceedings, he may be deprived of the whole or a part of his costs

- where the successful party raises issues or makes allegations improperly or unreasonably, the arbitrator may not only deprive him of his costs but may order him to pay the whole or a part of the unsuccessful party's costs

- where the successful party recovers significantly less than he claims, this of itself provides no justification for not awarding him all of his costs

- matters which may justify not awarding a successful party all of his costs include gross exaggeration of the claim, an offer by the unsuccessful party to compromise which the other party has unreasonably failed to accept, and extravagance in the conduct of the hearing.

OFFERS TO SETTLE

Principles

It is a fact that the majority of arbitrations settle before a final award; that is, the parties agree to compromise their dispute on agreed terms. The very existence of the arbitration proceedings acts as a catalyst to persuade each party to take a more realistic view of their chances of success.

In larger cases the amount of costs incurred by each party on legal and expert fees is a very significant item of expenditure and it is possible, where parties are intransigent, for costs to exceed the amount awarded or possibly even the amount in dispute. Arbitration is a commercial way to resolve disputes and therefore it is no surprise that the parties will wish to act commercially.

As costs can be so significant, the parties will wish to protect their position in costs. They do this by making offers to compromise claims made against them, but under cover of **privilege**. This means that the existence of the offer cannot be disclosed to anyone other than the parties themselves and in particular not to the arbitrator.

The principle behind the making of offers is that if a party achieves less by continuing with the arbitration to an award than he would have achieved by accepting an offer made before the award, it is unjust to require the party making the offer to pay the costs of the other party from the time when the offer should have been accepted. Further, justice demands that the party who should have accepted the offer at the time it was made, should pay not only his own but also the costs of the other party from the date when the offer should have been accepted.

In court offers to settle are dealt with by the offeror **paying the amount offered into court**. The other party then has 21 days to accept the offer by taking the money out of court; if it does not take the money out within 21 days, it has to seek the leave of the court to do so on terms imposed by the judge.

There is no equivalent to payment into court in arbitration; no money changes hands; the offer is purely a paper transaction. There are three common ways in which an offer to settle can be made in arbitration—**open offer, sealed offer** and **Calderbank offer.**

Open offers

Open offers are letters from one party to the other making an offer to compromise the dispute or part of it, in respect of which no privilege is sought or claimed or privilege has been waived. Open offers are not helpful for arbitrators as they are likely to be in the bundle of papers sent to him. The very fact that he knows the content of an offer might influence him in his decision. Even if it did not, an impartial observer might conclude that he was likely to be influenced by its contents. As discussed in earlier chapters, an arbitrator has to develop the ability to **put things out of his mind** and open offers are a prime example.

Open offers are fortunately very rare in commercial cases, but they are a common feature of consumer arbitrations carried out on a **documents only** basis. For example in a holiday arbitration, it is quite common for the papers to contain an offer by the holiday company to compromise the dispute by an offer of vouchers giving a discount off a future holiday, or by a cash offer. The arbitrator must put these offers out of his mind until he comes to consider the question of costs.

Sealed offers

Sealed offers are without prejudice offers of which both parties are aware. At some time during the hearing, before the arbitrator goes away to write his award, he will be given a sealed envelope and be asked not to open it until he has completed all of the substantive parts of his award but before he comes to deal with costs. The envelope will contain a copy of the offer.

When the arbitrator has completed his award on liability and quantum, including interest, he will open the envelope before he deals with costs.

This is a very old-fashioned method of dealing with offers to settle in arbitration and is rarely used today. The disadvantages are less than with an open offer, but the very existence of an envelope may influence the arbitrator to think that a claim has more merit than the evidence would have led him to believe it has, and therefore to be influenced to make an award in the claimant's favour because he knows there is an offer to settle. There also may be perceived to be a temptation for an arbitrator to open the envelope before he should do, or for an arbitrator to alter his award on substantive issues after he has opened the envelope and seen the offer.

These potential disadvantages can be reduced by the parties telling the arbitrator that the envelope might contain an offer or it might contain a note saying that there is no offer.

A normal **without prejudice offer,** which is not treated as a sealed offer or qualified as a Calderbank offer, cannot be disclosed to the arbitrator at any time and is therefore usually incapable of offering any protection in costs.

Calderbank offers

This type of offer is so called after a court case *Calderbank* v. *Calderbank*[1] involving a divorce settlement between Mr and Mrs Calderbank. The facts are unimportant save that the case gave rise to approval of a special type of offer to settle which can be identified by the words **"without prejudice save as to costs"** prominently displayed on it.

The offer is privileged and remains privileged until the arbitrator is asked to deal with costs when it loses its privilege and becomes an open document. It is an exception to the rule that no further evidence can be adduced once the arbitrator has made his award. The way it works is this:

- the offer is made on a "without prejudice save as to costs" basis, with a period of time given for acceptance, usually 21 days

- the offer is not accepted and the case proceeds to a hearing

- at the hearing the parties adduce all of their evidence and argument on liability, quantum and interest but do not make submissions on costs

- the arbitrator is asked to make a partial award on liability and quantum only but not to deal with costs

- the arbitrator makes his partial award

- the hearing is then reconvened and submissions are made on costs; the Calderbank offers will then be given to the arbitrator

- the arbitrator produces his award on costs, either as a further partial award or as his final award.

Calderbank offers are now the best and preferred method of dealing with offers to settle in arbitration. They have the following significant advantages:

- the arbitrator knows nothing of the offer until he has already made a final decision by award on the substantive issues between the parties: there can therefore be no temptation to be influenced by an offer nor can it be perceived that he might be so influenced

1 [1975] 3 All ER 333.

- Unlike a payment into court, the offeror does not have to find the cash at the time of the offer.

Features of a Calderbank offer

The following are typical features of a Calderbank offer letter:

- it is prominently marked "without prejudice save as to costs"

- it offers to pay a specified amount of money (or more unusually to perform some act) in full and final settlement of all or a specified part of the disputes between the parties in arbitration

- the offer includes interest up to the date of the offer and during the period for acceptance

- the offer is open for acceptance for (usually) a period of 21 days from the date of the offer—shorter periods are often used if the offer is made during the course of the hearing or less than 21 days prior to its commencement

- the offeror offers to pay the recoverable costs of the party receiving the offer up to the date of the offer and in addition to pay the recoverable costs of considering the offer; such costs to be determined by the arbitrator if not agreed

- following expiry of the period for acceptance, the offer will remain open for acceptance but on the following terms: interest will only run until the expiry of the period for acceptance; the party in receipt of the offer must agree to pay the offeror's costs from the expiration of the period for acceptance until the date of acceptance of the offer; there is commonly a condition that such costs are to be paid on an indemnity basis (that is, all costs actually incurred are recoverable unless they are unreasonable)

- in order to tempt acceptance of the offer, an offeror may sometimes set down a formula by which the offer reduces by a set amount each week after the expiry of the initial period for acceptance.

It is a feature of English law that an offer can be withdrawn at any time prior to acceptance; it is possible, therefore, to withdraw an offer to settle prior to acceptance.

If circumstances demand, a second or subsequent Calderbank offer can be made.

THE EFFECT ON COSTS OF AN OFFER TO SETTLE

Offer less than the amount awarded

If the award is for a sum greater than the amount offered, then the offer will have no effect on the costs award. The party in receipt of the offer was justified in rejecting the offer and continuing with the arbitration.

The only matter which might need to be considered is that great care must be taken to compare the offer and the award on a like for like basis. This can be best illustrated by example.

The respondent offers the sum of £100,000 to settle on 1 April 1997. The claimant rejects the offer and continues on with the arbitration and eventually on 1 October 1999 obtains an award for £120,000. On the face of it the claimant has been justified in rejecting the offer and continuing with the arbitration as he has been awarded 20 per cent more money than he was offered.

The award in October 1999 will contain interest and therefore the true comparison is the offer against the sum which would have been awarded at the time the offer was made. Therefore to make a proper comparison the sum of £120,000 awarded in October 1999 has to be reduced to April 1997 levels. Let us say that the average rate of interest awarded during that period is 10 per cent compound with annual rests. If the £120,000 awarded is reduced to April 1997 levels, the equivalent amount awarded at that date would have been in the order of £94,450. The offer in April 1997 was £100,000.

Thus, if a true like for like comparison is made, the offer actually exceeds the award and therefore should have been accepted in April 1997.

An **offer that is almost as much as the amount awarded** when compared on a like for like basis will not have any effect on costs. The comparison between the offer and the award should be strict; near enough is not good enough. Any consideration of what costs might have been recoverable should also have no effect on the comparison which is made.[2]

---

2 *Everglade Maritime Inc* v. *Schiffahrtsgesellschaft Detlef von Appen mbH ("The Maria")* [1992] 3 All ER 851.

For example, recoverable costs will usually be in the order of 75 per cent of the actual costs incurred, the other 25 per cent or thereabouts being unrecoverable. Let us say, comparing like with like, that an offer was £100,000 and the amount awarded was £105,000. On the face of it the winning party was justified in rejecting the offer of £100,000 because it has achieved a better result by continuing. Let us say that the winning party's costs after it rejected the offer were £30,000. When those costs are assessed to see how much is recoverable, it may be that 25 per cent will prove to be unrecoverable, namely £7,500. Therefore it could be argued that the winner received less in cash terms, having taken into account the issue of unrecoverable costs, than it would have received had it accepted the original offer of £100,000.

Attractive as that approach might appear, the decision in "*The Maria*"[3] is that costs should be ignored when an arbitrator considers whether an offer is of such magnitude that it has an impact on the costs award.

Offer equal to or greater than the sum awarded

If, applying the like for like comparison outlined above, the offer is equal to or greater than the amount awarded, then the offer should have been accepted when it was made, nothing has been gained by continuing; all of the costs incurred since the offer should have been accepted have, in effect, been wasted and unnecessary.

In his award the arbitrator will adopt the following principles in awarding costs:

• the party in receipt of the offer will be awarded its costs up to the date of the receipt of the offer

• that party will also be awarded its costs of considering the offer

• with the exception of the costs of considering the offer, all costs from the date of receipt of the offer will be awarded to the offeror.

When a party is awarded costs, it is entitled to receive its own recoverable costs. The definition of recoverable costs is dealt with below. In addition the other party will have to bear its own costs.

3 *Supra.*

OFFERS WHERE THERE IS A CLAIM AND COUNTERCLAIM

The general position on awarding costs where there is a claim and counterclaim has been dealt with in Chapter 11.

Where there is a claim and counterclaim, an offer may be an attempt to compromise the claim, the counterclaim or both. If, for example, the offer solely relates to the counterclaim and does not mention the claim, then for costs purposes precisely the same tests apply as outlined above except the comparison is between the amount awarded on the counterclaim and the offer; the amount awarded on the claim is ignored.

There are however many occasions when an offer will be a single sum which is offered in an attempt to compromise both claim and counterclaim together. The normal procedure in awarding costs on claim and counterclaim is for the arbitrator first to decide whether the counterclaim really is a cause of action in itself and is not merely a set-off to the claim. If it is a cause of action in itself, then costs are normally awarded separately on claim and counterclaim.

A net offer dealing with claim and counterclaim does not therefore sit happily with this standard procedure as the offer is for the net balance as between claim and counterclaim. It may be possible to argue that a net offer between claim and counterclaim is not effective for costs protection because the recipient must be able to know what sum is offered on the claim and what sum is being allowed on the counterclaim.

In the author's view such an argument is not likely to succeed before the courts and it is likely that an offer on claim and counterclaim, which exceeds the net balance between the amounts awarded on claim and counterclaim, will be effective as costs protection. This runs contrary to the accepted practice of individual costs awards on claim and counterclaim.

THE EFFECT OF AMENDMENTS TO PLEADINGS OR STATEMENTS OF CASE ON OFFERS PREVIOUSLY MADE

An offer is deemed to be made on the basis of the case as currently pleaded at the date of the offer. If a pleading is subsequently amended and the offeror considers that in the light of the amended case it should increase its offer, it may do so providing it acts within a reasonable time after the amended pleadings have been served. **Costs protection will be backdated until the date for acceptance of the previous offer.**

Should this happen, a new Calderbank offer should be made on terms that the increased offer arises solely out of the amendment to pleadings. It will state that in addition to the amount offered, the offeror will pay the recoverable costs of the other party up to the date for acceptance of the most recent offer made before the amendment to pleadings. The offer will again remain open for acceptance for a stated period, usually 21 days.

PARTIES' COSTS

The legal or other costs of the parties will include **costs incurred since the notice of arbitration** was given and **may include costs incurred prior to that date** if the **sole or dominant reason** for incurring those costs was **in contemplation of arbitration**.

Parties' costs will include:

- solicitors' costs, expenses and disbursements

- similar costs in respect of a lay advocate (if a solicitor is not engaged)

- experts' costs, expenses and disbursements

- expenses of witnesses, but not salaries of in-house staff

- barristers' fees, brief fees and refreshers (the brief fee will be payable not long before the hearing starts and will include the fees for preparation and attendance at the first day of the hearing— refreshers are the daily amounts paid for barristers' attendance at the hearing after the first day)

- costs of hiring hearing rooms and expenses of a similar nature

- the costs of transcription services, shorthand writers, translation services, video conferencing and the like

- the costs of or incidental to any proceedings to determine the amount of the recoverable costs of the arbitration.

If a party to an arbitration seeks the **intervention of the court** in connection with arbitral proceedings, then the costs incurred in connection with the court proceedings are normally dealt with by the court and do not form part of the costs of the arbitration.

It is important that all those involved in arbitration keep very careful records of their time and expenses as at some time in the future their costs may come under scrutiny to see if they represent the amounts which can be recovered from the party ordered to pay the costs.

FEES AND EXPENSES OF ARBITRAL INSTITUTIONS

In many arbitrations there will be no costs of any arbitral institution. However it is common for appointments to be made by arbitral institution appointors. Those institutions will charge a fee for the appointment process, which will, of course, have been paid by the claimant when he requested an appointment. Such fees are part of the **costs of the arbitration** under the definition in **Section 59** of the Arbitration Act 1996.

Other arbitrations are administered by arbitral institutions who carry out most of the administrative tasks for the arbitrator and leave him to deal with contentious matters, the hearing and the award. A fee is charged for this service, which is often based on a percentage of the amount in dispute; both parties may be charged half each, or where the respondent will not pay the claimant may have to bear the whole cost. Examples are arbitrations carried out under the rules of the London Court of International Arbitration or the International Chamber of Commerce in Paris.

ARBITRATORS' FEES AND EXPENSES

The fees and expenses of the arbitrator will include:

• all fees incurred since appointment for his time, either on a daily or hourly rate basis or a combination of the two—only exceptionally will arbitrators charge on an *ad valorem* basis (fees based on a percentage of the amount in dispute)

- general expenses including any incidental expenses expressly not included in the hourly or daily rate

- travelling and hotel expenses

- translation services, if paid for by the arbitrator

- transcription costs, if paid for by the arbitrator, but only if the parties have expressly agreed that a transcription service should be provided

- the fees and expenses of tribunal-appointed experts or legal advisers

- the fees and expenses of any technical assessor

- the costs of or incidental to any proceedings to determine the amount of the recoverable costs of the arbitration.

If the **arbitrator is made a respondent to any application to the court** arising out of or in connection with the arbitration, any costs incurred in connection with the court proceedings will be dealt with by the court and will not form part of the costs of the arbitration.

COSTS OF THE ARBITRATION

As stated in the introduction to this chapter, the costs of the arbitration includes the parties' costs, the costs of any arbitral institution and the arbitrator's costs. Thus when the arbitrator deals with costs in his award he is including all of those three elements of costs.

INTERLOCUTORY COSTS

In Chapter 8 the subject of interlocutory costs was dealt with. It may be remembered that in respect of each order for directions the arbitrator will deal with costs. He may say any of the following:

- **costs in the arbitration**—this means that the costs of and in connection with that application and order will be awarded as part of the costs which **follow the event.** Other expressions which mean exactly the same are **costs in the cause** and **costs in the reference**

* **costs to be borne and paid by the claimant (respondent) in any event**—this might be shortened to **respondent's (claimant's) costs in any event**—this means that whatever the outcome of the arbitration, the costs of and in connection with that application and order will be paid by the claimant (respondent)

* **costs of, thrown away and consequential on the amendment shall be paid in any event by the claimant (respondent)**— this order has a similar effect to the last example and means that whatever the outcome of the arbitration the costs of, thrown away and consequential on the amendment to pleadings or statement of case will be paid by the claimant (respondent)

* **claimant's (respondent's) costs in the arbitration**—this means that if the claimant (respondent) is finally successful, the costs of and in connection with that application and order will be awarded as part of the costs which follow the event, but if that party is not successful, the claimant (respondent) will **not** have to pay the costs of the other party in connection with that application and order

* **no order for costs**—this means that whichever party is successful, the costs of and in connection with that application and order will not be recoverable by or against either party

* **costs reserved**—this means that the arbitrator has not yet decided how these costs should be allocated and will deal with them at a later date.

When the arbitrator deals with costs in any award, he must be careful to review all of his interlocutory orders and to make specific provision in the award confirming all unusual interlocutory costs orders.

DETERMINING THE RECOVERABLE COSTS OF THE PARTIES

This subject is covered in **Section 63** of the Arbitration Act 1996.

Determination of recoverable costs is, for practical purposes, a small arbitration in its own right. The arbitrator will have made his award on the substantive issues and will have awarded which party is to pay which proportion of the costs.

In determining the recoverable costs of the parties, the arbitrator will determine the amount of money each party is entitled to receive from the other in costs.

The parties are **free to come to an agreement** as to what costs of the arbitration are recoverable; the majority of recoverable costs applications will be resolved by agreement.

The **court has no power to determine the recoverable costs** unless the arbitrator does not determine the recoverable costs himself. In other words, the court is there only as a backstop.

Arbitrator's order for directions

After the award on the substantive issues, any party whose costs, in principle, are recoverable from the other party, either in whole or in part, will apply to the arbitrator for directions for the process of determination of the recoverable costs. After hearing both parties, usually by written representations, or exceptionally at a meeting called for the purpose, the arbitrator will set a timetable for the procedure to be followed. The following will be a typical arbitrator's **order for directions** in a case where part of the claimant's and part of the respondent's recoverable costs are to be determined:

- Not later than 3 May 1998 each party shall submit its respective **bills of costs** and a copy thereof to me and upon receipt of bills of costs from both parties I shall thereafter forthwith serve each party with a copy of the other's bill.

- Not later than 28 days from service of the respective bills of costs each party shall serve on the other a **notice of objection** to the bill of costs of the other party, setting out in detail the basis of objection to each amount challenged.

- Not later than 14 days from service of the respective Notices of Objection each party may serve a **notice in reply**.

- There will be a hearing on determination of recoverable costs with a time estimate of two days to be held at my offices on 2 and 3 July 1998. I will assess the bills on an item by item basis.

- I will publish a **partial award on recoverable costs** with costs of the process of determination of recoverable costs reserved for a final award on recoverable costs. All awards will be reasoned.

- Costs in the determination of recoverable costs process.

- Liberty to either party to apply.

Bills of costs

Each party will then prepare its own bill of costs. Unlike court procedure, there is no set format for the bill of costs in arbitration. The bill of costs must set down the work done, when it was done and who did it. The fees of counsel must be set out, including the brief fee and any refreshers (discussed above). The fees of experts are usually claimed as disbursements, but as expert's fees are often so significant in arbitration, they too must be set out in detail as described above. All other disbursements and expenses will be set out.

The bill of costs will show the hourly or daily rates claimed for each person identified on the bill of costs and if the rates have changed during the period the case has been running the dates of change must be shown.

Solicitors often charge at an hourly rate agreed with their client which is subject to a percentage uplift for what is known as "care and control". The percentage uplift will be 50 per cent—60 per cent on a simple case to perhaps 100 per cent on a complex case. In a solicitor's bill of costs, the percentage uplifts claimed for each type of work must be identified.

The amounts claimed in a bill of costs may not necessarily be identical to the amounts invoiced to the client, but it is a valid objection to a bill of costs to establish that individual items claimed are in excess of the amounts invoiced to the client. In other words, no party can recover more than he has actually paid or is legally due to pay. This is known as the **"indemnity principle"**. This principle has recently been reinforced by the Court of Appeal.[4]

---

4 *The General of Berne Insurance Company* v. *Jardine Reinsurance Management Limited* (12 February 1998, CA), *The Times,* 20 February 1998.

Notices of objection

There are a series of common objections to bills of costs:

• the hours spent are excessive

• work has been duplicated between fee earners

• the hourly rate claimed is too high

• the mark up for care and control is too high

• the cost of counsel is not justified

• the cost of leading counsel (QC) is not justified

• part of the work was unnecessary

• the costs claimed were not incurred on matters in respect of which the party who has prepared the bill was successful in costs.

Notices in reply

Notices in reply respond to the notices of objection.

Hearing on determination of recoverable costs

At this hearing the parties are usually represented by costs drafts-men, who are specialists in presenting bills of costs and objections to them. Costs draftsmen work primarily in the courts where the process of determining recoverable costs is known as **taxation**.

The presentation to the arbitrator is by oral submissions supplementing the written bills of costs, objections and replies. There is no oral evidence at hearings on recoverable costs, save in the most exceptional circumstances. Only those elements of the bills of costs that are in dispute are covered.

Each bill of costs, where there is a dispute, is examined item by item. Usually the hourly rates will be covered first as they will apply to many items in the bills of costs. Unlike a typical hearing on the substantive issues, the arbitrator will make his decision immediately on each point argued before him and will explain his decision and where necessary his reasoning orally and extemporarily. After hourly rates, the arbitrator will consider argument on all other items page by page and item by item, giving his decision on each point after he has heard both sides.

Thus at the end of the hearing on determination of recoverable costs, each party and the arbitrator will be able to work out exactly what amount has been determined as the recoverable costs.

Value Added Tax

If both parties are registered for VAT, no VAT will be shown or claimed on the bills of costs, as both parties will have recovered any VAT charged to them. If, however, the successful party is not registered for VAT, then the VAT which will have been incurred on professional fees will not be recoverable from HM Customs and Excise, and is therefore correctly claimable as part of the bill of costs.

Award on recoverable costs

The arbitrator will usually ask the parties to agree the amount of money he has awarded on the basis of his extemporary decisions at the hearing on recoverable costs. The arbitrator will normally, unless the parties otherwise agree having heard the reasons given orally, set out his reasons in the award on recoverable costs.

Subject to the right of the parties to agree otherwise, the arbitrator is required by **Section 63 (3)** of the Arbitration Act 1996 to state in his award the basis on which he has acted and the items of claimed recoverable costs and the amount referable to each. By "basis on which he acted", the Arbitration Act means the test that is applied to each item of claimed costs to see whether it is recoverable and if so in what amount.

The standard tests are set out in **Section 63 (5)** of the Act:

- the recoverable costs of the arbitration shall be determined on the basis that there shall be allowed a reasonable amount in respect of all costs reasonably incurred, and

- any doubt as to whether costs were reasonably incurred or were reasonable in amount shall be resolved in favour of the paying party.

Only in the most exceptional circumstances will any other test be applied. If in such exceptional case the arbitrator is persuaded that he should adopt a more generous basis of determining recoverable costs, it will usually be on the following lines:

• the recoverable costs of the arbitration shall be determined on the basis that there shall be allowed all costs incurred except where unreasonable in amount or unreasonably incurred, and

• any doubt as to whether costs were unreasonably incurred or were unreasonable in amount shall be resolved in favour of the receiving party.

Finally the arbitrator will order one party to pay to the other the net balance of the recoverable costs he has awarded.

Costs of determining the recoverable costs

The normal rule is that the receiving party, namely the party whose bill is being assessed, is entitled to receive his costs of the determination process from the paying party. However even this can be complicated by the paying party making an offer to settle the bill of costs at an amount higher than the amount of recoverable costs awarded by the arbitrator.

As with the Calderbank procedure described above, the paying party will make an offer in writing which is headed "without prejudice save as to costs of determining the recoverable costs of the arbitration". Similar considerations apply as to Calderbank offers to settle the substantive issues in the arbitration as discussed above, but with one significant exception. The arbitrator will normally deprive the successful party of his costs of the process of determining the recoverable costs from the time when he should have reasonably accepted the offer to settle the amount of recoverable costs. However, it is only in exceptional circumstances that an arbitrator will order the successful party to pay any of the costs of the unsuccessful party even from the date when the offer to settle should have been accepted.[5]

In such circumstances, the effect will often be that from the date the offer should have been accepted, the arbitrator will make no award as to the parties' costs of determining the recoverable costs.

5 *Chrulew and others* v. *Borm-Reid & Co (a firm)* [1992] 1 All ER 953.

It is because of the possibility of offers to settle the costs that the arbitrator refers to a partial award on recoverable costs in his order for directions on determining recoverable costs. The arbitrator's final award on recoverable costs will deal with the costs of determining the recoverable costs. That award will bring the whole arbitration to an end.

Determination of recoverable costs by the court

The court can only become involved if the arbitrator fails to determine the recoverable costs himself. Even then any party may make an application to the court which has two options:

• it can determine the recoverable costs of the arbitration on such basis as it thinks fit, (but unless it determines otherwise, is bound to follow the basis set out in Section 63 (5) of the Act) or

• it can order that the recoverable costs of the arbitration be determined by such means and upon such terms as it may specify.

This second option indicates that the court has power to delegate the determination of the recoverable costs, perhaps to an experienced arbitrator not involved in the case.

DETERMINING THE ARBITRATOR'S RECOVERABLE FEES AND EXPENSES

This issue needs to be addressed from two directions:

• the arbitrator's personal entitlement to fees and expenses

• the amount of the arbitrator's fees and expenses that can be recovered as between the parties.

The arbitrator's personal entitlement to fees and expenses

The principles are as follows:

• if the arbitrator has made any agreement with the parties as to the rate of his remuneration or any other terms, then such agreement is sacrosanct and will not be altered by the court

- subject to the first point, the arbitrator is entitled to such reasonable fees and expenses (if any) as are appropriate in the circumstances (**Section 28 (1)** of the Arbitration Act 1996)

- any party may apply to the court which may order that the amount of the arbitrator's fees and expenses shall be considered and adjusted by such means and upon such terms as it may direct (**Section 28 (2)**)

- the court may order any excessive amounts already paid to the arbitrator to be refunded, but shall not do so unless it is shown that it is reasonable in the circumstances to order repayment (**Section 28 (3)**)

- the arbitrator may refuse to deliver an award except on full payment of his fees (**Section 56 (1)**)

- in such cases, before taking up the award, any party can apply to the court for the arbitrator's fees and expenses properly payable to be determined and the court shall do so by such means and upon such terms as it may direct (**Section 56 (2) (b)**).

Thus the court has power to determine the amount of the recoverable fees and expenses that the arbitrator may receive under both **Section 28 (2)** and **Section 56 (2)** of the Arbitration Act 1996. The arbitrator has no power to determine conclusively his own entitlement to fees and expenses.

The amount of the arbitrator's fees and expenses that can be recovered as between the parties

The amount of the arbitrator's fees and expenses that can be recovered as between the parties may not necessarily be the same amount as the arbitrator is entitled to recover personally. The process of determining the recoverable fees and the expenses of the arbitrator as between the parties is covered in **Section 64** of the Arbitration Act 1996.

The parties are free to agree the amount of the arbitrator's fees and expenses that are recoverable as between the parties. If they do not agree, the recoverable costs shall include, in respect of the fees and expenses of the arbitrator, only such reasonable fees and expenses as are appropriate in the circumstances (**Section 64 (1)**).

Any party which is not content may make an application to the court which has two options under **Section 64 (2)**:

- it can determine the recoverable fees and expenses of the arbitrators as between the parties or

- it can order that the recoverable fees and expenses of the arbitrators as between the parties be determined by such means and upon such terms as it may specify.

As before, this second option indicates that the court has power to delegate the determination of the recoverable costs, perhaps to an experienced arbitrator not involved in the case.

POWER TO LIMIT RECOVERABLE COSTS

This power has been discussed in Chapter 7 under item 33 of the agenda for the preliminary meeting.

Under **Section 65** of the Arbitration Act 1996 the arbitrator, unless the parties otherwise agree, may direct that the recoverable costs of the arbitration, or of any part of the arbitral proceedings, shall be limited to a specified amount which may be subject to subsequent review.

Section 59 establishes that the "costs of the arbitration" include the arbitrator's fees and expenses. Thus it might appear that if the arbitrator does limit or cap recoverable costs, he is also capping his own entitlement to fees and expenses. That is not a correct interpretation in the author's view because the relevant Section, namely **Section 64** of the Arbitration Act, does not cover the arbitrator's personal entitlement to fees and expenses, but rather covers the amount of the arbitrator's fees and expenses that can be recovered as between the parties.

Thus it is correct that unless the arbitrator qualifies that the cap on recoverable costs applies only to the legal or other costs of the parties, the cap may have the effect of preventing one party recovering against the other the full amount of the arbitrator's fees and expenses. The arbitrator's personal entitlement to fees and expenses is covered by **Section 28**.

The difficult question for arbitrators is to determine the level of the cap on recoverable costs. Experience will no doubt yield clues, but each case is likely to be unique and therefore any blanket formula is not likely to be appropriate in all cases. It has been suggested that a starting point might be to limit recoverable costs to 35 per cent of the amount in dispute.

CHAPTER 13

OTHER TYPES OF ARBITRATION

DOCUMENTS-ONLY ARBITRATIONS

Many arbitrations, perhaps a substantial majority in terms of numbers, proceed on the basis of exchange of written documents only. The arbitrator may hold a preliminary meeting, although there are many cases where even this does not happen. The parties will be ordered to prepare written submissions in turn. First the claimant will prepare a statement of claim and submissions and attach to it copies of all of the documents he intends to rely on; this will be followed by the respondent's defence and any counterclaim and submissions, which will also be accompanied by all of the documents he intends to rely on. Finally the claimant will have an opportunity to submit a written reply and, if appropriate, a defence to counterclaim, with any additional submissions, again accompanied by any further documents he wishes to rely on.

Once these written exchanges are complete, the arbitrator proceeds immediately to write his award on the basis of the submissions and documents in his possession. If the arbitrator needs clarification on any point, he may write to the parties to seek that clarification, but generally he will make his decision without further reference to the parties.

Documents-only arbitrations are used where limitation of costs is an important or overriding factor, such as in consumer disputes. It is also suitable in commercial contracts where there are no disputes of fact and the arbitrator has to decide on the interpretation of a document or decide a point of law.

Where there are conflicts of fact, documents-only arbitrations are difficult to operate, as the arbitrator does not have the benefit of seeing a witness cross-examined under oath or affirmation. Unless a witness's statement can be corroborated by contemporaneous documents it is very difficult to know which witness to believe if they are telling conflicting stories. It is said that one word-processor can lie as well as the next one.

Thus, if an arbitrator is asked to proceed on a documents-only basis, he will normally ask if there are likely to be any conflicts of fact. If there are likely to be such conflicts, and that is true of the majority of cases, then the arbitrator will usually insist on a hearing, in the absence of a contrary agreement between the parties.

COMMODITY—"LOOK-SNIFF" ARBITRATIONS

There are many disputes, particularly in the commodity field, that are purely disputes of quality. Does this shipment of grain comply with the specification and the agreed sample? Or does this machine tool produce components to meet the required tolerances and specification? Or does this plasterwork comply with the contractual requirements? Or does this consignment of coffee beans comply with the agreed quality sample?

These and many other questions of pure quality are best resolved by experts in the field. In such an arbitration, the parties will disclose to the arbitrator the relevant documents setting out the required specification and may show him the agreed sample. He will then look at the item or consignment in dispute and using his knowledge of the commodity and his experience will decide whether it complies with the requirements or not.

He may be asked to decide whether the material should be rejected in its entirety or whether it should be paid for at a lower price, and if so, what price.

Thus in these types of cases, the arbitrator is not making his decision on the basis of the evidence of the parties, he is looking or sniffing, using his own experience and knowledge, and coming to a decision based on his own opinion.

This type of case is the prime exception to the rule that an arbitrator should not normally take into account his own opinions unless he has explained those opinions to the parties and given them an opportunity to deal with them in evidence or submissions.

COUNTY COURT SMALL CLAIMS ARBITRATIONS

Most smaller civil court actions will be commenced in the county court. Parties have an option to request determination by arbitration and arbitration may be imposed by the district judge if he considers it appropriate. At the time of going to press, if a person issues a county court summons for less than £3,000 in England or Wales, £1,000 in Northern Ireland or £750 in Scotland, the case is automatically heard by a district judge as an arbitration instead of a normal court action.

However county court small claims arbitration is quite different from other forms of commercial arbitration. It is a creature of the **County Courts Act 1984** and is not governed by the Arbitration Act 1996—see **Section 92**. County court small claims arbitration essentially proceeds on an inquisitorial basis with the judge personally examining the parties or their witnesses. It is essentially informal in character and is intended to provide a cheap and effective way of disposing of small civil claims.

STATUTORY ARBITRATIONS

Many statutes, that is, Acts of Parliament, provide for disputes arising in respect of matters covered by that legislation to be resolved by arbitration. The main distinction between statutory arbitration and most other forms of arbitration is that the arbitration reference does not arise out of a contractual agreement between the parties but as a statutory obligation.

Examples of statutes which provide for certain disputes to be resolved by arbitration are:

• Agricultural Holdings Act 1986

• Agricultural Tenancies Act 1995

• Arbitration (International Investment Disputes) Act 1966

• Aircraft and Shipbuilding Industries Act 1977

• Building Societies Act 1986

• Channel Tunnel Act 1987

• Friendly Societies Act 1992

• Highways Act 1980

• Trade Union and Labour Relations (Consolidation) Act 1992

Section 94 of the Arbitration Act 1996 provides for Part I of the Act to apply to every statutory arbitration subject to certain exceptions which are set out in **Sections 95 to 98** inclusive.

One example of the exceptions is that an arbitrator under a statutory arbitration cannot rule on his own jurisdiction save as to whether the arbitration reference properly comes under the statute in question.

CONSUMER ARBITRATION AGREEMENTS

Consumers enter into contracts when they purchase durables, such as a television, perhaps on hire purchase, or when they engage a local tradesman to attend to some domestic emergency. Often those contracts will be in writing and they may be asked to sign an agreement with the back of the form covered in minuscule printing setting out the terms of the contract; few consumers bother to read such terms before signing.

Parliament passed the **Unfair Terms in Consumer Contracts Regulations 1994**, under which consumers are released from contract terms which are "unfair". An "unfair" term is one which is imposed on the consumer and unreasonably restricts their rights under the contract.

The Arbitration Act 1996, **Section 89**, provides that terms which constitute an arbitration agreement will, in certain circumstances, automatically be regarded as unfair.

Section 91 (1) of the Arbitration Act 1996 provides that if an arbitration agreement relates to a claim for an amount of money below a certain limit, it is automatically unfair. That limit is currently £3,000.

If the reference to arbitration relates to a claim in which the amount in dispute is over £3,000, it may or may not be unfair, according to the individual circumstances. If the arbitration agreement is held to distort the balance of rights and obligations between the parties to the detriment of the consumer, it may be regarded as unfair.

The effect is therefore that a consumer is not bound by an arbitration agreement which is automatically unfair or which may be held to be unfair and if the other party to the contract commences an arbitration against him, the consumer can rely on the Unfair Terms in Consumer Contracts Regulations 1994 to avoid the arbitration. Equally a consumer does not have to commence an arbitration if he has a dispute under a contract and the arbitration agreement comes under the definition of "unfair".

There is, however, nothing to prevent a consumer commencing or continuing with an arbitration if he so chooses; he merely cannot be compelled to do so in certain circumstances.

The Department of Trade and Industry have published a very helpful guide on this subject entitled "**Arbitration for Consumers and Small Businesses—Guide to the Arbitration Act 1996**".[1]

TRADE SCHEME ARBITRATIONS

The Chartered Institute of Arbitrators has many administered arbitration schemes affecting particular trades, industries and professions. These schemes have their own arbitration rules which modify certain non-mandatory Sections of the Arbitration Act 1996. The purpose of the Schemes is to resolve disputes in particular consumer fields; the most well known of the arbitration schemes is that run for the Association of British Travel Agents (ABTA) which provides a cheap and efficient means for resolving disputes between holidaymakers and package holiday companies.

The scheme rules are specifically adapted for the relevant trade or industry. Consumers only pay a small registration fee to refer their dispute to arbitration; the member of the trade organisation is obliged to pay a larger fee to the Chartered Institute, part of which goes to the arbitrator appointed and part is retained by the Chartered Institute for its administration.

If a dispute is referred to arbitration, the Chartered Institute collects the relevant fees and then arranges for each party in turn

1 Published by DTI Publications—ref: DTI/Pub 2605/1k/2/97/NP.URN 97/250.

to make written representations and to send in copies of all relevant documents. When all of the documents have been collected, the President or a Vice-President of the Chartered Institute of Arbitrators will appoint an arbitrator who has been specially trained and selected for suitability for appointment under that scheme.

The parties are notified of the appointment and the Chartered Institute sends to the arbitrator all of the documents it has received from the parties. The arbitrator will make his decision on documents only and when his award is made it is sent to the Chartered Institute for onward transmission to the parties.

Some of the Arbitration Schemes operated by the Chartered Institute of Arbitrators are:

- Association of British Introduction Agencies

- Association of British Travel Agents (ABTA)

- Automobile Association

- British Telecom

- Cellnet

- Coal Authority

- Denplan (dental insurance scheme)

- Glass and Glazing Federation (GGF)—(double glazing and replacement windows)

- National Association of Funeral Directors

- National House Building Council (NHBC)

- Personal Insurance Arbitration Service (PIAS)

- Post Office

- British Rail

- Royal Institution of Chartered Surveyors (RICS)

- Welsh Water.

ARBITRATION ACT 1996

General principles

1. The provisions of this Part are founded on the following principles, and shall be construed accordingly—

    (a) the object of arbitration is to obtain the fair resolution of disputes by an impartial tribunal without unnecessary delay or expense;

    (b) the parties should be free to agree how their disputes are resolved, subject only to such safeguards as are necessary in the public interest;

    (c) in matters governed by this Part the court should not intervene except as provided by this Part.

Scope of application of provisions

2.—(1) The provisions of this Part apply where the seat of the arbitration is in England and Wales or Northern Ireland.

(2) The following sections apply even if the seat of the arbitration is outside England and Wales or Northern Ireland or no seat has been designated or determined—

    (a) sections 9 to 11 (stay of legal proceedings, etc.), and

    (b) section 66 (enforcement of arbitral awards).

(3) The powers conferred by the following sections apply even if the seat of the arbitration is outside England and Wales or Northern Ireland or no seat has been designated or determined—

    (a) section 43 (securing the attendance of witnesses), and

    (b) section 44 (court powers exercisable in support of arbitral proceedings);

but the court may refuse to exercise any such power if, in the opinion of the court, the fact that the seat of the arbitration is outside England and Wales or Northern Ireland, or that when designated or determined the seat is likely to be outside England and Wales or Northern Ireland, makes it inappropriate to do so.

(4) The court may exercise a power conferred by any provision of this Part not mentioned in subsection (2) or (3) for the purpose of supporting the arbitral process where—

(a) no seat of the arbitration has been designated or determined, and

(b) by reason of a connection with England and Wales or Northern Ireland the court is satisfied that it is appropriate to do so.

(5) Section 7 (separability of arbitration agreement) and section 8 (death of a party) apply where the law applicable to the arbitration agreement is the law of England and Wales or Northern Ireland even if the seat of the arbitration is outside England and Wales or Northern Ireland or has not been designated or determined.

The seat of the arbitration

3. In this Part "the seat of the arbitration" means the juridical seat of the arbitration designated—

(a) by the parties to the arbitration agreement, or

(b) by any arbitral or other institution or person vested by the parties with powers in that regard, or

(c) by the arbitral tribunal if so authorised by the parties,

or determined, in the absence of any such designation, having regard to the parties' agreement and all the relevant circumstances.

Mandatory and non-mandatory provisions

4.—(1) The mandatory provisions of this Part are listed in Schedule 1 and have effect notwithstanding any agreement to the contrary.

(2) The other provisions of this Part (the "non-mandatory provisions") allow the parties to make their own arrangements by agreement but provide rules which apply in the absence of such agreement.

(3) The parties may make such arrangements by agreeing to the application of institutional rules or providing any other means by which a matter may be decided.

(4) It is immaterial whether or not the law applicable to the parties' agreement is the law of England and Wales or, as the case may be, Northern Ireland.

(5) The choice of a law other than the law of England and Wales or Northern Ireland as the applicable law in respect of a matter provided for by a non-mandatory provision of this Part is equivalent to an agreement making provision about that matter.

For this purpose an applicable law determined in accordance with the parties' agreement, or which is objectively determined in the absence of any express or implied choice, shall be treated as chosen by the parties.

Agreements to be in writing

5.—(1) The provisions of this Part apply only where the arbitration agreement is in writing, and any other agreement between the parties as to any matter is effective for the purposes of this Part only if in writing.

The expressions "agreement", "agree" and "agreed" shall be construed accordingly.

(2) There is an agreement in writing—
   (a) if the agreement is made in writing (whether or not it is signed by the parties),
   (b) if the agreement is made by exchange of communications in writing, or
   (c) if the agreement is evidenced in writing.

(3) Where parties agree otherwise than in writing by reference to terms which are in writing, they make an agreement in writing.

(4) An agreement is evidenced in writing if an agreement made otherwise than in writing is recorded by one of the parties, or by a third party, with the authority of the parties to the agreement.

(5) An exchange of written submissions in arbitral or legal proceedings in which the existence of an agreement otherwise than in writing is alleged by one party against another party and not denied by the other party in his response constitutes as between those parties an agreement in writing to the effect alleged.

(6) References in this Part to anything being written or in writing include its being recorded by any means.

The arbitration agreement

Definition of arbitration agreement

6.—(1) In this Part an "arbitration agreement" means an agreement to submit to arbitration present or future disputes (whether they are contractual or not).

(2) The reference in an agreement to a written form of arbitration clause or to a document containing an arbitration clause constitutes an arbitration agreement if the reference is such as to make that clause part of the agreement.

Separability of arbitration agreement

7. Unless otherwise agreed by the parties, an arbitration agreement which forms or was intended to form part of another agreement (whether or not in writing) shall not be regarded as invalid, non-existent or ineffective because that other agreement is invalid, or did not come into existence or has become ineffective, and it shall for that purpose be treated as a distinct agreement.

Whether agreement discharged by death of a party

8.—(1) Unless otherwise agreed by the parties, an arbitration agreement is not discharged by the death of a party and may be enforced by or against the personal representatives of that party.

(2) Subsection (1) does not affect the operation of any enactment or rule of law by virtue of which a substantive right or obligation is extinguished by death.

Stay of legal proceedings

Stay of legal proceedings

9.—(1) A party to an arbitration agreement against whom legal proceedings are brought (whether by way of claim or counterclaim) in respect of a matter which under the agreement is to be referred to arbitration may (upon notice to the other parties to the proceedings) apply to the court in which the proceedings have been brought to stay the proceedings so far as they concern that matter.

(2) An application may be made notwithstanding that the matter is to be referred to arbitration only after the exhaustion of other dispute resolution procedures.

(3) An application may not be made by a person before taking the appropriate procedural step (if any) to acknowledge the legal proceedings against him or after he has taken any step in those proceedings to answer the substantive claim.

(4) On an application under this section the court shall grant a stay unless satisfied that the arbitration agreement is null and void, inoperative, or incapable of being performed.

(5) If the court refuses to stay the legal proceedings, any provision that an award is a condition precedent to the bringing of legal proceedings in respect of any matter is of no effect in relation to those proceedings.

Reference of interpleader issue to arbitration

10.—(1) Where in legal proceedings relief by way of interpleader is granted and any issue between the claimants is one in respect of which there is an arbitration agreement between them, the court granting the relief shall direct that the issue be determined in accordance with the agreement unless the circumstances are such that proceedings brought by a claimant in respect of the matter would not be stayed.

(2) Where subsection (1) applies but the court does not direct that the issue be determined in accordance with the arbitration agreement, any provision that an award is a condition precedent to the bringing of legal proceedings in respect of any matter shall not affect the determination of that issue by the court.

Retention of security where Admiralty proceedings stayed

11.—(1) Where Admiralty proceedings are stayed on the ground that the dispute in question should be submitted to arbitration, the court granting the stay may, if in those proceedings property has been arrested or bail or other security has been given to prevent or obtain release from arrest—

(a) order that the property arrested be retained as security for the satisfaction of any award given in the arbitration in respect of that dispute, or

(b) order that the stay of those proceedings be conditional on the provision of equivalent security for the satisfaction of any such award.

(2) Subject to any provision made by rules of court and to any necessary modifications, the same law and practice shall apply in relation to property retained in pursuance of an order as would apply if it were held for the purposes of proceedings in the court making the order.

Commencement of arbitral proceedings

Power of court to extend time for beginning arbitral proceedings, etc.

12.—(1) Where an arbitration agreement to refer future disputes to arbitration provides that a claim shall be barred, or the claimant's right extinguished, unless the claimant takes within a time fixed by the agreement some step—

   (a) to begin arbitral proceedings, or
   (b) to begin other dispute resolution procedures which must be exhausted before arbitral proceedings can be begun,

the court may by order extend the time for taking that step.

(2) Any party to the arbitration agreement may apply for such an order (upon notice to the other parties), but only after a claim has arisen and after exhausting any available arbitral process for obtaining an extension of time.

(3) The court shall make an order only if satisfied—

   (a) that the circumstances are such as were outside the reasonable contemplation of the parties when they agreed the provision in question, and that it would be just to extend the time, or
   (b) that the conduct of one party makes it unjust to hold the other party to the strict terms of the provision in question.

(4) The court may extend the time for such period and on such terms as it thinks fit, and may do so whether or not the time previously fixed (by agreement or by a previous order) has expired.

(5) An order under this section does not affect the operation of the Limitation Acts (see section 13).

(6) The leave of the court is required for any appeal from a decision of the court under this section.

Application of Limitation Acts

13.—(1) The Limitation Acts apply to arbitral proceedings as they apply to legal proceedings.

(2) The court may order that in computing the time prescribed by the Limitation Acts for the commencement of proceedings (including arbitral proceedings) in respect of a dispute which was the subject matter—

   (a) of an award which the court orders to be set aside or declares to be of no effect, or
   (b) of the affected part of an award which the court orders to be set

aside in part, or declares to be in part of no effect,
the period between the commencement of the arbitration and the date of
the order referred to in paragraph (a) or (b) shall be excluded.

(3) In determining for the purposes of the Limitation Acts when a cause
of action accrued, any provision that an award is a condition precedent to
the bringing of legal proceedings in respect of a matter to which an
arbitration agreement applies shall be disregarded.

(4) In this Part "the Limitation Acts" means—

    (a) in England and Wales, the Limitation Act 1980, the Foreign
        Limitation Periods Act 1984 and any other enactment (whenever
        passed) relating to the limitation of actions;

    (b) in Northern Ireland, the Limitation (Northern Ireland) Order
        1989, the Foreign Limitation Periods (Northern Ireland) Order
        1985 and any other enactment (whenever passed) relating to the
        limitation of actions.

Commencement of arbitral proceedings

14.—(1) The parties are free to agree when arbitral proceedings are to
be regarded as commenced for the purposes of this Part and for the
purposes of the Limitation Acts.

(2) If there is no such agreement the following provisions apply.

(3) Where the arbitrator is named or designated in the arbitration agreement, arbitral proceedings are commenced in respect of a matter when one
party serves on the other party or parties a notice in writing requiring him
or them to submit that matter to the person so named or designated.

(4) Where the arbitrator or arbitrators are to be appointed by the parties,
arbitral proceedings are commenced in respect of a matter when one party
serves on the other party or parties notice in writing requiring him or them
to appoint an arbitrator or to agree to the appointment of an arbitrator in
respect of that matter.

(5) Where the arbitrator or arbitrators are to be appointed by a person
other than a party to the proceedings, arbitral proceedings are commenced
in respect of a matter when one party gives notice in writing to that person
requesting him to make the appointment in respect of that matter.

The arbitral tribunal

The arbitral tribunal

15.—(1) The parties are free to agree on the number of arbitrators to
form the tribunal and whether there is to be a chairman or umpire.

(2) Unless otherwise agreed by the parties, an agreement that the
number of arbitrators shall be two or any other even number shall be
understood as requiring the appointment of an additional arbitrator as
chairman of the tribunal.

(3) If there is no agreement as to the number of arbitrators, the tribunal
shall consist of a sole arbitrator.

Procedure for appointment of arbitrators

16.—(1) The parties are free to agree on the procedure for appointing the arbitrator or arbitrators, including the procedure for appointing any chairman or umpire.

(2) If or to the extent that there is no such agreement, the following provisions apply.

(3) If the tribunal is to consist of a sole arbitrator, the parties shall jointly appoint the arbitrator not later than 28 days after service of a request in writing by either party to do so.

(4) If the tribunal is to consist of two arbitrators, each party shall appoint one arbitrator not later than 14 days after service of a request in writing by either party to do so.

(5) If the tribunal is to consist of three arbitrators—

    (a) each party shall appoint one arbitrator not later than 14 days after service of a request in writing by either party to do so, and

    (b) the two so appointed shall forthwith appoint a third arbitrator as the chairman of the tribunal.

(6) If the tribunal is to consist of two arbitrators and an umpire—

    (a) each party shall appoint one arbitrator not later than 14 days after service of a request in writing by either party to do so, and

    (b) the two so appointed may appoint an umpire at any time after they themselves are appointed and shall do so before any substantive hearing or forthwith if they cannot agree on a matter relating to the arbitration.

(7) In any other case (in particular, if there are more than two parties) section 18 applies as in the case of a failure of the agreed appointment procedure.

Power in case of default to appoint sole arbitrator

17.—(1) Unless the parties otherwise agree, where each of two parties to an arbitration agreement is to appoint an arbitrator and one party ("the party in default") refuses to do so, or fails to do so within the time specified, the other party, having duly appointed his arbitrator, may give notice in writing to the party in default that he proposes to appoint his arbitrator to act as sole arbitrator.

(2) If the party in default does not within 7 clear days of that notice being given—

    (a) make the required appointment, and

    (b) notify the other party that he has done so,

the other party may appoint his arbitrator as sole arbitrator whose award shall be binding on both parties as if he had been so appointed by agreement.

(3) Where a sole arbitrator has been appointed under subsection (2), the party in default may (upon notice to the appointing party) apply to the court which may set aside the appointment.

(4) The leave of the court is required for any appeal from a decision of the court under this section.

Failure of appointment procedure

18.—(1) The parties are free to agree what is to happen in the event of a failure of the procedure for the appointment of the arbitral tribunal.

There is no failure if an appointment is duly made under section 17 (power in case of default to appoint sole arbitrator), unless that appointment is set aside.

(2) If or to the extent that there is no such agreement any party to the arbitration agreement may (upon notice to the other parties) apply to the court to exercise its powers under this section.

(3) Those powers are—

    (a) to give directions as to the making of any necessary appointments;

    (b) to direct that the tribunal shall be constituted by such appointments (or any one or more of them) as have been made;

    (c) to revoke any appointments already made;

    (d) to make any necessary appointments itself.

(4) An appointment made by the court under this section has effect as if made with the agreement of the parties.

(5) The leave of the court is required for any appeal from a decision of the court under this section.

Court to have regard to agreed qualifications

19. In deciding whether to exercise, and in considering how to exercise, any of its powers under section 16 (procedure for appointment of arbitrators) or section 18 (failure of appointment procedure), the court shall have due regard to any agreement of the parties as to the qualifications required of the arbitrators.

Chairman

20.—(1) Where the parties have agreed that there is to be a chairman, they are free to agree what the functions of the chairman are to be in relation to the making of decisions, orders and awards.

(2) If or to the extent that there is no such agreement, the following provisions apply.

(3) Decisions, orders and awards shall be made by all or a majority of the arbitrators (including the chairman).

(4) The view of the chairman shall prevail in relation to a decision, order or award in respect of which there is neither unanimity nor a majority under subsection (3).

Umpire

21.—(1) Where the parties have agreed that there is to be an umpire, they are free to agree what the functions of the umpire are to be, and in particular—

    (a) whether he is to attend the proceedings, and

    (b) when he is to replace the other arbitrators as the tribunal with power to make decisions, orders and awards.

(2) If or to the extent that there is no such agreement, the following provisions apply.

(3) The umpire shall attend the proceedings and be supplied with the same documents and other materials as are supplied to the other arbitrators.

(4) Decisions, orders and awards shall be made by the other arbitrators unless and until they cannot agree on a matter relating to the arbitration.

In that event they shall forthwith give notice in writing to the parties and the umpire, whereupon the umpire shall replace them as the tribunal with power to make decisions, orders and awards as if he were sole arbitrator.

(5) If the arbitrators cannot agree but fail to give notice of that fact, or if any of them fails to join in the giving of notice, any party to the arbitral proceedings may (upon notice to the other parties and to the tribunal) apply to the court which may order that the umpire shall replace the other arbitrators as the tribunal with power to make decisions, orders and awards as if he were sole arbitrator.

(6) The leave of the court is required for any appeal from a decision of the court under this section.

Decision-making where no chairman or umpire

22.—(1) Where the parties agree that there shall be two or more arbitrators with no chairman or umpire, the parties are free to agree how the tribunal is to make decisions, orders and awards.

(2) If there is no such agreement, decisions, orders and awards shall be made by all or a majority of the arbitrators.

Revocation of arbitrator's authority

23.—(1) The parties are free to agree in what circumstances the authority of an arbitrator may be revoked.

(2) If or to the extent that there is no such agreement the following provisions apply.

(3) The authority of an arbitrator may not be revoked except—

    (a) by the parties acting jointly, or

    (b) by an arbitral or other institution or person vested by the parties with powers in that regard.

(4) Revocation of the authority of an arbitrator by the parties acting jointly must be agreed in writing unless the parties also agree (whether or not in writing) to terminate the arbitration agreement.

(5) Nothing in this section affects the power of the court—

(a) to revoke an appointment under section 18 (powers exercisable in case of failure of appointment procedure), or

(b) to remove an arbitrator on the grounds specified in section 24.

Power of court to remove arbitrator

24.—(1) A party to arbitral proceedings may (upon notice to the other parties, to the arbitrator concerned and to any other arbitrator) apply to the court to remove an arbitrator on any of the following grounds—

(a) that circumstances exist that give rise to justifiable doubts as to his impartiality;

(b) that he does not possess the qualifications required by the arbitration agreement;

(c) that he is physically or mentally incapable of conducting the proceedings or there are justifiable doubts as to his capacity to do so;

(d) that he has refused or failed—

(i) properly to conduct the proceedings, or

(ii) to use all reasonable despatch in conducting the proceedings or making an award, and that substantial injustice has been or will be caused to the applicant.

(2) If there is an arbitral or other institution or person vested by the parties with power to remove an arbitrator, the court shall not exercise its power of removal unless satisfied that the applicant has first exhausted any available recourse to that institution or person.

(3) The arbitral tribunal may continue the arbitral proceedings and make an award while an application to the court under this section is pending.

(4) Where the court removes an arbitrator, it may make such order as it thinks fit with respect to his entitlement (if any) to fees or expenses, or the repayment of any fees or expenses already paid.

(5) The arbitrator concerned is entitled to appear and be heard by the court before it makes any order under this section.

(6) The leave of the court is required for any appeal from a decision of the court under this section.

Resignation of arbitrator

25.—(1) The parties are free to agree with an arbitrator as to the consequences of his resignation as regards—

(a) his entitlement (if any) to fees or expenses, and

(b) any liability thereby incurred by him.

(2) If or to the extent that there is no such agreement the following provisions apply.

(3) An arbitrator who resigns his appointment may (upon notice to the parties) apply to the court—

(a) to grant him relief from any liability thereby incurred by him, and

(b) to make such order as it thinks fit with respect to his entitlement (if any) to fees or expenses or the repayment of any fees or expenses already paid.

(4) If the court is satisfied that in all the circumstances it was reasonable for the arbitrator to resign, it may grant such relief as is mentioned in subsection (3)(a) on such terms as it thinks fit.

(5) The leave of the court is required for any appeal from a decision of the court under this section.

Death of arbitrator or person appointing him

26.—(1) The authority of an arbitrator is personal and ceases on his death.

(2) Unless otherwise agreed by the parties, the death of the person by whom an arbitrator was appointed does not revoke the arbitrator's authority.

Filling of vacancy, etc

27.—(1) Where an arbitrator ceases to hold office, the parties are free to agree—

  (a) whether and if so how the vacancy is to be filled,

  (b) whether and if so to what extent the previous proceedings should stand, and

  (c) what effect (if any) his ceasing to hold office has on any appointment made by him (alone or jointly).

(2) If or to the extent that there is no such agreement, the following provisions apply.

(3) The provisions of sections 16 (procedure for appointment of arbitrators) and 18 (failure of appointment procedure) apply in relation to the filling of the vacancy as in relation to an original appointment.

(4) The tribunal (when reconstituted) shall determine whether and if so to what extent the previous proceedings should stand.

This does not affect any right of a party to challenge those proceedings on any ground which had arisen before the arbitrator ceased to hold office.

(5) His ceasing to hold office does not affect any appointment by him (alone or jointly) of another arbitrator, in particular any appointment of a chairman or umpire.

Joint and several liability of parties to arbitrators for fees and expenses

28.—(1) The parties are jointly and severally liable to pay to the arbitrators such reasonable fees and expenses (if any) as are appropriate in the circumstances.

(2) Any party may apply to the court (upon notice to the other parties and to the arbitrators) which may order that the amount of the arbitrators' fees and expenses shall be considered and adjusted by such means and upon such terms as it may direct.

(3) If the application is made after any amount has been paid to the arbitrators by way of fees or expenses, the court may order the repayment of such amount (if any) as is shown to be excessive, but shall not do so unless it is shown that it is reasonable in the circumstances to order repayment.

(4) The above provisions have effect subject to any order of the court under section 24(4) or 25(3)(b) (order as to entitlement to fees or expenses in case of removal or resignation of arbitrator).

(5) Nothing in this section affects any liability of a party to any other party to pay all or any of the costs of the arbitration (see sections 59 to 65) or any contractual right of an arbitrator to payment of his fees and expenses.

(6) In this section references to arbitrators include an arbitrator who has ceased to act and an umpire who has not replaced the other arbitrators.

Immunity of arbitrator

29.—(1) An arbitrator is not liable for anything done or omitted in the discharge or purported discharge of his functions as arbitrator unless the act or omission is shown to have been in bad faith.

(2) Subsection (1) applies to an employee or agent of an arbitrator as it applies to the arbitrator himself.

(3) This section does not affect any liability incurred by an arbitrator by reason of his resigning (but see section 25).

Jurisdiction of the arbitral tribunal

Competence of tribunal to rule on its own jurisdiction

30.—(1) Unless otherwise agreed by the parties, the arbitral tribunal may rule on its own substantive jurisdiction, that is, as to—
- (a) whether there is a valid arbitration agreement,
- (b) whether the tribunal is properly constituted, and
- (c) what matters have been submitted to arbitration in accordance with the arbitration agreement.

(2) Any such ruling may be challenged by any available arbitral process of appeal or review or in accordance with the provisions of this Part.

Objection to substantive jurisdiction of tribunal

31.—(1) An objection that the arbitral tribunal lacks substantive jurisdiction at the outset of the proceedings must be raised by a party not later than the time he takes the first step in the proceedings to contest the merits of any matter in relation to which he challenges the tribunal's jurisdiction.

A party is not precluded from raising such an objection by the fact that he has appointed or participated in the appointment of an arbitrator.

(2) Any objection during the course of the arbitral proceedings that the arbitral tribunal is exceeding its substantive jurisdiction must be made as

soon as possible after the matter alleged to be beyond its jurisdiction is raised.

(3) The arbitral tribunal may admit an objection later than the time specified in subsection (1) or (2) if it considers the delay justified.

(4) Where an objection is duly taken to the tribunal's substantive jurisdiction and the tribunal has power to rule on its own jurisdiction, it may—

    (a) rule on the matter in an award as to jurisdiction, or

    (b) deal with the objection in its award on the merits.

If the parties agree which of these courses the tribunal should take, the tribunal shall proceed accordingly.

(5) The tribunal may in any case, and shall if the parties so agree, stay proceedings whilst an application is made to the court under section 32 (determination of preliminary point of jurisdiction).

Determination of preliminary point of jurisdiction

32.—(1) The court may, on the application of a party to arbitral proceedings (upon notice to the other parties), determine any question as to the substantive jurisdiction of the tribunal.

A party may lose the right to object (see section 73).

(2) An application under this section shall not be considered unless—

    (a) it is made with the agreement in writing of all the other parties to the proceedings, or

    (b) it is made with the permission of the tribunal and the court is satisfied—

        (i) that the determination of the question is likely to produce substantial savings in costs,

        (ii) that the application was made without delay, and

        (iii) that there is good reason why the matter should be decided by the court.

(3) An application under this section, unless made with the agreement of all the other parties to the proceedings, shall state the grounds on which it is said that the matter should be decided by the court.

(4) Unless otherwise agreed by the parties, the arbitral tribunal may continue the arbitral proceedings and make an award while an application to the court under this section is pending.

(5) Unless the court gives leave, no appeal lies from a decision of the court whether the conditions specified in subsection (2) are met.

(6) The decision of the court on the question of jurisdiction shall be treated as a judgment of the court for the purposes of an appeal.

But no appeal lies without the leave of the court which shall not be given unless the court considers that the question involves a point of law which is one of general importance or is one which for some other special reason should be considered by the Court of Appeal.

The arbitral proceedings

General duty of the tribunal

33.—(1) The tribunal shall—

(a) act fairly and impartially as between the parties, giving each party a reasonable opportunity of putting his case and dealing with that of his opponent, and

(b) adopt procedures suitable to the circumstances of the particular case, avoiding unnecessary delay or expense, so as to provide a fair means for the resolution of the matters falling to be determined.

(2) The tribunal shall comply with that general duty in conducting the arbitral proceedings, in its decisions on matters of procedure and evidence and in the exercise of all other powers conferred on it.

Procedural and evidential matters

34.—(1) It shall be for the tribunal to decide all procedural and evidential matters, subject to the right of the parties to agree any matter.

(2) Procedural and evidential matters include—

(a) when and where any part of the proceedings is to be held;

(b) the language or languages to be used in the proceedings and whether translations of any relevant documents are to be supplied;

(c) whether any and if so what form of written statements of claim and defence are to be used, when these should be supplied and the extent to which such statements can be later amended;

(d) whether any and if so which documents or classes of documents should be disclosed between and produced by the parties and at what stage;

(e) whether any and if so what questions should be put to and answered by the respective parties and when and in what form this should be done;

(f) whether to apply strict rules of evidence (or any other rules) as to the admissibility, relevance or weight of any material (oral, written or other) sought to be tendered on any matters of fact or opinion, and the time, manner and form in which such material should be exchanged and presented;

(g) whether and to what extent the tribunal should itself take the initiative in ascertaining the facts and the law;

(h) whether and to what extent there should be oral or written evidence or submissions.

(3) The tribunal may fix the time within which any directions given by it are to be complied with, and may if it thinks fit extend the time so fixed (whether or not it has expired).

Consolidation of proceedings and concurrent hearings

35.—(1) The parties are free to agree—

(a) that the arbitral proceedings shall be consolidated with other arbitral proceedings, or

(b) that concurrent hearings shall be held,

on such terms as may be agreed.

(2) Unless the parties agree to confer such power on the tribunal, the tribunal has no power to order consolidation of proceedings or concurrent hearings.

Legal or other representation

36. Unless otherwise agreed by the parties, a party to arbitral proceedings may be represented in the proceedings by a lawyer or other person chosen by him.

Power to appoint experts, legal advisers or assessors

37.—(1) Unless otherwise agreed by the parties—

(a) the tribunal may—

(i) appoint experts or legal advisers to report to it and the parties, or

(ii) appoint assessors to assist it on technical matters,

and may allow any such expert, legal adviser or assessor to attend the proceedings and

(b) the parties shall be given a reasonable opportunity to comment on any information, opinion or advice offered by any such person.

(2) The fees and expenses of an expert, legal adviser or assessor appointed by the tribunal for which the arbitrators are liable are expenses of the arbitrators for the purposes of this Part.

General powers exercisable by the tribunal

38.—(1) The parties are free to agree on the powers exercisable by the arbitral tribunal for the purposes of and in relation to the proceedings.

(2) Unless otherwise agreed by the parties the tribunal has the following powers.

(3) The tribunal may order a claimant to provide security for the costs of the arbitration. This power shall not be exercised on the ground that the claimant is—

(a) an individual ordinarily resident outside the United Kingdom, or

(b) a corporation or association incorporated or formed under the law of a country outside the United Kingdom, or whose central management and control is exercised outside the United Kingdom.

(4) The tribunal may give directions in relation to any property which is the subject of the proceedings or as to which any question arises in the proceedings, and which is owned by or is in the possession of a party to the proceedings—

(a) for the inspection, photographing, preservation, custody or detention of the property by the tribunal, an expert or a party, or

(b) ordering that samples be taken from, or any observation be made of or experiment conducted upon, the property.

(5) The tribunal may direct that a party or witness shall be examined on oath or affirmation, and may for that purpose administer any necessary oath or take any necessary affirmation.

(6) The tribunal may give directions to a party for the preservation for the purposes of the proceedings of any evidence in his custody or control.

Power to make provisional awards

39.—(1) The parties are free to agree that the tribunal shall have power to order on a provisional basis any relief which it would have power to grant in a final award.

(2) This includes, for instance, making—

(a) a provisional order for the payment of money or the disposition of property as between the parties, or

(b) an order to make an interim payment on account of the costs of the arbitration.

(3) Any such order shall be subject to the tribunal's final adjudication and the tribunal's final award, on the merits or as to costs, shall take account of any such order.

(4) Unless the parties agree to confer such power on the tribunal, the tribunal has no such power.

This does not affect its powers under section 47 (awards on different issues, etc).

General duty of parties

40.—(1) The parties shall do all things necessary for the proper and expeditious conduct of the arbitral proceedings.

(2) This includes—

(a) complying without delay with any determination of the tribunal as to procedural or evidential matters, or with any order or directions of the tribunal, and

(b) where appropriate, taking without delay any necessary steps to obtain a decision of the court on a preliminary question of jurisdiction or law (see sections 32 and 45).

Powers of tribunal in case of party's default

41.—(1) The parties are free to agree on the powers of the tribunal in case of a party's failure to do something necessary for the proper and expeditious conduct of the arbitration.

(2) Unless otherwise agreed by the parties, the following provisions apply.

(3) If the tribunal is satisfied that there has been inordinate and inex-

cusable delay on the part of the claimant in pursuing his claim and that the delay—

    (a) gives rise, or is likely to give rise, to a substantial risk that it is not possible to have a fair resolution of the issues in that claim, or

    (b) has caused, or is likely to cause, serious prejudice to the respondent,

the tribunal may make an award dismissing the claim.

(4) If without showing sufficient cause a party—

    (a) fails to attend or be represented at an oral hearing of which due notice was given, or

    (b) where matters are to be dealt with in writing, fails after due notice to submit written evidence or make written submissions,

the tribunal may continue the proceedings in the absence of that party or, as the case may be, without any written evidence or submissions on his behalf, and may make an award on the basis of the evidence before it.

(5) If without showing sufficient cause a party fails to comply with any order or directions of the tribunal, the tribunal may make a peremptory order to the same effect, prescribing such time for compliance with it as the tribunal considers appropriate.

(6) If a claimant fails to comply with a peremptory order of the tribunal to provide security for costs, the tribunal may make an award dismissing his claim.

(7) If a party fails to comply with any other kind of peremptory order, then, without prejudice to section 42 (enforcement by court of tribunal's peremptory orders), the tribunal may do any of the following—

    (a) direct that the party in default shall not be entitled to rely upon any allegation or material which was the subject matter of the order;

    (b) draw such adverse inferences from the act of non-compliance as the circumstances justify;

    (c) proceed to an award on the basis of such materials as have been properly provided to it;

    (d) make such order as it thinks fit as to the payment of costs of the arbitration incurred in consequence of the non-compliance.

Powers of court in relation to arbitral proceedings

Enforcement of peremptory orders of tribunal

42.—(1) Unless otherwise agreed by the parties, the court may make an order requiring a party to comply with a peremptory order made by the tribunal.

(2) An application for an order under this section may be made—

    (a) by the tribunal (upon notice to the parties),

    (b) by a party to the arbitral proceedings with the permission of the tribunal (and upon notice to the other parties), or

    (c) where the parties have agreed that the powers of the court under this section shall be available.

(3) The court shall not act unless it is satisfied that the applicant has exhausted any available arbitral process in respect of failure to comply with the tribunal's order.

(4) No order shall be made under this section unless the court is satisfied that the person to whom the tribunal's order was directed has failed to comply with it within the time prescribed in the order or, if no time was prescribed, within a reasonable time.

(5) The leave of the court is required for any appeal from a decision of the court under this section.

Securing the attendance of witnesses

43.—(1) A party to arbitral proceedings may use the same court procedures as are available in relation to legal proceedings to secure the attendance before the tribunal of a witness in order to give oral testimony or to produce documents or other material evidence.

(2) This may only be done with the permission of the tribunal or the agreement of the other parties.

(3) The court procedures may only be used if—
    (a) the witness is in the United Kingdom, and
    (b) the arbitral proceedings are being conducted in England and Wales or, as the case may be, Northern Ireland.

(4) A person shall not be compelled by virtue of this section to produce any document or other material evidence which he could not be compelled to produce in legal proceedings.

Court powers exercisable in support of arbitral proceedings

44.—(1) Unless otherwise agreed by the parties, the court has for the purposes of and in relation to arbitral proceedings the same power of making orders about the matters listed below as it has for the purposes of and in relation to legal proceedings.

(2) Those matters are—
    (a) the taking of the evidence of witnesses;
    (b) the preservation of evidence;
    (c) making orders relating to property which is the subject of the proceedings or as to which any question arises in the proceedings—
        (i) for the inspection, photographing, preservation, custody or detention of the property, or
        (ii) ordering that samples be taken from, or any observation be made of or experiment conducted upon, the property;
    and for that purpose authorising any person to enter any premises in the possession or control of a party to the arbitration;
    (d) the sale of any goods the subject of the proceedings;
    (e) the granting of an interim injunction or the appointment of a receiver.

(3) If the case is one of urgency, the court may, on the application of a party or proposed party to the arbitral proceedings, make such orders as it

thinks necessary for the purpose of preserving evidence or assets.

(4) If the case is not one of urgency, the court shall act only on the application of a party to the arbitral proceedings (upon notice to the other parties and to the tribunal) made with the permission of the tribunal or the agreement in writing of the other parties.

(5) In any case the court shall act only if or to the extent that the arbitral tribunal, and any arbitral or other institution or person vested by the parties with power in that regard, has no power or is unable for the time being to act effectively.

(6) If the court so orders, an order made by it under this section shall cease to have effect in whole or in part on the order of the tribunal or of any such arbitral or other institution or person having power to act in relation to the subject-matter of the order.

(7) The leave of the court is required for any appeal from a decision of the court under this section.

Determination of preliminary point of law

45.—(1) Unless otherwise agreed by the parties, the court may on the application of a party to arbitral proceedings (upon notice to the other parties) determine any question of law arising in the course of the proceedings which the court is satisfied substantially affects the rights of one or more of the parties.

An agreement to dispense with reasons for the tribunal's award shall be considered an agreement to exclude the court's jurisdiction under this section.

(2) An application under this section shall not be considered unless—

    (a) it is made with the agreement of all the other parties to the proceedings, or

    (b) it is made with the permission of the tribunal and the court is satisfied—

        (i) that the determination of the question is likely to produce substantial savings in costs, and

        (ii) that the application was made without delay.

(3) The application shall identify the question of law to be determined and, unless made with the agreement of all the other parties to the proceedings, shall state the grounds on which it is said that the question should be decided by the court.

(4) Unless otherwise agreed by the parties, the arbitral tribunal may continue the arbitral proceedings and make an award while an application to the court under this section is pending.

(5) Unless the court gives leave, no appeal lies from a decision of the court whether the conditions specified in subsection (2) are met.

(6) The decision of the court on the question of law shall be treated as a judgment of the court for the purposes of an appeal.

But no appeal lies without the leave of the court which shall not be given unless the court considers that the question is one of general importance, or is one which for some other special reason should be considered by the Court of Appeal.

The award

Rules applicable to substance of dispute

46.—(1) The arbitral tribunal shall decide the dispute—
  (a) in accordance with the law chosen by the parties as applicable to the substance of the dispute, or
  (b) if the parties so agree, in accordance with such other considerations as are agreed by them or determined by the tribunal.

(2) For this purpose the choice of the laws of a country shall be understood to refer to the substantive laws of that country and not its conflict of laws rules.

(3) If or to the extent that there is no such choice or agreement, the tribunal shall apply the law determined by the conflict of laws rules which it considers applicable.

Awards on different issues, etc.

47.—(1) Unless otherwise agreed by the parties, the tribunal may make more than one award at different times on different aspects of the matters to be determined.

(2) The tribunal may, in particular, make an award relating—
  (a) to an issue affecting the whole claim, or
  (b) to a part only of the claims or cross-claims submitted to it for decision.

(3) If the tribunal does so, it shall specify in its award the issue, or the claim or part of a claim, which is the subject matter of the award.

Remedies

48.—(1) The parties are free to agree on the powers exercisable by the arbitral tribunal as regards remedies.

(2) Unless otherwise agreed by the parties, the tribunal has the following powers.

(3) The tribunal may make a declaration as to any matter to be determined in the proceedings.

(4) The tribunal may order the payment of a sum of money, in any currency.

(5) The tribunal has the same powers as the court—
  (a) to order a party to do or refrain from doing anything;
  (b) to order specific performance of a contract (other than a contract relating to land);
  (c) to order the rectification, setting aside or cancellation of a deed or other document.

Interest

49.—(1) The parties are free to agree on the powers of the tribunal as regards the award of interest.

(2) Unless otherwise agreed by the parties the following provisions apply.

(3) The tribunal may award simple or compound interest from such dates, at such rates and with such rests as it considers meets the justice of the case—

(a) on the whole or part of any amount awarded by the tribunal, in respect of any period up to the date of the award;

(b) on the whole or part of any amount claimed in the arbitration and outstanding at the commencement of the arbitral proceedings but paid before the award was made, in respect of any period up to the date of payment.

(4) The tribunal may award simple or compound interest from the date of the award (or any later date) until payment, at such rates and with such rests as it considers meets the justice of the case, on the outstanding amount of any award (including any award of interest under subsection (3) and any award as to costs).

(5) References in this section to an amount awarded by the tribunal include an amount payable in consequence of a declaratory award by the tribunal.

(6) The above provisions do not affect any other power of the tribunal to award interest.

Extension of time for making award

50.—(1) Where the time for making an award is limited by or in pursuance of the arbitration agreement, then, unless otherwise agreed by the parties, the court may in accordance with the following provisions by order extend that time.

(2) An application for an order under this section may be made—

(a) by the tribunal (upon notice to the parties), or

(b) by any party to the proceedings (upon notice to the tribunal and the other parties),

but only after exhausting any available arbitral process for obtaining an extension of time.

(3) The court shall only make an order if satisfied that a substantial injustice would otherwise be done.

(4) The court may extend the time for such period and on such terms as it thinks fit, and may do so whether or not the time previously fixed (by or under the agreement or by a previous order) has expired.

(5) The leave of the court is required for any appeal from a decision of the court under this section.

Settlement

51.—(1) If during arbitral proceedings the parties settle the dispute, the following provisions apply unless otherwise agreed by the parties.

(2) The tribunal shall terminate the substantive proceedings and, if so requested by the parties and not objected to by the tribunal, shall record the settlement in the form of an agreed award.

(3) An agreed award shall state that it is an award of the tribunal and shall have the same status and effect as any other award on the merits of the case.

(4) The following provisions of this Part relating to awards (sections 52 to 58) apply to an agreed award.

(5) Unless the parties have also settled the matter of the payment of the costs of the arbitration, the provisions of this Part relating to costs (sections 59 to 65) continue to apply.

Form of award

52.—(1) The parties are free to agree on the form of an award.

(2) If or to the extent that there is no such agreement, the following provisions apply.

(3) The award shall be in writing signed by all the arbitrators or all those assenting to the award.

(4) The award shall contain the reasons for the award unless it is an agreed award or the parties have agreed to dispense with reasons.

(5) The award shall state the seat of the arbitration and the date when the award is made.

Place where award treated as made

53. Unless otherwise agreed by the parties, where the seat of the arbitration is in England and Wales or Northern Ireland, any award in the proceedings shall be treated as made there, regardless of where it was signed, despatched or delivered to any of the parties.

Date of award

54.—(1) Unless otherwise agreed by the parties, the tribunal may decide what is to be taken to be the date on which the award was made.

(2) In the absence of any such decision, the date of the award shall be taken to be the date on which it is signed by the arbitrator or, where more than one arbitrator signs the award, by the last of them.

Notification of award

55.—(1) The parties are free to agree on the requirements as to notification of the award to the parties.

(2) If there is no such agreement, the award shall be notified to the

parties by service on them of copies of the award, which shall be done without delay after the award is made.

(3) Nothing in this section affects section 56 (power to withhold award in case of non-payment).

Power to withhold award in case of non-payment

56.—(1) The tribunal may refuse to deliver an award to the parties except upon full payment of the fees and expenses of the arbitrators.

(2) If the tribunal refuses on that ground to deliver an award, a party to the arbitral proceedings may (upon notice to the other parties and the tribunal) apply to the court, which may order that—

- (a) the tribunal shall deliver the award on the payment into court by the applicant of the fees and expenses demanded, or such lesser amount as the court may specify,
- (b) the amount of the fees and expenses properly payable shall be determined by such means and upon such terms as the court may direct, and
- (c) out of the money paid into court there shall be paid out such fees and expenses as may be found to be properly payable and the balance of the money (if any) shall be paid out to the applicant.

(3) For this purpose the amount of fees and expenses properly payable is the amount the applicant is liable to pay under section 28 or any agreement relating to the payment of the arbitrators.

(4) No application to the court may be made where there is any available arbitral process for appeal or review of the amount of the fees or expenses demanded.

(5) References in this section to arbitrators include an arbitrator who has ceased to act and an umpire who has not replaced the other arbitrators.

(6) The above provisions of this section also apply in relation to any arbitral or other institution or person vested by the parties with powers in relation to the delivery of the tribunal's award.

As they so apply, the references to the fees and expenses of the arbitrators shall be construed as including the fees and expenses of that institution or person.

(7) The leave of the court is required for any appeal from a decision of the court under this section.

(8) Nothing in this section shall be construed as excluding an application under section 28 where payment has been made to the arbitrators in order to obtain the award.

Correction of award or additional award

57.—(1) The parties are free to agree on the powers of the tribunal to correct an award or make an additional award.

(2) If or to the extent there is no such agreement, the following provisions apply.

(3) The tribunal may on its own initiative or on the application of a party—
- (a) correct an award so as to remove any clerical mistake or error arising from an accidental slip or omission or clarify or remove any ambiguity in the award, or
- (b) make an additional award in respect of any claim (including a claim for interest or costs) which was presented to the tribunal but was not dealt with in the award.

These powers shall not be exercised without first affording the other parties a reasonable opportunity to make representations to the tribunal.

(4) Any application for the exercise of those powers must be made within 28 days of the date of the award or such longer period as the parties may agree.

(5) Any correction of an award shall be made within 28 days of the date the application was received by the tribunal or, where the correction is made by the tribunal on its own initiative, within 28 days of the date of the award or, in either case, such longer period as the parties may agree.

(6) Any additional award shall be made within 56 days of the date of the original award or such longer period as the parties may agree.

(7) Any correction of an award shall form part of the award.

Effect of award

58.—(1) Unless otherwise agreed by the parties, an award made by the tribunal pursuant to an arbitration agreement is final and binding both on the parties and on any persons claiming through or under them.

(2) This does not affect the right of a person to challenge the award by any available arbitral process of appeal or review or in accordance with the provisions of this Part.

Costs of the arbitration

Costs of the arbitration

59.—(1) References in this Part to the costs of the arbitration are to—
- (a) the arbitrators' fees and expenses,
- (b) the fees and expenses of any arbitral institution concerned, and
- (c) the legal or other costs of the parties.

(2) Any such reference includes the costs of or incidental to any proceedings to determine the amount of the recoverable costs of the arbitration (see section 63).

Agreement to pay costs in any event

60. An agreement which has the effect that a party is to pay the whole or part of the costs of the arbitration in any event is only valid if made after the dispute in question has arisen.

Award of costs

61.—(1) The tribunal may make an award allocating the costs of the arbitration as between the parties, subject to any agreement of the parties.

(2) Unless the parties otherwise agree, the tribunal shall award costs on the general principle that costs should follow the event except where it appears to the tribunal that in the circumstances this is not appropriate in relation to the whole or part of the costs.

Effect of agreement or award about costs

62. Unless the parties otherwise agree, any obligation under an agreement between them as to how the costs of the arbitration are to be borne, or under an award allocating the costs of the arbitration, extends only to such costs as are recoverable.

The recoverable costs of the arbitration

63.—(1) The parties are free to agree what costs of the arbitration are recoverable.

(2) If or to the extent there is no such agreement, the following provisions apply.

(3) The tribunal may determine by award the recoverable costs of the arbitration on such basis as it thinks fit.

If it does so, it shall specify—

    (a) the basis on which it has acted, and

    (b) the items of recoverable costs and the amount referable to each.

(4) If the tribunal does not determine the recoverable costs of the arbitration, any party to the arbitral proceedings may apply to the court (upon notice to the other parties) which may—

    (a) determine the recoverable costs of the arbitration on such basis as it thinks fit, or

    (b) order that they shall be determined by such means and upon such terms as it may specify.

(5) Unless the tribunal or the court determines otherwise—

    (a) the recoverable costs of the arbitration shall be determined on the basis that there shall be allowed a reasonable amount in respect of all costs reasonably incurred, and

    (b) any doubt as to whether costs were reasonably incurred or were reasonable in amount shall be resolved in favour of the paying party.

(6) The above provisions have effect subject to section 64 (recoverable fees and expenses of arbitrators).

(7) Nothing in this section affects any right of the arbitrators, any expert, legal adviser or assessor appointed by the tribunal, or any arbitral institution, to payment of their fees and expenses.

Recoverable fees and expenses of arbitrators

64.—(1) Unless otherwise agreed by the parties, the recoverable costs of the arbitration shall include in respect of the fees and expenses of the arbitrators only such reasonable fees and expenses as are appropriate in the circumstances.

(2) If there is any question as to what reasonable fees and expenses are appropriate in the circumstances, and the matter is not already before the court on an application under section 63(4), the court may on the application of any party (upon notice to the other parties)–

   (a) determine the matter, or
   (b) order that it be determined by such means and upon such terms as the court may specify.

(3) Subsection (1) has effect subject to any order of the court under section 24(4) or 25(3)(b) (order as to entitlement to fees or expenses in case of removal or resignation of arbitrator).

(4) Nothing in this section affects any right of the arbitrator to payment of his fees and expenses.

Power to limit recoverable costs

65.—(1) Unless otherwise agreed by the parties, the tribunal may direct that the recoverable costs of the arbitration, or of any part of the arbitral proceedings, shall be limited to a specified amount.

(2) Any direction may be made or varied at any stage, but this must be done sufficiently in advance of the incurring of costs to which it relates, or the taking of any steps in the proceedings which may be affected by it, for the limit to be taken into account.

Powers of the court in relation to award

Enforcement of the award

66.—(1) An award made by the tribunal pursuant to an arbitration agreement may, by leave of the court, be enforced in the same manner as a judgment or order of the court to the same effect.

(2) Where leave is so given, judgment may be entered in terms of the award.

(3) Leave to enforce an award shall not be given where, or to the extent that, the person against whom it is sought to be enforced shows that the tribunal lacked substantive jurisdiction to make the award.

The right to raise such an objection may have been lost (see section 73).

(4) Nothing in this section affects the recognition or enforcement of an award under any other enactment or rule of law, in particular under Part II of the Arbitration Act 1950 (enforcement of awards under Geneva Convention) or the provisions of Part III of this Act relating to the recognition and enforcement of awards under the New York Convention or by an action on the award.

Challenging the award: substantive jurisdiction

67.—(1) A party to arbitral proceedings may (upon notice to the other parties and to the tribunal) apply to the court—

    (a) challenging any award of the arbitral tribunal as to its substantive jurisdiction or

    (b) for an order declaring an award made by the tribunal on the merits to be of no effect, in whole or in part, because the tribunal did not have substantive jurisdiction.

A party may lose the right to object (see section 73) and the right to apply is subject to the restrictions in section 70(2) and (3).

(2) The arbitral tribunal may continue the arbitral proceedings and make a further award while an application to the court under this section is pending in relation to an award as to jurisdiction.

(3) On an application under this section challenging an award of the arbitral tribunal as to its substantive jurisdiction, the court may by order—

    (a) confirm the award,

    (b) vary the award, or

    (c) set aside the award in whole or in part.

(4) The leave of the court is required for any appeal from a decision of the court under this section.

Challenging the award: serious irregularity

68.—(1) A party to arbitral proceedings may (upon notice to the other parties and to the tribunal) apply to the court challenging an award in the proceedings on the ground of serious irregularity affecting the tribunal, the proceedings or the award.

A party may lose the right to object (see section 73) and the right to apply is subject to the restrictions in section 70(2) and (3).

(2) Serious irregularity means an irregularity of one or more of the following kinds which the court considers has caused or will cause substantial injustice to the applicant—

    (a) failure by the tribunal to comply with section 33 (general duty of tribunal);

    (b) the tribunal exceeding its powers (otherwise than by exceeding its substantive jurisdiction: see section 67);

    (c) failure by the tribunal to conduct the proceedings in accordance with the procedure agreed by the parties;

    (d) failure by the tribunal to deal with all the issues that were put to it;

    (e) any arbitral or other institution or person vested by the parties with powers in relation to the proceedings or the award exceeding its powers;

    (f) uncertainty or ambiguity as to the effect of the award;

    (g) the award being obtained by fraud or the award or the way in which it was procured being contrary to public policy;

    (h) failure to comply with the requirements as to the form of the award or

    (i) any irregularity in the conduct of the proceedings or in the award which is admitted by the tribunal or by any arbitral or other institution or person vested by the parties with powers in relation to the proceedings or the award.

(3) If there is shown to be serious irregularity affecting the tribunal, the proceedings or the award, the court may—

    (a) remit the award to the tribunal, in whole or in part, for reconsideration,

    (b) set the award aside in whole or in part, or

    (c) declare the award to be of no effect, in whole or in part.

The court shall not exercise its power to set aside or to declare an award to be of no effect, in whole or in part, unless it is satisfied that it would be inappropriate to remit the matters in question to the tribunal for reconsideration.

(4) The leave of the court is required for any appeal from a decision of the court under this section.

Appeal on point of law

69.—(1) Unless otherwise agreed by the parties, a party to arbitral proceedings may (upon notice to the other parties and to the tribunal) appeal to the court on a question of law arising out of an award made in the proceedings.

An agreement to dispense with reasons for the tribunal's award shall be considered an agreement to exclude the court's jurisdiction under this section.

(2) An appeal shall not be brought under this section except—

    (a) with the agreement of all the other parties to the proceedings, or

    (b) with the leave of the court.

The right to appeal is also subject to the restrictions in section 70(2) and (3).

(3) Leave to appeal shall be given only if the court is satisfied—

    (a) that the determination of the question will substantially affect the rights of one or more of the parties,

    (b) that the question is one which the tribunal was asked to determine,

    (c) that, on the basis of the findings of fact in the award—

        (i) the decision of the tribunal on the question is obviously wrong, or

        (ii) the question is one of general public importance and the decision of the tribunal is at least open to serious doubt, and

    (d) that, despite the agreement of the parties to resolve the matter by arbitration, it is just and proper in all the circumstances for the court to determine the question.

(4) An application for leave to appeal under this section shall identify the question of law to be determined and state the grounds on which it is alleged that leave to appeal should be granted.

(5) The court shall determine an application for leave to appeal under this section without a hearing unless it appears to the court that a hearing is required.

(6) The leave of the court is required for any appeal from a decision of the court under this section to grant or refuse leave to appeal.

(7) On an appeal under this section the court may by order—

(a) confirm the award,

(b) vary the award,

(c) remit the award to the tribunal, in whole or in part, for reconsideration in the light of the court's determination, or

(d) set aside the award in whole or in part.

The court shall not exercise its power to set aside an award, in whole or in part, unless it is satisfied that it would be inappropriate to remit the matters in question to the tribunal for reconsideration.

(8) The decision of the court on an appeal under this section shall be treated as a judgment of the court for the purposes of a further appeal.

But no such appeal lies without the leave of the court which shall not be given unless the court considers that the question is one of general importance or is one which for some other special reason should be considered by the Court of Appeal.

Challenge or appeal: supplementary provisions

70.—(1) The following provisions apply to an application or appeal under section 67, 68 or 69.

(2) An application or appeal may not be brought if the applicant or appellant has not first exhausted—

(a) any available arbitral process of appeal or review, and

(b) any available recourse under section 57 (correction of award or additional award).

(3) Any application or appeal must be brought within 28 days of the date of the award or, if there has been any arbitral process of appeal or review, of the date when the applicant or appellant was notified of the result of that process.

(4) If on an application or appeal it appears to the court that the award—

(a) does not contain the tribunal's reasons, or

(b) does not set out the tribunal's reasons in sufficient detail to enable the court properly to consider the application or appeal,

the court may order the tribunal to state the reasons for its award in sufficient detail for that purpose.

(5) Where the court makes an order under subsection (4), it may make such further order as it thinks fit with respect to any additional costs of the arbitration resulting from its order.

(6) The court may order the applicant or appellant to provide security for the costs of the application or appeal, any may direct that the application or appeal be dismissed if the order is not complied with.

The power to order security for costs shall not be exercised on the ground that the applicant or appellant is—

(a) an individual ordinarily resident outside the United Kingdom, or
(b) a corporation or association incorporated or formed under the law of a country outside the United Kingdom, or whose central management and control is exercised outside the United Kingdom.

(7) The court may order that any money payable under the award shall be brought into court or otherwise secured pending the determination of the application or appeal, and may direct that the application or appeal be dismissed if the order is not complied with.

(8) The court may grant leave to appeal subject to conditions to the same or similar effect as an order under subsection (6) or (7).

This does not affect the general discretion of the court to grant leave subject to conditions.

Challenge or appeal: effect of order of court

71.—(1) The following provisions have effect where the court makes an order under section 67, 68 or 69 with respect to an award.

(2) Where the award is varied, the variation has effect as part of the tribunal's award.

(3) Where the award is remitted to the tribunal, in whole or in part, for reconsideration, the tribunal shall make a fresh award in respect of the matters remitted within three months of the date of the order for remission or such longer or shorter period as the court may direct.

(4) Where the award is set aside or declared to be of no effect, in whole or in part, the court may also order that any provision that an award is a condition precedent to the bringing of legal proceedings in respect of a matter to which the arbitration agreement applies, is of no effect as regards the subject matter of the award or, as the case may be, the relevant part of the award.

Miscellaneous

Saving for rights of person who takes no part in proceedings

72.—(1) A person alleged to be a party to arbitral proceedings but who takes no part in the proceedings may question—
(a) whether there is a valid arbitration agreement,
(b) whether the tribunal is properly constituted, or
(c) what matters have been submitted to arbitration in accordance with the arbitration agreement,
by proceedings in the court for a declaration or injunction or other appropriate relief.

(2) He also has the same right as a party to the arbitral proceedings to challenge an award—
(a) by an application under section 67 on the ground of lack of substantive jurisdiction in relation to him, or
(b) by an application under section 68 on the ground of serious

irregularity (within the meaning of that section) affecting him; and section 70(2) (duty to exhaust arbitral procedures) does not apply in his case.

Loss of right to object

73.—(1) If a party to arbitral proceedings takes part, or continues to take part, in the proceedings without making, either forthwith or within such time as is allowed by the arbitration agreement or the tribunal or by any provision of this Part, any objection—

(a) that the tribunal lacks substantive jurisdiction,

(b) that the proceedings have been improperly conducted,

(c) that there has been a failure to comply with the arbitration agreement or with any provision of this Part, or

(d) that there has been any other irregularity affecting the tribunal or the proceedings,

he may not raise that objection later, before the tribunal or the court, unless he shows that, at the time he took part or continued to take part in the proceedings, he did not know and could not with reasonable diligence have discovered the grounds for the objection.

(2) Where the arbitral tribunal rules that it has substantive jurisdiction and a party to arbitral proceedings who could have questioned that ruling—

(a) by any available arbitral process of appeal or review, or

(b) by challenging the award,

does not do so, or does not do so within the time allowed by the arbitration agreement or any provision of this Part, he may not object later to the tribunal's substantive jurisdiction on any ground which was the subject of that ruling.

Immunity of arbitral institutions, etc

74.—(1) An arbitral or other institution or person designated or requested by the parties to appoint or nominate an arbitrator is not liable for anything done or omitted in the discharge or purported discharge of that function unless the act or omission is shown to have been in bad faith.

(2) An arbitral or other institution or person by whom an arbitrator is appointed or nominated is not liable, by reason of having appointed or nominated him, for anything done or omitted by the arbitrator (or his employees or agents) in the discharge or purported discharge of his functions as arbitrator.

(3) The above provisions apply to an employee or agent of an arbitral or other institution or person as they apply to the institution or person himself.

Charge to secure payment of solicitors' costs

75. The powers of the court to make declarations and orders under section 73 of the Solicitors Act 1974 or Article 71H of the Solicitors

(Northern Ireland) Order 1976 (power to charge property recovered in the proceedings with the payment of solicitors' costs) may be exercised in relation to arbitral proceedings as if those proceedings were proceedings in the court.

Supplementary

Service of notices, etc

76.—(1) The parties are free to agree on the manner of service of any notice or other document required or authorised to be given or served in pursuance of the arbitration agreement or for the purposes of the arbitral proceedings.

(2) If or to the extent that there is no such agreement the following provisions apply.

(3) A notice or other document may be served on a person by any effective means.

(4) If a notice or other document is addressed, pre-paid and delivered by post—

    (a) to the addressee's last known principal residence or, if he is or has been carrying on a trade, profession or business, his last known principal business address, or

    (b) where the addressee is a body corporate, to the body's registered or principal office,

it shall be treated as effectively served.

(5) This section does not apply to the service of documents for the purposes of legal proceedings, for which provision is made by rules of court.

(6) References in this Part to a notice or other document include any form of communication in writing and references to giving or serving a notice or other document shall be construed accordingly.

Powers of court in relation to service of documents

77.—(1) This section applies where service of a document on a person in the manner agreed by the parties, or in accordance with provisions of section 76 having effect in default of agreement, is not reasonably practicable.

(2) Unless otherwise agreed by the parties, the court may make such order as it thinks fit—

    (a) for service in such manner as the court may direct, or

    (b) dispensing with service of the document.

(3) Any party to the arbitration agreement may apply for an order, but only after exhausting any available arbitral process for resolving the matter.

(4) The leave of the court is required for any appeal from a decision of the court under this section.

Reckoning periods of time

78.—(1) The parties are free to agree on the method of reckoning periods of time for the purposes of any provision agreed by them or any provision of this Part having effect in default of such agreement.

(2) If or to the extent there is no such agreement, periods of time shall be reckoned in accordance with the following provisions.

(3) Where the act is required to be done within a specified period after or from a specified date, the period begins immediately after that date.

(4) Where the act is required to be done a specified number of clear days after a specified date, at least that number of days must intervene between the day on which the act is done and that date.

(5) Where the period is a period of seven days or less which would include a Saturday, Sunday or a public holiday in the place where anything which has to be done within the period falls to be done, that day shall be excluded.

In relation to England and Wales or Northern Ireland, a "public holiday" means Christmas Day, Good Friday or a day which under the Banking and Financial Dealings Act 1971 is a bank holiday.

Power of court to extend time limits relating to arbitral proceedings

79.—(1) Unless the parties otherwise agree, the court may by order extend any time limit agreed by them in relation to any matter relating to the arbitral proceedings or specified in any provision of this Part having effect in default of such agreement.

This section does not apply to a time limit to which section 12 applies (power of court to extend time for beginning arbitral proceedings, etc).

(2) An application for an order may be made—

  (a) by any party to the arbitral proceedings (upon notice to the other parties and to the tribunal), or

  (b) by the arbitral tribunal (upon notice to the parties).

(3) The court shall not exercise its power to extend a time limit unless it is satisfied—

  (a) that any available recourse to the tribunal, or to any arbitral or other institution or person vested by the parties with power in that regard, has first been exhausted, and

  (b) that a substantial injustice would otherwise be done.

(4) The court's power under this section may be exercised whether or not the time has already expired.

(5) An order under this section may be made on such terms as the court thinks fit.

(6) The leave of the court is required for any appeal from a decision of the court under this section.

Notice and other requirements in connection with legal proceedings

80.—(1) References in this Part to an application, appeal or other step in relation to legal proceedings being taken "upon notice" to the other parties to the arbitral proceedings, or to the tribunal, are to such notice of the originating process as is required by rules of court and do not impose any separate requirement.

(2) Rules of court shall be made—
   (a) requiring such notice to be given as indicated by any provision of this Part, and
   (b) as to the manner, form and content of any such notice.

(3) Subject to any provision made by rules of court, a requirement to give notice to the tribunal of legal proceedings shall be construed—
   (a) if there is more than one arbitrator, as a requirement to give notice to each of them and
   (b) if the tribunal is not fully constituted, as a requirement to give notice to any arbitrator who has been appointed.

(4) References in this Part to making an application or appeal to the court within a specified period are to the issue within that period of the appropriate originating process in accordance with rules of court.

(5) Where any provision of this Part requires an application or appeal to be made to the court within a specified time, the rules of court relating to the reckoning of periods, the extending or abridging of periods, and the consequences of not taking a step within the period prescribed by the rules, apply in relation to that requirement.

(6) Provision may be made by rules of court amending the provisions of this Part—
   (a) with respect to the time within which any application or appeal to the court must be made,
   (b) so as to keep any provision made by this Part in relation to arbitral proceedings in step with the corresponding provision of rules of court applying in relation to proceedings in the court, or
   (c) so as to keep any provision made by this Part in relation to legal proceedings in step with the corresponding provision of rules of court applying generally in relation to proceedings in the court.

(7) Nothing in this section affects the generality of the power to make rules of court.

Saving for certain matters governed by common law

81.—(1) Nothing in this Part shall be construed as excluding the operation of any rule of law consistent with the provisions of this Part, in particular, any rule of law as to—
   (a) matters which are not capable of settlement by arbitration;
   (b) the effect of an oral arbitration agreement or
   (c) the refusal of recognition or enforcement of an arbitral award on grounds of public policy.

(2) Nothing in this Act shall be construed as reviving any jurisdiction of the court to set aside or remit an award on the ground of errors of fact or law on the face of the award.

Minor definitions

82.—(1) In this Part—

"arbitrator", unless the context otherwise requires, includes an umpire;

"available arbitral process", in relation to any matter, includes any process of appeal to or review by an arbitral or other institution or person vested by the parties with powers in relation to that matter;

"claimant", unless the context otherwise requires, includes a counter-claimant, and related expressions shall be construed accordingly;

"dispute" includes any difference;

"enactment" includes an enactment contained in Northern Ireland legislation;

"legal proceedings" means civil proceedings in the High Court or a county court;

"peremptory order" means an order made under section 41(5) or made in exercise of any corresponding power conferred by the parties;

"premises" includes land, buildings, moveable structures, vehicles, vessels, aircraft and hovercraft;

"question of law" means—

(a) for a court in England and Wales, a question of the law of England and Wales, and

(b) for a court in Northern Ireland, a question of the law of Northern Ireland;

"substantive jurisdiction", in relation to an arbitral tribunal, refers to the matters specified in section 30(1)(a) to (c), and references to the tribunal exceeding its substantive jurisdiction shall be construed accordingly.

(2) References in this Part to a party to an arbitration agreement include any person claiming under or through a party to the agreement.

Index of defined expressions: Part I

83. In this Part the expressions listed below are defined or otherwise explained by the provisions indicated—

agreement, agree and agreed	section 5(1)
agreement in writing	section 5(2) to (5)
arbitration agreement	sections 6 and 5(1)
arbitrator	section 82(1)
available arbitral process	section 82(1)
claimant	section 82(1)
commencement (in relation to arbitral proceedings)	section 14

costs of the arbitration	section 59
the court	section 105
dispute	section 82(1)
enactment	section 82(1)
legal proceedings	section 82(1)
Limitation Acts	section 13(4)
notice (or other document)	section 76(6)
party—	
—in relation to an arbitration agreement	section 82(2)
—where section 106(2) or (3) applies	section 106(4)
peremptory order	section 82(1) (and see section 41(5))
premises	section 82(1)
question of law	section 82(1)
recoverable costs	sections 63 and 64
seat of the arbitration	section 3
serve and service (of notice or other document)	section 76(6)
substantive jurisdiction (in relation to an arbitral tribunal)	section 82(1) (and see section 30(1)(a) to (c))
upon notice (to the parties or the tribunal)	section 80
written and in writing	section 5(6)

Transitional provisions

84.—(1) The provisions of this Part do not apply to arbitral proceedings commenced before the date on which this Part comes into force.

(2) They apply to arbitral proceedings commenced on or after that date under an arbitration agreement whenever made.

(3) The above provisions have effect subject to any transitional provision made by an order under section 109(2) (power to include transitional provisions in commencement order).

PART II. OTHER PROVISIONS RELATING TO ARBITRATION

Domestic arbitration agreements

Modification of Part I in relation to domestic arbitration agreement

85.—(1) In the case of a domestic arbitration agreement the provisions of Part I are modified in accordance with the following sections.

(2) For this purpose a "domestic arbitration agreement" means an arbitration agreement to which none of the parties is—

(a) an individual who is a national of, or habitually resident in, a state other than the United Kingdom, or

(b) a body corporate which is incorporated in, or whose central control and management is exercised in, a state other than the United Kingdom,

and under which the seat of the arbitration (if the seat has been designated or determined) is in the United Kingdom.

(3) In subsection (2) "arbitration agreement" and "seat of the arbitration" have the same meaning as in Part I (see sections 3, 5(1) and 6).

Staying of legal proceedings

86.—(1) In section 9 (stay of legal proceedings), subsection (4) (stay unless the arbitration agreement is null and void, inoperative, or incapable of being performed) does not apply to a domestic arbitration agreement.

(2) On an application under that section in relation to a domestic arbitration agreement the court shall grant a stay unless satisfied—

(a) that the arbitration agreement is null and void, inoperative, or incapable of being performed, or

(b) that there are other sufficient grounds for not requiring the parties to abide by the arbitration agreement.

(3) The court may treat as a sufficient ground under subsection (2)(b) the fact that the applicant is or was at any material time not ready and willing to do all things necessary for the proper conduct of the arbitration or of any other dispute resolution procedures required to be exhausted before resorting to arbitration.

(4) For the purposes of this section the question whether an arbitration agreement is a domestic arbitration agreement shall be determined by reference to the facts at the time the legal proceedings are commenced.

Effectiveness of agreement to exclude court's jurisdiction

87.—(1) In the case of a domestic arbitration agreement any agreement to exclude the jurisdiction of the court under—

(a) section 45 (determination of preliminary point of law), or

(b) section 69 (challenging the award: appeal on point of law),

is not effective unless entered into after the commencement of the arbitral proceedings in which the question arises or the award is made.

(2) For this purpose the commencement of the arbitral proceedings has the same meaning as in Part I (see section 14).

(3) For the purposes of this section the question whether an arbitration agreement is a domestic arbitration agreement shall be determined by reference to the facts at the time the agreement is entered into.

Power to repeal or amend sections 85 to 87

88.—(1) The Secretary of State may by order repeal or amend the provisions of sections 85 to 87.

(2) An order under this section may contain such supplementary, incidental and transitional provisions as appear to the Secretary of State to be appropriate.

(3) An order under this section shall be made by statutory instrument and no such order shall be made unless a draft of it has been laid before and approved by a resolution of each House of Parliament.

Consumer arbitration agreements

Application of unfair terms regulations to consumer arbitration agreements

89.—(1) The following sections extend the application of the Unfair Terms in Consumer Contracts Regulations 1994 in relation to a term which constitutes an arbitration agreement.

For this purpose "arbitration agreement" means an agreement to submit to arbitration present or future disputes or differences (whether or not contractual).

(2) In those sections "the Regulations" mean those regulations and includes any regulations amending or replacing those regulations.

(3) Those sections apply whatever the law applicable to the arbitration agreement.

Regulations apply where consumer is a legal person

90. The Regulations apply where the consumer is a legal person as they apply where the consumer is a natural person.

Arbitration agreement unfair where modest amount sought

91.—(1) A term which constitutes an arbitration agreement is unfair for the purposes of the Regulations so far as it relates to a claim for a pecuniary remedy which does not exceed the amount specified by order for the purposes of this section.

(2) Orders under this section may make different provision for different cases and for different purposes.

(3) The power to make orders under this section is exercisable—
   (a) for England and Wales, by the Secretary of State with the concurrence of the Lord Chancellor,
   (b) for Scotland, by the Secretary of State with the concurrence of the Lord Advocate, and
   (c) for Northern Ireland, by the Department of Economic Development for Northern Ireland with the concurrence of the Lord Chancellor.

(4) Any such order for England and Wales or Scotland shall be made by statutory instrument which shall be subject to annulment in pursuance of a resolution of either House of Parliament.

(5) Any such order for Northern Ireland shall be a statutory rule for the

purposes of the Statutory Rules (Northern Ireland) Order 1979 and shall be subject to negative resolution, within the meaning of section 41(6) of the Interpretation Act (Northern Ireland) Order 1954.

Small claims arbitration in the county court

Exclusion of Part I in relation to small claims arbitration in the county court

92. Nothing in Part I of this Act applies to arbitration under section 64 of the County Courts Act 1984.

Appointment of judges as arbitrators

Appointment of judges as arbitrators

93.—(1) A judge of the Commercial Court or an official referee may, if in all the circumstances he thinks fit, accept appointment as a sole arbitrator or as umpire by or by virtue of an arbitration agreement.

(2) A judge of the Commercial Court shall not do so unless the Lord Chief Justice has informed him that, having regard to the state of business in the High Court and the Crown Court, he can be made available.

(3) An official referee shall not do so unless the Lord Chief Justice has informed him that, having regard to the state of official referees' business, he can be made available.

(4) The fees payable for the services of a judge of the Commercial Court or official referee as arbitrator or umpire shall be taken in the High Court.

(5) In this section—
   "arbitration agreement" has the same meaning as in Part I and
   "official referee" means a person nominated under section 68(1)(a) of the Supreme Court Act 1981 to deal with official referees' business.

(6) The provisions of Part I of this Act apply to arbitration before a person appointed under this section with the modifications specified in Schedule 2.

Statutory arbitrations

Application of Part I to statutory arbitrations

94.—(1) The provisions of Part I apply to every arbitration under an enactment (a "statutory arbitration"), whether the enactment was passed or made before or after the commencement of this Act, subject to the adaptations and exclusions specified in sections 95 to 98.

(2) The provisions of Part I do not apply to a statutory arbitration if or to the extent that their application—
   (a) is inconsistent with the provisions of the enactment concerned, with any rules or procedure authorised or recognised by it, or
   (b) is excluded by any other enactment.

(3) In this section and the following provisions of this Part "enactment"—

(a) in England and Wales, includes an enactment contained in sub-ordinate legislation within the meaning of the Interpretation Act 1978;

(b) in Northern Ireland, means a statutory provision within the meaning of section 1(f) of the Interpretation Act (Northern Ireland) 1954.

General adaptation of provisions in relation to statutory arbitrations

95.—(1) The provisions of Part I apply to a statutory arbitration—

(a) as if the arbitration were pursuant to an arbitration agreement and as if the enactment were that agreement, and

(b) as if the persons by and against whom a claim subject to arbitration in pursuance of the enactment may be or has been made were parties to that agreement.

(2) Every statutory arbitration shall be taken to have its seat in England and Wales or, as the case may be, in Northern Ireland.

Specific adaptations of provisions in relation to statutory arbitrations

96.—(1) The following provisions of Part I apply to a statutory arbitration with the following adaptations.

(2) In section 30(1) (competence of tribunal to rule on its own jurisdiction), the reference in paragraph (a) to whether there is a valid arbitration agreement shall be construed as a reference to whether the enactment applies to the dispute or difference in question.

(3) Section 35 (consolidation of proceedings and concurrent hearings) applies only so as to authorise the consolidation of proceedings, or concurrent hearings in proceedings, under the same enactment.

(4) Section 46 (rules applicable to substance of dispute) applies with the omission of subsection (1)(b) (determination in accordance with considerations agreed by parties).

Provisions excluded from applying to statutory arbitrations

97. The following provisions of Part I do not apply in relation to a statutory arbitration—

(a) section 8 (whether agreement discharged by death of a party);

(b) section 12 (power of court to extend agreed time limits);

(c) sections 9(5), 10(2) and 71(4) (restrictions on effect of provision that award condition precedent to right to bring legal proceedings).

Power to make further provision by regulations

98.—(1) The Secretary of State may make provision by regulations for adapting or excluding any provision of Part I in relation to statutory arbitrations in general or statutory arbitrations of any particular description.

(2) The power is exercisable whether the enactment concerned is passed or made before or after the commencement of this Act.

(3) Regulations under this section shall be made by statutory instrument which shall be subject to annulment in pursuance of a resolution of either House of Parliament.

PART III. RECOGNITION AND ENFORCEMENT OF CERTAIN FOREIGN AWARDS

Enforcement of Geneva Convention awards

Continuation of Part II of the Arbitration Act 1950

99. Part II of the Arbitration Act 1950 (enforcement of certain foreign awards) continues to apply in relation to foreign awards within the meaning of that Part which are not also New York Convention awards.

Recognition and enforcement of New York Convention awards

New York Convention awards

100.—(1) In this Part a "New York Convention award" means an award made, in pursuance of an arbitration agreement, in the territory of a state (other than the United Kingdom) which is a party to the New York Convention.

(2) For the purposes of subsection (1) and of the provisions of this Part relating to such awards—

(a) "arbitration agreement" means an arbitration agreement in writing, and

(b) an award shall be treated as made at the seat of the arbitration, regardless of where it was signed, despatched or delivered to any of the parties.

In this subsection "agreement in writing" and "seat of the arbitration" have the same meaning as in Part I.

(3) If Her Majesty by Order in Council declares that a state specified in the Order is a party to the New York Convention, or is a party in respect of any territory so specified, the Order shall, while in force, be conclusive evidence of that fact.

(4) In this section "the New York Convention" means the Convention on the Recognition and Enforcement of Foreign Arbitral Awards adopted by the United Nations Conference on International Commercial Arbitration on 10th June 1958.

Recognition and enforcement of awards

101.—(1) A New York Convention award shall be recognised as binding on the persons as between whom it was made, and may accordingly be relied on by those persons by way of defence, set-off or otherwise in any legal proceedings in England and Wales or Northern Ireland.

(2) A New York Convention award may, by leave of the court, be enforced in the same manner as a judgment or order of the court to the same effect.

As to the meaning of "the court" see section 105.

(3) Where leave is so given, judgment may be entered in terms of the award.

Evidence to be produced by party seeking recognition or enforcement

102.—(1) A party seeking the recognition or enforcement of a New York Convention award must produce—

    (a) the duly authenticated original award or a duly certified copy of it, and

    (b) the original arbitration agreement or a duly certified copy of it.

(2) If the award or agreement is in a foreign language, the party must also produce a translation of it certified by an official or sworn translator or by a diplomatic or consular agent.

Refusal of recognition or enforcement

103.—(1) Recognition or enforcement of a New York Convention award shall not be refused except in the following cases.

(2) Recognition or enforcement of the award may be refused if the person against whom it is invoked proves—

    (a) that a party to the arbitration agreement was (under the law applicable to him) under some incapacity;

    (b) that the arbitration agreement was not valid under the law to which the parties subjected it or, failing any indication thereon, under the law of the country where the award was made;

    (c) that he was not given proper notice of the appointment of the arbitrator or of the arbitration proceedings or was otherwise unable to present his case;

    (d) that the award deals with a difference not contemplated by or not falling within the terms of the submission to arbitration or contains decisions on matters beyond the scope of the submission to arbitration (but see subsection (4));

    (e) that the composition of the arbitral tribunal or the arbitral procedure was not in accordance with the agreement of the parties or, failing such agreement, with the law of the country in which the arbitration took place;

    (f) that the award has not yet become binding on the parties, or has been set aside or suspended by a competent authority of the country in which, or under the law of which, it was made.

(3) Recognition or enforcement of the award may also be refused if the award is in respect of a matter which is not capable of settlement by arbitration, or if it would be contrary to public policy to recognise or enforce the award.

(4) An award which contains decisions on matters not submitted to arbitration may be recognised or enforced to the extent that it contains decisions on matters submitted to arbitration which can be separated from those on matters not so submitted.

(5) Where an application for the setting aside or suspension of the award has been made to such a competent authority as is mentioned in subsection (2)(f), the court before which the award is sought to be relied upon may, if it considers it proper, adjourn the decision on the recognition or enforcement of the award.

It may also on the application of the party claiming recognition or enforcement of the award order the other party to give suitable security.

Saving for other bases of recognition or enforcement

104. Nothing in the preceding provisions of this Part affects any right to rely upon or enforce a New York Convention award at common law or under section 66.

PART IV. GENERAL PROVISIONS

Meaning of "the court": jurisdiction of High Court and county court

105.—(1) In this Act "the court" means the High Court or a county court, subject to the following provisions.

(2) The Lord Chancellor may by order make provision—
- (a) allocating proceedings under this Act to the High Court or to county courts or
- (b) specifying proceedings under this Act which may be commenced or taken only in the High Court or in a county court.

(3) The Lord Chancellor may by order make provision requiring proceedings of any specified description under this Act in relation to which a county court has jurisdiction to be commenced or taken in one or more specified county courts.

Any jurisdiction so exercisable by a specified county court is exercisable throughout England and Wales or, as the case may be, Northern Ireland.

(4) An order under this section—
- (a) may differentiate between categories of proceedings by reference to such criteria as the Lord Chancellor sees fit to specify, and
- (b) may make such incidental or transitional provision as the Lord Chancellor considers necessary or expedient.

(5) An order under this section for England and Wales shall be made by statutory instrument which shall be subject to annulment in pursuance of a resolution of either House of Parliament.

(6) An order under this section for Northern Ireland shall be a statutory rule for the purposes of the Statutory Rules (Northern Ireland) Order 1979 which shall be subject to annulment in pursuance of a resolution of either House of Parliament in like manner as a statutory instrument and section 5 of the Statutory Instruments Act 1946 shall apply accordingly.

Crown application

106.—(1) Part I of this Act applies to any arbitration agreement to which Her Majesty, either in right of the Crown or of the Duchy of Lancaster or otherwise, or the Duke of Cornwall, is a party.

(2) Where Her Majesty is party to an arbitration agreement otherwise than in right of the Crown, Her Majesty shall be represented for the purposes of any arbitral proceedings—

    (a) where the agreement was entered into by Her Majesty in right of the Duchy of Lancaster, by the Chancellor of the Duchy or such person as he may appoint, and

    (b) in any other case, by such person as Her Majesty may appoint in writing under the Royal Sign Manual.

(3) Where the Duke of Cornwall is party to an arbitration agreement, he shall be represented for the purposes of any arbitral proceedings by such person as he may appoint.

(4) References in Part I to a party or the parties to the arbitration agreement or to arbitral proceedings shall be construed, where subsection (2) or (3) applies, as references to the person representing Her Majesty or the Duke of Cornwall.

Consequential amendments and repeals

107.—(1) The enactments specified in Schedule 3 are amended in accordance with that Schedule, the amendments being consequential on the provisions of this Act.

(2) The enactments specified in Schedule 4 are repealed to the extent specified.

Extent

108.—(1) The provisions of this Act extend to England and Wales and, except as mentioned below, to Northern Ireland.

(2) The following provisions of Part II do not extend to Northern Ireland—
section 92 (exclusion of Part I in relation to small claims arbitration in the county court), and
section 93 and Schedule 2 (appointment of judges as arbitrators).

(3) Sections 89, 90 and 91 (consumer arbitration agreements) extend

to Scotland and the provisions of Schedules 3 and 4 (consequential amendments and repeals) extend to Scotland as far as they relate to enactments which so extend, subject as follows.

(4) The repeal of the Arbitration Act 1975 extends only to England and Wales and Northern Ireland.

Commencement

109.—(1) The provisions of this Act come into force on such day as the Secretary of State may appoint by order made by statutory instrument, and different days may be appointed for different purposes.

(2) An order under subsection (1) may contain such transitional provisions as appear to the Secretary of State to be appropriate.

Short title

110. This Act may be cited as the Arbitration Act 1996.

SCHEDULE 1. MANDATORY PROVISIONS OF PART I
SECTION 4(1)

sections 9 to 11 (stay of legal proceedings);
section 12 (power of court to extend agreed time limits);
section 13 (application of Limitation Acts);
section 24 (power of court to remove arbitrator);
section 26(1) (effect of death of arbitrator);
section 28 (liability of parties for fees and expenses of arbitrators);
section 29 (immunity of arbitrator);
section 31 (objection to substantive jurisdiction of tribunal);
section 32 (determination of preliminary point of jurisdiction);
section 33 (general duty of tribunal);
section 37(2) (items to be treated as expenses of arbitrators);
section 40 (general duty of parties);
section 43 (securing the attendance of witnesses);
section 56 (power to withhold award in case of non-payment);
section 60 (effectiveness of agreement for payment of costs in any event);
section 66 (enforcement of award);
sections 67 and 68 (challenging the award: substantive jurisdiction and serious irregularity), and sections 70 and 71 (supplementary provisions effect of order of court) so far as relating to those sections;
section 72 (saving for rights of person who takes no part in proceedings);
section 73 (loss of right to object);
section 74 (immunity of arbitral institutions, etc.);
section 75 (charge to secure payment of solicitors' costs).

SCHEDULE 2. MODIFICATIONS OF PART I IN RELATION TO JUDGE-ARBITRATORS SECTION 93(6)

Introductory

1. In this Schedule "judge-arbitrator" means a judge of the Commercial Court or official referee appointed as arbitrator or umpire under section 93.

General

2.—(1) Subject to the following provisions of this Schedule, references in Part I to the court shall be construed in relation to a judge-arbitrator, or in relation to the appointment of a judge-arbitrator, as references to the Court of Appeal.

(2) The references in sections 32(6), 45(6) and 69(8) to the Court of Appeal shall in such a case be construed as references to the House of Lords.

Arbitrator's fees

3.—(1) The power of the court in section 28(2) to order consideration and adjustment of the liability of a party for the fees of an arbitrator may be exercised by a judge-arbitrator.

(2) Any such exercise of the power is subject to the powers of the Court of Appeal under sections 24(4) and 25(3)(b) (directions as to entitlement to fees or expenses in case of removal or resignation).

Exercise of court powers in support of arbitration

4.—(1) Where the arbitral tribunal consists of or includes a judge-arbitrator the powers of the court under sections 42 to 44 (enforcement of peremptory orders, summoning witnesses, and other court powers) are exercisable by the High Court and also by the judge-arbitrator himself.

(2) Anything done by a judge-arbitrator in the exercise of those powers shall be regarded as done by him in his capacity as judge of the High Court and have effect as if done by that court.

Nothing in this sub-paragraph prejudices any power vested in him as arbitrator or umpire.

Extension of time for making award

5.—(1) The power conferred by section 50 (extension of time for making award) is exercisable by the judge-arbitrator himself.

(2) Any appeal from a decision of a judge-arbitrator under that section lies to the Court of Appeal with the leave of that court.

Withholding award in case of non-payment

6.—(1) The provisions of paragraph 7 apply in place of the provisions of section 56 (power to withhold award in the case of non-payment) in relation to the withholding of an award for non-payment of the fees and expenses of a judge-arbitrator.

(2) This does not affect the application of section 56 in relation to the delivery of such an award by an arbitral or other institution or person vested by the parties with powers in relation to the delivery of the award.

7.—(1) A judge-arbitrator may refuse to deliver an award except upon payment of the fees and expenses mentioned in section 56(1).

(2) The judge-arbitrator may, on an application by a party to the arbitral proceedings, order that if he pays into the High Court the fees and expenses demanded, or such lesser amount as the judge-arbitrator may specify—

    (a) the award shall be delivered,

    (b) the amount of the fees and expenses properly payable shall be determined by such means and upon such terms as he may direct, and

    (c) out of the money paid into court there shall be paid out such fees and expenses as may be found to be properly payable and the balance of the money (if any) shall be paid out to the applicant.

(3) For this purpose the amount of fees and expenses properly payable is the amount the applicant is liable to pay under section 28 or any agreement relating to the payment of the arbitrator.

(4) No application to the judge-arbitrator under this paragraph may be made where there is any available arbitral process for appeal or review of the amount of the fees or expenses demanded.

(5) Any appeal from a decision of a judge-arbitrator under this paragraph lies to the Court of Appeal with the leave of that court.

(6) Where a party to arbitral proceedings appeals under sub-paragraph (5), an arbitrator is entitled to appear and be heard.

Correction of award or additional award

8. Subsections (4) to (6) of section 57 (correction of award or additional award: time limit for application or exercise of power) do not apply to a judge-arbitrator.

Costs

9. Where the arbitral tribunal consists of or includes a judge-arbitrator the powers of the court under section 63(4) (determination of recoverable costs) shall be exercised by the High Court.

10.—(1) The power of the court under section 64 to determine an arbitrator's reasonable fees and expenses may be exercised by a judge-arbitrator.

(2) Any such exercise of the power is subject to the powers of the Court of Appeal under sections 24(4) and 25(3)(b) (directions as to entitlement to fees or expenses in case of removal or resignation).

Enforcement of award

11. The leave of the court required by section 66 (enforcement of award) may in the case of an award of a judge-arbitrator be given by the judge-arbitrator himself.

Solicitors' costs

12. The powers of the court to make declarations and orders under the provisions applied by section 75 (power to charge property recovered in arbitral proceedings with the payment of solicitors' costs) may be exercised by the judge-arbitrator.

Powers of court in relation to service of documents

13.—(1) The power of the court under section 77(2) (powers of court in relation to service of documents) is exercisable by the judge-arbitrator.

(2) Any appeal from a decision of a judge-arbitrator under that section lies to the Court of Appeal with the leave of that court.

Powers of court to extend time limits relating to arbitral proceedings

14.—(1) The power conferred by section 79 (power of court to extend time limits relating to arbitral proceedings) is exercisable by the judge-arbitrator himself.

(2) Any appeal from a decision of a judge-arbitrator under that section lies to the Court of Appeal with the leave of that court.

SCHEDULE 3. CONSEQUENTIAL AMENDMENTS
SECTION 107(1)

Merchant Shipping Act 1894 (c.60)

1. In section 496 of the Merchant Shipping Act 1894 (provisions as to deposits by owners of goods), after subsection (4) insert—

"(5) In subsection (3) the expression 'legal proceedings' includes arbitral proceedings and as respects England and Wales and Northern Ireland the provisions of section 14 of the Arbitration Act 1996 apply to determine when such proceedings are commenced.".

Stannaries Court (Abolition) Act 1896 (c.45)

2. In section 4(1) of the Stannaries Court (Abolition) Act 1896 (references of certain disputes to arbitration), for the words from "tried before" to "any such reference" substitute "referred to arbitration before himself or before an arbitrator agreed on by the parties or an officer of the court".

Tithe Act 1936 (c.43)

3. In section 39(1) of the Tithe Act 1936 (proceedings of Tithe Redemption Commission)–
   (a) for "the Arbitration Acts 1889 to 1934" substitute "Part I of the Arbitration Act 1996";
   (b) for paragraph (e) substitute—
       "(e) the making of an application to the court to determine a preliminary point of law and the bringing of an appeal to the court on a point of law;";
   (c) for "the said Acts" substitute "Part I of the Arbitration Act 1996".

Education Act 1944 (c.31)

4. In section 75(2) of the Education Act 1944 (proceedings of Independent School Tribunals) for "the Arbitration Acts 1889 to 1934" substitute "Part I of the Arbitration Act 1996".

Commonwealth Telegraphs Act 1949 (c.39)

5. In section 8(2) of the Commonwealth Telegraphs Act 1949 (proceedings of referees under the Act) for "the Arbitration Acts 1889 to 1934, or the Arbitration Act (Northern Ireland) 1937," substitute "Part I of the Arbitration Act 1996".

Lands Tribunal Act 1949 (c.42)

6. In section 3 of the Lands Tribunal Act 1949 (proceedings before the Lands Tribunal)–
   (a) in subsection (6)(c) (procedural rules: power to apply Arbitration Acts), and
   (b) in subsection (8) (exclusion of Arbitration Acts except as applied by rules),
for "the Arbitration Acts 1889 to 1934" substitute "Part I of the Arbitration Act 1996".

Wireless Telegraphy Act 1949 (c.54)

7. In the Wireless Telegraphy Act 1949, Schedule 2 (procedure of appeals tribunal), in paragraph 3(1)–
   (a) for the words "the Arbitration Acts 1889 to 1934" substitute "Part I of the Arbitration Act 1996";
   (b) after the word "Wales" insert "or Northern Ireland" and
   (c) for "the said Acts" substitute "Part I of that Act".

Patents Act 1949 (c.87)

8. In section 67 of the Patents Act 1949 (proceedings as to infringement of pre-1978 patents referred to comptroller), for "The Arbitration Acts 1889 to 1934" substitute "Part I of the Arbitration Act 1996".

National Health Service (Amendment) Act 1949 (c.93)

9. In section 7(8) of the National Health Service (Amendment) Act 1949 (arbitration in relation to hardship arising from the National Health Service Act 1946 or the Act), for "the Arbitration Acts 1889 to 1934" substitute "Part I of the Arbitration Act 1996" and for "the said Acts" substitute "Part I of that Act".

Arbitration Act 1950 (c.27)

10. In section 36(1) of the Arbitration Act 1950 (effect of foreign awards enforceable under Part II of that Act) for "section 26 of this Act" substitute "section 66 of the Arbitration Act 1996".

Interpretation Act (Northern Ireland) 1954 (c.33 (N.I.))

11. In section 46(2) of the Interpretation Act (Northern Ireland) 1954 (miscellaneous definitions), for the definition of "arbitrator" substitute—

" 'arbitrator' has the same meaning as in Part I of the Arbitration Act 1996;".

Agricultural Marketing Act 1958 (c.47)

12. In section 12(1) of the Agricultural Marketing Act 1958 (application of provisions of Arbitration Act 1950)–
   (a) for the words from the beginning to "shall apply" substitute "Sections 45 and 69 of the Arbitration Act 1996 (which relate to the determination by the court of questions of law) and section 66 of that Act (enforcement of awards) apply" and
   (b) for "an arbitration" substitute "arbitral proceedings".

Carriage by Air Act 1961 (c.27)

13.—(1) The Carriage by Air Act 1961 is amended as follows.
   (2) In section 5(3) (time for bringing proceedings)–
   (a) for "an arbitration" in the first place where it occurs substitute "arbitral proceedings" and
   (b) for the words from "and subsections (3) and (4)" to the end substitute "and the provisions of section 14 of the Arbitration Act 1996 apply to determine when such proceedings are commenced.".
   (3) In section 11(c) (application of section 5 to Scotland)—

(a) for "subsections (3) and (4)" substitute "the provisions of section 14 of the Arbitration Act 1996" and
(b) for "an arbitration" substitute "arbitral proceedings".

Factories Act 1961 (c.34)

14. In the Factories Act 1961, for section 171 (application of Arbitration Act 1950), substitute—

"*Application of the Arbitration Act 1996*
171. Part I of the Arbitration Act 1996 does not apply to proceedings under this Act except in so far as it may be applied by regulations made under this Act.".

Clergy Pensions Measure 1961 (No. 3)

15. In the Clergy Pensions Measure 1961, section 38(4) (determination of questions), for the words "The Arbitration Act 1950" substitute "Part I of the Arbitration Act 1996".

Transport Act 1962 (c.46)

16.—(1) The Transport Act 1962 is amended as follows.
(2) In section 74(6)(f) (proceedings before referees in pension disputes), for the words "the Arbitration Act 1950" substitute "Part I of the Arbitration Act 1996".
(3) In section 81(7) (proceedings before referees in compensation disputes), for the words "the Arbitration Act 1950" substitute "Part I of the Arbitration Act 1996".
(4) In Schedule 7, Part IV (pensions), in paragraph 17(5) for the words "the Arbitration Act 1950" substitute "Part I of the Arbitration Act 1996".

Corn Rents Act 1963 (c.14)

17. In the Corn Rents Act 1963, section 1(5) (schemes for apportioning corn rents, etc.), for the words "the Arbitration Act 1950" substitute "Part I of the Arbitration Act 1996".

Plant Varieties and Seeds Act 1964 (c.14)

18. In section 10(6) of the Plant Varieties and Seeds Act 1964 (meaning of "arbitration agreement"), for "the meaning given by section 32 of the Arbitration Act 1950" substitute "the same meaning as in Part I of the Arbitration Act 1996".

Lands Tribunal and Compensation Act (Northern Ireland) 1964 (c.29 (N.I.))

19. In section 9 of the Lands Tribunal and Compensation Act (Northern Ireland) 1964 (proceedings of Lands Tribunal), in subsection (3) (where Tribunal acts as arbitrator) for "the Arbitration Act (Northern Ireland) 1937" substitute "Part I of the Arbitration Act 1996".

Industrial and Provident Societies Act 1965 (c.12)

20.—(1) Section 60 of the Industrial and Provident Societies Act 1965 is amended as follows.

(2) In subsection (8) (procedure for hearing disputes between society and member, etc.)–

- (a) in paragraph (a) for "the Arbitration Act 1950" substitute "Part I of the Arbitration Act 1996" and
- (b) in paragraph (b) omit "by virtue of section 12 of the said Act of 1950".

(3) For subsection (9) substitute—

"(9) The court or registrar to whom any dispute is referred under subsections (2) to (7) may at the request of either party state a case on any question of law arising in the dispute for the opinion of the High Court or, as the case may be, the Court of Session".

Carriage of Goods by Road Act 1965 (c.37)

21. In section 7(2) of the Carriage of Goods by Road Act 1965 (arbitrations: time at which deemed to commence), for paragraphs (a) and (b) substitute—

"(a) as respects England and Wales and Northern Ireland, the pro-visions of section 14(3) to (5) of the Arbitration Act 1996 (which determine the time at which an arbitration is commenced) apply;".

Factories Act (Northern Ireland) 1965 (c.20 (N.I.))

22. In section 171 of the Factories Act (Northern Ireland) 1965 (application of Arbitration Act), for "The Arbitration Act (Northern Ireland) 1937" substitute "Part I of the Arbitration Act 1996".

Commonwealth Secretariat Act 1966 (c.10)

23. In section 1(3) of the Commonwealth Secretariat Act 1966 (contracts with Commonwealth Secretariat to be deemed to contain pro-vision for arbitration), for "the Arbitration Act 1950 and the Arbitration Act (Northern Ireland) 1937" substitute "Part I of the Arbitration Act 1996".

Arbitration (International Investment Disputes) Act 1966 (c.41)

24. In the Arbitration (International Investment Disputes) Act 1966, for section 3 (application of Arbitration Act 1950 and other enactments) substitute—

"Application of provisions of Arbitration Act 1996
3.—(1) The Lord Chancellor may by order direct that any of the provisions contained in sections 36 and 38 to 44 of the Arbitration Act 1996 (provisions concerning the conduct of arbitral proceedings, etc.) shall apply to such proceedings pursuant to the Convention as are specified in the order with or without any modifications or exceptions specified in the order.

(2) Subject to subsection (1), the Arbitration Act 1996 shall not apply to proceedings pursuant to the Convention, but this subsection shall not be taken as affecting section 9 of that Act (stay of legal proceedings in respect of matter subject to arbitration).

(3) An order made under this section—
    (a) may be varied or revoked by a subsequent order so made, and
    (b) shall be contained in a statutory instrument.".

Poultry Improvement Act (Northern Ireland) 1968 (c.12 (N.I.))

25. In paragraph 10(4) of the Schedule to the Poultry Improvement Act (Northern Ireland) 1968 (reference of disputes), for "The Arbitration Act (Northern Ireland) 1937" substitute "Part I of the Arbitration Act 1996".

Industrial and Provident Societies Act (Northern Ireland) 1969 (c.24 (N.I.))

26.—(1) Section 69 of the Industrial and Provident Societies Act (Northern Ireland) 1969 (decision of disputes) is amended as follows.

(2) In subsection (7) (decision of disputes)–
    (a) in the opening words, omit the words from "and without preju-dice" to "1937";
    (b) at the beginning of paragraph (a) insert "without prejudice to any powers exercisable by virtue of Part I of the Arbitration Act 1996," and
    (c) in paragraph (b) omit "the registrar or" and "registrar or" and for the words from "as might have been granted by the High Court" to the end substitute "as might be granted by the registrar".

(3) For subsection (8) substitute—

"(8) The court or registrar to whom any dispute is referred under subsections (2) to (6) may at the request of either party state a case on any question of law arising in the dispute for the opinion of the High Court.".

Health and Personal Social Services (Northern Ireland) Order 1972 (N.I. 14)

27. In Article 105(6) of the Health and Personal Social Services (Northern Ireland) Order 1972 (arbitrations under the Order), for "the Arbitration Act (Northern Ireland) 1937" substitute "Part I of the Arbitration Act 1996".

Consumer Credit Act 1974 (c.39)

28.—(1) Section 146 of the Consumer Credit Act 1974 is amended as follows.

(2) In subsection (2) (solicitor engaged in contentious business), for "section 86(1) of the Solicitors Act 1957" substitute "section 87(1) of the Solicitors Act 1974".

(3) In subsection (4) (solicitor in Northern Ireland engaged in contentious business), for the words from "business done" to "Administration of Estates (Northern Ireland) Order 1979" substitute "contentious business (as defined in Article 3(2) of the Solicitors (Northern Ireland) Order 1976.".

Friendly Societies Act 1974 (c.46)

29.—(1) The Friendly Societies Act 1974 is amended as follows.

(2) For section 78(1) (statement of case) substitute—

"(1) Any arbitrator, arbiter or umpire to whom a dispute falling within section 76 above is referred under the rules of a registered society or branch may at the request of either party state a case on any question of law arising in the dispute for the opinion of the High Court or, as the case may be, the Court of Session.".

(3) In section 83(3) (procedure on objections to amalgamations etc. of friendly societies), for "the Arbitration Act 1950 or, in Northern Ireland, the Arbitration Act (Northern Ireland) 1937" substitute "Part I of the Arbitration Act 1996".

Industry Act 1975 (c.68)

30. In Schedule 3 to the Industry Act (arbitration of disputes relating to vesting and compensation orders), in paragraph 14 (application of certain provisions of Arbitration Acts)–

    (a) for "the Arbitration Act 1950 or, in Northern Ireland, the Arbitration Act (Northern Ireland) 1937" substitute "Part I of the Arbitration Act 1996", and

    (b) for "that Act" substitute "that Part".

Industrial Relations (Northern Ireland) Order 1976 (N.I. 16)

31. In Article 59(9) of the Industrial Relations (Northern Ireland) Order 1976 (proceedings of industrial tribunal), for "The Arbitration Act

(Northern Ireland) 1937" substitute "Part I of the Arbitration Act 1996".

Aircraft and Shipbuilding Industries Act 1977 (c.3)

32. In Schedule 7 to the Aircraft and Shipbuilding Industries Act 1977 (procedure of Arbitration Tribunal), in paragraph 2–
    (a) for "the Arbitration Act 1950 or, in Northern Ireland, the Arbitration Act (Northern Ireland) 1937" substitute "Part I of the Arbitration Act 1996", and
    (b) for "that Act" substitute "that Part".

Patents Act 1977 (c.37)

33. In section 130 of the Patents Act 1977 (interpretation), in subsection (8) (exclusion of Arbitration Act) for "The Arbitration Act 1950" substitute "Part I of the Arbitration Act 1996".

Judicature (Northern Ireland) Act 1978 (c.23)

34.—(1) The Judicature (Northern Ireland) Act 1978 is amended as follows.

(2) In section 35(2) (restrictions on appeals to the Court of Appeal), after paragraph (f) insert—

"(fa) except as provided by Part I of the Arbitration Act 1996, from any decision of the High Court under that Part;".

(3) In section 55(2) (rules of court), after paragraph (c) insert—

"(cc) providing for any prescribed part of the jurisdiction of the High Court in relation to the trial of any action involving matters of account to be exercised in the prescribed manner by a person agreed by the parties and for the remuneration of any such person;".

Health and Safety at Work (Northern Ireland) Order 1978 (N.I. 9)

35. In Schedule 4 to the Health and Safety at Work (Northern Ireland) Order 1978 (licensing provisions), in paragraph 3, for "The Arbitration Act (Northern Ireland) 1937" substitute "Part I of the Arbitration Act 1996".

County Courts (Northern Ireland) Order 1980 (N.I. 3)

36.—(1) The County Courts (Northern Ireland) Order 1980 is amended as follows.

(2) In Article 30 (civil jurisdiction exercisable by district judge)–
    (a) for paragraph (2) substitute—

"(2) Any order, decision or determination made by a district judge under this Article (other than one made in dealing with a claim by way of arbitration under paragraph (3)) shall be embodied in a decree which for all purposes (including the right of appeal under Part VI) shall have the like effect as a decree pronounced by a county court judge.";

(b) for paragraphs (4) and (5) substitute—

"(4) Where in any action to which paragraph (1) applies the claim is dealt with by way of arbitration under paragraph (3)–

(a) any award made by the district judge in dealing with the claim shall be embodied in a decree which for all purposes (except the right of appeal under Part VI) shall have the like effect as a decree pronounced by a county court judge;

(b) the district judge may, and shall if so required by the High Court, state for the determination of the High Court any question of law arising out of an award so made;

(c) except as provided by sub-paragraph (b), any award so made shall be final and

(d) except as otherwise provided by county court rules, no costs shall be awarded in connection with the action.

(5) Subject to paragraph (4), county court rules may—

(a) apply any of the provisions of Part I of the Arbitration Act 1996 to arbitrations under paragraph (3) with such modifications as may be prescribed;

(b) prescribe the rules of evidence to be followed on any arbitration under paragraph (3) and, in particular, make provision with respect to the manner of taking and questioning evidence.

(5A) Except as provided by virtue of paragraph (5)(a), Part I of the Arbitration Act 1996 shall not apply to an arbitration under paragraph (3).".

(3) After Article 61 insert—

"Appeals from decisions under Part I of Arbitration Act 1996

61A.—(1) Article 61 does not apply to a decision of a county court judge made in the exercise of the jurisdiction conferred by Part I of the Arbitration Act 1996.

(2) Any party dissatisfied with a decision of the county court made in the exercise of the jurisdiction conferred by any of the following provisions of Part I of the Arbitration Act 1996, namely—

(a) section 32 (question as to substantive jurisdiction of arbitral tribunal);

(b) section 45 (question of law arising in course of arbitral proceedings);

(c) section 67 (challenging award of arbitral tribunal substantive jurisdiction);

(d) section 68 (challenging award of arbitral tribunal serious irregularity);

(e) section 69 (appeal on point of law),

may, subject to the provisions of that Part, appeal from that decision to the Court of Appeal.

(3) Any party dissatisfied with any decision of a county court made in the exercise of the jurisdiction conferred by any other provision of Part I of the Arbitration Act 1996 may, subject to the provisions of that Part, appeal from that decision to the High Court.

(4) The decision of the Court of Appeal on an appeal under paragraph (2) shall be final.".

Supreme Court Act 1981 (c.54)

37.—(1) The Supreme Court Act 1981 is amended as follows.

(2) In section 18(1) (restrictions on appeals to the Court of Appeal), for paragraph (g) substitute—

"(g) except as provided by Part I of the Arbitration Act 1996, from any decision of the High Court under that Part;".

(3) In section 151 (interpretation, etc.), in the definition of "arbitration agreement", for "the Arbitration Act 1950 by virtue of section 32 of that Act;" substitute "Part I of the Arbitration Act 1996;".

Merchant Shipping (Liner Conferences) Act 1982 (c.37)

38. In section 7(5) of the Merchant Shipping (Liner Conferences) Act 1982 (stay of legal proceedings), for the words from "section 4(1)" to the end substitute "section 9 of the Arbitration Act 1996 (which also provides for the staying of legal proceedings).".

Agricultural Marketing (Northern Ireland) Order 1982 (N.I. 12)

39. In Article 14 of the Agricultural Marketing (Northern Ireland) Order 1982 (application of provisions of Arbitration Act (Northern Ireland) 1937)–
   (a) for the words from the beginning to "shall apply" substitute "Section 45 and 69 of the Arbitration Act 1996 (which relate to the determination by the court of questions of law) and section 66 of that Act (enforcement of awards)" apply and
   (b) for "an arbitration" substitute "arbitral proceedings".

Mental Health Act 1983 (c.20)

40. In section 78 of the Mental Health Act 1983 (procedure of Mental Health Review Tribunals), in subsection (9) for "The Arbitration Act 1950" substitute "Part I of the Arbitration Act 1996".

Registered Homes Act 1984 (c.23)

41. In section 43 of the Registered Homes Act 1984 (procedure of Registered Homes Tribunals), in subsection (3) for "The Arbitration Act 1950" substitute "Part I of the Arbitration Act 1996".

Housing Act 1985 (c.68)

42. In section 47(3) of the Housing Act 1985 (agreement as to determination of matters relating to service charges) for "section 32 of the Arbitration Act 1950" substitute "Part I of the Arbitration Act 1996".

Landlord and Tenant Act 1985 (c.70)

43. In section 19(3) of the Landlord and Tenant Act 1985 (agreement as to determination of matters relating to service charges), for "section 32 of the Arbitration Act 1950" substitute "Part I of the Arbitration Act 1996".

Credit Unions (Northern Ireland) Order 1985 (N.I. 12)

44.—(1) Article 72 of the Credit Unions (Northern Ireland) Order 1985 (decision of disputes) is amended as follows.

(2) In paragraph (7)—

    (a) in the opening words, omit the words from "and without prejudice" to "1937";

    (b) at the beginning of sub-paragraph (a) insert "without prejudice to any powers exercisable by virtue of Part I of the Arbitration Act 1996," and

    (c) in sub-paragraph (b) omit "the registrar or" and "registrar or" and for the words from "as might have been granted by the High Court" to the end substitute "as might be granted by the registrar".

(3) For paragraph (8) substitute—

"(8) The court or registrar to whom any dispute is referred under paragraphs (2) to (6) may at the request of either party state a case on any question of law arising in the dispute for the opinion of the High Court.".

Agricultural Holdings Act 1986 (c.5)

45. In section 84(1) of the Agricultural Holdings Act 1986 (provisions relating to arbitration), for "the Arbitration Act 1950" substitute "Part I of the Arbitration Act 1996".

Insolvency Act 1986 (c.45)

46. In the Insolvency Act 1986, after section 349 insert—

"Arbitration agreements to which bankrupt is party.

349A.—(1) This section applies where a bankrupt had become party to a contract containing an arbitration agreement before the commencement of his bankruptcy.

(2) If the trustee in bankruptcy adopts the contract, the arbitration agreement is enforceable by or against the trustee in relation to matters arising from or connected with the contract.

(3) If the trustee in bankruptcy does not adopt the contract and a matter to which the arbitration agreement applies requires to be determined in connection with or for the purposes of the bankruptcy proceedings—

(a) the trustee with the consent of the creditors' committee, or

(b) any other party to the agreement,

may apply to the court which may, if it thinks fit in all the circumstances of the case, order that the matter be referred to arbitration in accordance with the arbitration agreement.

(4) In this section—

'arbitration agreement' has the same meaning as in Part I of the Arbitration Act 1996 and 'the court' means the court which has jurisdiction in the bankruptcy proceedings.".

Building Societies Act 1986 (c.53)

47. In Part II of Schedule 14 to the Building Societies Act 1986 (settlement of disputes: arbitration), in paragraph 5(6) for "the Arbitration Act 1950 and the Arbitration Act 1979 or, in Northern Ireland, the Arbitration Act (Northern Ireland) 1937" substitute "Part I of the Arbitration Act 1996".

Mental Health (Northern Ireland) Order 1986 (N.I. 4)

48. In Article 83 of the Mental Health (Northern Ireland) Order 1986 (procedure of Mental Health Review Tribunal), in paragraph (8) for "The Arbitration Act (Northern Ireland) 1937" substitute "Part I of the Arbitration Act 1996".

Multilateral Investment Guarantee Agency Act 1988 (c.8)

49. For section 6 of the Multilateral Investment Guarantee Agency Act 1988 (application of Arbitration Act) substitute—

"Application of Arbitration Act

6.—(1) The Lord Chancellor may by order made by statutory instrument direct that any of the provisions of sections 36 and 38 to 44 of the Arbitration Act 1996 (provisions in relation to the conduct of the arbitral proceedings, etc.) apply, with such modifications or exceptions as are specified in the order, to such arbitration proceedings pursuant to Annex II to the Convention as are specified in the order.

(2) Except as provided by an order under subsection (1) above, no

provision of Part I of the Arbitration Act 1996 other than section 9 (stay of legal proceedings) applies to any such proceedings.".

Copyright, Designs and Patents Act 1988 (c.48)

50. In section 150 of the Copyright, Designs and Patents Act 1988 (Lord Chancellor's power to make rules for Copyright Tribunal), for subsection (2) substitute—

"(2) The rules may apply in relation to the Tribunal, as respects proceedings in England and Wales or Northern Ireland, any of the provisions of Part I of the Arbitration Act 1996.".

Fair Employment (Northern Ireland) Act 1989 (c.32)

51. In the Fair Employment (Northern Ireland) Act 1989, section 5(7) (procedure of Fair Employment Tribunal), for "The Arbitration Act (Northern Ireland) 1937" substitute "Part I of the Arbitration Act 1996".

Limitation (Northern Ireland) Order 1989 (N.I. 11)

52. In Article 2(2) of the Limitation (Northern Ireland) Order 1989 (interpretation), in the definition of "arbitration agreement", for "the Arbitration Act (Northern Ireland) 1937" substitute "Part I of the Arbitration Act 1996".

Insolvency (Northern Ireland) Order 1989 (N.I. 19)

53. In the Insolvency (Northern Ireland) Order 1989, after Article 320 insert—

"*Arbitration agreements to which bankrupt is party*
320A.—(1) This Article applies where a bankrupt had become party to a contract containing an arbitration agreement before the commencement of his bankruptcy.

(2) If the trustee in bankruptcy adopts the contract, the arbitration agreement is enforceable by or against the trustee in relation to matters arising from or connected with the contract.

(3) If the trustee in bankruptcy does not adopt the contract and a matter to which the arbitration agreement applies requires to be determined in connection with or for the purposes of the bankruptcy proceedings—

(a) the trustee with the consent of the creditors' committee, or

(b) any other party to the agreement,

may apply to the court which may, if it thinks fit in all the circumstances of the case, order that the matter be referred to arbitration in accordance with the arbitration agreement.

(4) In this Article—

'arbitration agreement' has the same meaning as in Part I of the

Arbitration Act 1996 and 'the court' means the court which has jurisdiction in the bankruptcy proceedings.".

Social Security Administration Act 1992 (c.5)

54. In section 59 of the Social Security Administration Act 1992 (procedure for inquiries, etc.), in subsection (7), for "The Arbitration Act 1950" substitute "Part I of the Arbitration Act 1996".

Social Security Administration (Northern Ireland) Act 1992 (c.8)

55. In section 57 of the Social Security Administration (Northern Ireland) Act 1992 (procedure for inquiries, etc.), in subsection (6) for "the Arbitration Act (Northern Ireland) 1937" substitute "Part I of the Arbitration Act 1996".

Trade Union and Labour Relations (Consolidation) Act 1992 (c.52)

56. In sections 212(5) and 263(6) of the Trade Union and Labour Relations (Consolidation) Act 1992 (application of Arbitration Act) for "the Arbitration Act 1950" substitute "Part I of the Arbitration Act 1996".

Industrial Relations (Northern Ireland) Order 1992 (N.I. 5)

57. In Articles 84(9) and 92(5) of the Industrial Relations (Northern Ireland) Order 1992 (application of Arbitration Act) for "The Arbitration Act (Northern Ireland) 1937" substitute "Part I of the Arbitration Act 1996".

Registered Homes (Northern Ireland) Order 1992 (N.I. 20)

58. In Article 33(3) of the Registered Homes (Northern Ireland) Order 1992 (procedure of Registered Homes Tribunal) for "The Arbitration Act (Northern Ireland) 1937" substitute "Part I of the Arbitration Act 1996".

Education Act 1993 (c.35)

59. In section 180(4) of the Education Act 1993 (procedure of Special Educational Needs Tribunal), for "The Arbitration Act 1950" substitute "Part I of the Arbitration Act 1996".

Roads (Northern Ireland) Order 1993 (N.I. 15)

60.—(1) The Roads (Northern Ireland) Order 1993 is amended as follows.

(2) In Article 131 (application of Arbitration Act) for "the Arbitration Act (Northern Ireland) 1937" substitute "Part I of the Arbitration Act 1996".

(3) In Schedule 4 (disputes), in paragraph 3(2) for "the Arbitration Act (Northern Ireland) 1937" substitute "Part I of the Arbitration Act 1996".

Merchant Shipping 1995 (c.21)

61. In Part II of Schedule 6 to the Merchant Shipping Act 1995 (provisions having effect in connection with Convention Relating to the Carriage of Passengers and Their Luggage by Sea), for paragraph 7 substitute—

"7. Article 16 shall apply to arbitral proceedings as it applies to an action and, as respects England and Wales and Northern Ireland, the provisions of section 14 of the Arbitration Act 1996 apply to determine for the purposes of that Article when an arbitration is commenced.".

Industrial Tribunals Act 1996 (c.17)

62. In section 6(2) of the Industrial Tribunals Act 1996 (procedure of industrial tribunals), for "The Arbitration Act 1950" substitute "Part I of the Arbitration Act 1996".

SCHEDULE 4. REPEALS (SECTION 107(2))

Chapter	Short title	Extent of repeal
1892 c. 43.	Military Lands Act 1892.	In section 21(b), the words "under the Arbitration Act 1889".
1922 c. 51.	Allotments Act 1922.	In section 21(3), the words "under the Arbitration Act 1889".
1937 c. 8 (N.I.).	Arbitration Act (Northern Ireland) 1937.	The whole Act.
1949 c. 54.	Wireless Telegraphy Act 1949.	In Schedule 2, paragraph 3(3).
1949 c. 97.	National Parks and Access to the Countryside Act 1949.	In section 18(4), the words from "Without prejudice" to "England or Wales".
1950 c. 27.	Arbitration Act 1950.	Part I. Section 42(3).
1958 c. 47.	Agricultural Marketing Act 1958.	Section 53(8).
1962 c. 46.	Transport Act 1962.	In Schedule 11, Part II, paragraph 7.
1964 c. 14.	Plant Varieties and Seeds Act 1964.	In section 10(4) the words from "or in section 9" to "three arbitrators)". Section 39(3)(b)(i).
1964 c. 29 (N.I.).	Lands Tribunal and Compensation Act (Northern Ireland) 1964.	In section 9(3) the words from "so, however, that" to the end.

Chapter	Short title	Extent of repeal
1965 c. 12.	Industrial and Provident Societies Act 1965.	In section 60(8)(b), the words "by virtue of section 12 of the said Act of 1950".
1965 c. 37.	Carriage of Goods by Road Act 1965.	Section 7(2)(b).
1965 c. 13 (N.I.).	New Towns Act (Northern Ireland) 1965.	In section 27(2), the words from "under and in accordance with" to the end.
1969 c. 24 (N.I.).	Industrial and Provident Societies Act (Northern Ireland) 1969.	In section 69(7)– (a) in the opening words, the words from "and without prejudice" to "1937"; (b) in paragraph (b), the words "the registrar or" and "registrar or".
1970 c. 31.	Administration of Justice Act 1970.	Section 4. Schedule 3.
1973 c. 41.	Fair Trading Act 1973.	Section 33(2)(d).
1973 N.I. 1.	Drainage (Northern Ireland) Order 1973.	In Article 15(4), the words from "under and in accordance" to the end. Article 40(4). In Schedule 7, in paragraph 9(2), the words from "under and in accordance" to the end.
1974 c. 47.	Solicitors Act 1974.	In section 87(1), in the definition of "contentious business", the words "appointed under the Arbitration Act 1950".
1975 c. 3.	Arbitration Act 1975.	The whole Act.
1975 c. 74.	Petroleum and Submarine Pipe-Lines Act 1975	In Part II of Schedule 2— (a) in model clause 40(2), the words "in accordance with the Arbitration Act 1950"; (b) in model clause 40(2B), the words "in accordance with the Arbitration Act (Northern Ireland) 1937". In Part II of Schedule 3, in model clause 38(2), the words "in accordance with the Arbitration Act 1950".
1976 N.I. 12.	Solicitors (Northern Ireland) Order 1976.	In Article 3(2), in the entry "contentious business", the words "appointed

Chapter	*Short title*	*Extent of repeal*
		under the Arbitration Act (Northern Ireland) 1937". Article 71H(3).
1977 c. 37.	Patents Act 1977.	In section 52(4) the words "section 21 of the Arbitration Act 1950 or, as the case may be, section 22 of the Arbitration Act (Northern Ireland) 1937 (statement of cases by arbitrators) but". Section 131(e).
1977 c. 38.	Administration of Justice Act 1977.	Section 17(2).
1978 c. 23.	Judicature (Northern Ireland) Act 1978.	In section 35(2), paragraph (g)(v). In Schedule 5, the amendment to the Arbitration Act 1950.
1979 c. 42.	Arbitration Act 1979.	The whole Act.
1980 c. 58.	Limitation Act 1980.	Section 34.
1980 N.I. 3.	County Courts (Northern Ireland) Order 1980.	Article 31(3).
1981 c. 54.	Supreme Court Act 1981.	Section 148.
1982 c. 27.	Civil Jurisdiction and Judgments Act 1982.	Section 25(3)(c) and (5).In section 26— (a) in subsection (1), the words "to arbitration or"; (b) in subsection (1)(a)(i), the words "arbitration or"; (c) in subsection (2), the words "arbitration or".
1982 c. 53.	Administration of Justice Act 1982.	Section 15(6). In Schedule 1, Part IV.
1984 c. 5.	Merchant Shipping Act 1984.	Section 4(8).
1984 c. 12.	Telecommunications Act 1984.	Schedule 2, paragraph 13(8).
1984 c. 16.	Foreign Limitation Periods Act 1984.	Section 5.
1984 c. 28.	County Courts Act 1984.	In Schedule 2, paragraph 70.
1985 c. 61.	Administration of Justice Act 1985.	Section 58. In Schedule 9, paragraph 15.
1985 c. 68.	Housing Act 1985.	In Schedule 18, in paragraph 6(2) the words from "and the Arbitration Act 1950" to the end.
1985 N.I. 12.	Credit Unions (Northern Ireland) Order 1985.	In Article 72(7)— (a) in the opening words, the words from "and

Chapter	Short title	Extent of repeal
		without prejudice" to "1937";
		(b) in sub-paragraph (b), the words "the registrar or" and "registrar or".
1986 c. 45.	Insolvency Act 1986.	In Schedule 14, the entry relating to the Arbitration Act 1950.
1988 c. 8.	Multilateral Investment Guarantee Agency Act 1988.	Section 8(3).
1988 c. 21.	Consumer Arbitration Agreements Act 1988.	The whole Act.
1989 N.I. 11.	Limitation (Northern Ireland) Order 1989.	Article 72. In Schedule 3, paragraph 1.
1989 N.I. 19.	Insolvency (Northern Ireland) Order 1989.	In Part II of Schedule 9, paragraph 66.
1990 c. 41.	Courts and Legal Services Act 1990.	Sections 99 and 101 to 103.
1991 N.I. 7.	Food Safety (Northern Ireland) Order 1991.	In Articles 8(8) and 11(10), the words from "and the provisions" to the end.
1992 c. 40.	Friendly Societies Act 1992.	In Schedule 16, paragraph 30(1).
1995 c. 8.	Agricultural Tenancies Act 1995.	Section 28(4).
1995 c. 21.	Merchant Shipping Act 1995.	Section 96(10). Section 264(9).
1995 c. 42.	Private International Law (Miscellaneous Provisions) Act 1995.	Section 3.

APPENDIX 2

ARBITRATION ACT 1996 (COMMENCEMENT NO. 1) ORDER 1996 (S.I. 1996/3146)

Made   16th December 1996

The Secretary of State, in exercise of the powers conferred on him by section 109 of the Arbitration Act 1996[a], hereby makes the following Order:

1. This Order may be cited as the Arbitration Act 1996 (Commencement No. 1) Order 1996.

2. The provisions of the Arbitration Act 1996 ("the Act") listed in Schedule 1 to this Order shall come into force on the day after this Order is made.

3. The rest of the Act, except sections 85 to 87, shall come into force on 31st January 1997.

4. The transitional provisions in Schedule 2 to this Order shall have effect.

John M. Taylor,
Parliamentary Under-Secretary of State
for Corporate and Consumer Affairs,
16th December 1996   Department of Trade and Industry

SCHEDULE 1   Article 2.

Section 91 so far as it relates to the power to make orders under the section.

Section 105.

Section 107(1) and paragraph 36 of Schedule 3, so far as relating to the provision that may be made by county court rules.

Section 107(2) and the reference in Schedule 4 to the County Courts

(a) 1996 c. 23.

(Northern Ireland) Order 1980[(a)] so far as relating to the above matter.

Sections 108 to 110.

SCHEDULE 2

Article 4.

1. In this Schedule:
   (a) "the appointed day" means the date specified in Article 3 of this Order;
   (b) "arbitration application" means any application relating to arbitration made by or in legal proceedings, whether or not arbitral proceedings have commenced;
   (c) "the old law" means the enactments specified in section 107 as they stood before their amendment or repeal by the Act.

2. The old law shall continue to apply to:
   (a) arbitral proceedings commenced before the appointed day;
   (b) arbitration applications commenced or made before the appointed day;
   (c) arbitration applications commenced or made on or after the appointed day relating to arbitral proceedings commenced before the appointed day
   and the provisions of the Act which would otherwise be applicable shall not apply.

3. The provisions of this Act brought into force by this Order shall apply to any other arbitration application.

4. In the application of paragraph (b) of subsection (1) of section 46 (provision for dispute to be decided in accordance with provisions other than law) to an arbitration agreement made before the appointed day, the agreement shall have effect in accordance with the rules of law (including any conflict of laws rules) as they stood immediately before the appointed day.

EXPLANATORY NOTE

(This note is not part of the Order)

With one exception, this Order brings into force the provisions of the Arbitration Act 1996. Those provisions necessary to enable the substantive provisions to be brought into force are commenced immediately. The substantive provisions come into force on 31st January 1997. Commencement is subject to transitional provisions designed to ensure continuity of legal proceedings and to preserve the current law on what

(a) 1980 N.I. 3.

are known as "honourable engagement" clauses in relation to existing agreements.

Sections 85 to 87, which make special provision in relation to domestic arbitration agreements, are not commenced.

APPENDIX 3

THE HIGH COURT AND COUNTY COURTS (ALLOCATION OF ARBITRATION PROCEEDINGS) ORDER 1996 (S.I. 1996/3215)

Made   19th December 1996

Laid before Parliament   20th December 1996

Coming into force   31st January 1997

The Lord Chancellor, in exercise of the powers conferred on him by section 105 of the Arbitration Act 1996[(a)], hereby makes the following Order:

1.—(1) This Order may be cited as the High Court and County Courts (Allocation of Arbitration Proceedings) Order 1996 and shall come into force on 31st January 1997.

(2) In this Order, "the Act" means the Arbitration Act 1996.

2.   Subject to articles 3 to 5, proceedings under the Act shall be commenced and taken in the High Court.

3.   Proceedings under section 9 of the Act (stay of legal proceedings) shall be commenced in the court in which the legal proceedings are pending.

4.   Proceedings under sections 66 and 101(2) (enforcement of awards) of the Act may be commenced in any county court.

5.—(1) Proceedings under the Act may be commenced and taken in the Central London County Court Business List.

(2) Where, in exercise of the powers conferred by sections 41 and 42 of the County Courts Act 1984[(b)] the High Court or the judge in charge of the Central London County Court Business List orders the transfer of proceedings under the Act which were commenced in the Central London

---

(a) 1996 c. 23.
(b) 1984 c. 28; sections 41 and 42 were substituted by the Courts and Legal Services Act 1990 (c. 41), section 2(2) and (3) and section 41 was amended by the Matrimonial and Family Proceedings Act 1984 (c. 42), Schedule 1 paragraph 3.

County Court Business List to the High Court, those proceedings shall be taken in the High Court.

(3) Where, in exercise of its powers under section 40(2) of the County Courts Act 1984[a] the High Court orders the transfer of proceedings under the Act which were commenced in the High Court to the Central London County Court Business List, those proceedings shall be taken in the Central London County Court Business List.

(4) In exercising the powers referred to in paragraphs (2) and (3) regard shall be had to the following criteria—

    (a) the financial substance of the dispute referred to arbitration, including the value of any claim or counterclaim;

    (b) the nature of the dispute referred to arbitration (for example, whether it arises out of a commercial or business transaction or relates to engineering, building or other construction work);

    (c) whether the proceedings are otherwise important and, in particular, whether they raise questions of importance to persons who are not parties, and

    (d) the balance of convenience points to having the proceedings taken in the Central London County Court Business List,

and, where the financial substance of the dispute exceeds £200,000, the proceedings shall be taken in the High Court unless the proceedings do not raise questions of general importance to persons who are not parties.

(5) In this article—

"the Central London County Court Business List" means the business list established at the Central London County Court by Order 48C of the County Court Rules 1981[b];

"value" shall be construed in accordance with articles 9 and 10 of the High Court and County Courts Jurisdiction Order 1991[c].

6. Nothing in this Order shall prevent the judge in charge of the commercial list (within the meaning of section 62(3) of the Supreme Court Act 1981[d]) from transferring proceedings under the Act to another list, court or Division of the High Court to which he has power to transfer proceedings and, where such an order is made, the proceedings may be taken in that list, court or Division as the case may be.

Dated 19th December 1996   *Mackay of Clashfern, C.*

    (a) 1984 c. 28; section 40 was substituted by the Courts and Legal Services Act 1990 (c. 41), section 2(1).

    (b) S.I. 1981/1687; the relevant amending instruments are S.I. 1994/1288 and 1996/3215.

    (c) S.I. 1991/724.

    (d) 1981 c. 54.

EXPLANATORY NOTE

(This note is not part of the Order)

This Order specifies the courts in which proceedings under the Arbitration Act 1996 may be commenced and allocates proceedings between the High Court and the Central London County Court.

THE RULES OF THE SUPREME COURT (AMENDMENT) 1996 (S.I. 1996/3219)

Made   19 December 1996

Laid before Parliament   20 December 1996

Coming into force   31 January 1997

We, the Supreme Court Rule Committee, having power under section 85 of the Supreme Court Act 1981[a] to make rules of court under section 60 of that Act and under section 84 of that Act for the purpose of regulating and prescribing the practice and procedure to be followed in the High Court and the civil division of the Court of Appeal, hereby exercise those powers as follows—

Citation, commencement and interpretation

1.—(1) These Rules may be cited as the Rules of the Supreme Court (Amendment) 1996 and shall come into force on 31 January 1997.

(2) In these Rules, an Order referred to by number means the Order so numbered in the Rules of the Supreme Court 1965[b] and a reference to Appendix A is a reference to Appendix A to those Rules.

Arbitration Act 1996

2. The Arrangement of Orders at the beginning of the Rules of the Supreme Court 1965 shall be amended, by substituting for the title to Order 73, the following "Applications relating to Arbitration".

(a) 1981 c.54; section 85 was amended by the Courts and Legal Services Act 1990 (c.41), Schedule 18, paragraph 36(1).
(b) S.I. 1965/1776; the relevant amending instruments are noted in footnotes to provisions in the body of the instrument.

3.   Order 11, rule 9(1) and (4)[a] shall be amended by omitting the words "Subject to Order 73, rule 7,".

4.   Order 59, rule 1A(7)(a)[b] shall be amended by inserting, after "1979", the words "or under section 69(7) of the Arbitration Act 1996[c]" and rule 1A(7)(b)(iii) shall be amended by inserting, after "section 1(2)", the words "or of section 69(7)of the said Act of 1996".

5.   For Order 73 there shall be substituted the following—

"ORDER 73

APPLICATIONS RELATING TO ARBITRATION

Introduction

This Order is divided into three Parts. Part I is concerned with applications to the Court relating to arbitration to which Part I of the Arbitration Act 1996 applies. Part II restates with some necessary adjustments provisions of the existing Order which are to be preserved. Part III is concerned with applications for enforcement under the earlier Arbitration Acts and under the 1996 Act.

The application of the Order to particular proceedings may be determined by reference to the following table. Column 1 shows the date on which arbitral proceedings (if any) were commenced. Column 2 shows the date of the application to the Court. Column 3 shows the appropriate Part of the Order for the application.

Column 1 *Date of arbitral proceedings*	Column 2 *Date of application to the Court*	Column 3 *Appropriate Part of Order 73*
not commenced	before 31 January 1997	Part II
before 31 January 1997	before 31 January 1997	Part II
not commenced	on or after 31 January 1997	Part I
before 31 January 1997	on or after 31 January 1997	Part II
on or after 31 January 1997	on or after 31 January 1997	Part I
on or after 31 January 1997	before 31 January 1997	Part II

(a) Order 11, rule 9 has been amended by S.I. 1979/1716, 1980/629, 2000 and 1983/1181.

(b) Order 59, rule 1A was added by S.I. 1988/1340 and amended by S.I. 1993/2133 and 1994/1975.

(c) 1996 c.23.

The other provisions of these rules apply to applications relating to arbitration subject to the provisions of this Order and only to the extent that they do not conflict with it.

See, for example, the following provisions of these rules for the following matters—
Order 10—service of originating process
Order 12—acknowledgement of service
Order 29—injunctions
Order 32—proceedings in chambers
Order 41—affidavits
Order 65—service of documents.

PART I

The overriding objective

1. This Part of this Order is founded on the general principles in section 1 of the Arbitration Act and shall be construed accordingly.

Meaning of arbitration application

2.—(1) Subject to paragraph (2), "arbitration application" means the following—
   (a) an application to the Court under the Arbitration Act;
   (b) proceedings to determine—
       (i) whether there is a valid arbitration agreement;
       (ii) whether an arbitrational tribunal is properly constituted;
       (iii) what matters have been submitted to arbitration in accordance with an arbitration agreement;
   (c) proceedings to declare that an award made by an arbitral tribunal is not binding on a party;
   (d) any other application affecting arbitration proceedings (whether instituted or anticipated) or to construe or affecting an arbitration agreement,
and includes the originating process by which an arbitration application is begun.

(2) In this Part of this Order, an arbitration application does not include proceedings to enforce an award—
   (a) to which Part III of this Order applies; or
   (b) by an action on the award.

Interpretation

3. In this Part—
"applicant" means the party making an arbitration application and references to respondent shall be construed accordingly;
"the Arbitration Act" means the Arbitration Act 1996 and any expressions used in this Order and in Part I of the Arbitration Act have the same meanings in this Order as they have in that Part of the Arbitration Act.

Form and content of arbitration application

4.—(1) An arbitration application must be in Form No. 8A in Appendix A.

(2) Every arbitration application must—
   (a) include a concise statement of
      (i) the remedy or relief claimed, and
      (ii) (where appropriate) the questions on which the applicant seeks the determination or direction of the Court;
   (b) give details of any arbitration award that is challenged by the applicant, showing the grounds for any such challenge;
   (c) where the applicant claims an order for costs, identify the respondent against whom the claim is made,
   (d) (where appropriate) specify the section of the Arbitration Act under which the application is brought; and
   (e) show that any statutory requirements have been satisfied including those set out, by way of example, in the Table Below.

Application made	Statutory requirements
section 9 (stay of legal proceedings)	see section 9(3)
section 12 (extensions of time for beginning arbitral proceedings)	see section 12(2)
section 18 (failure of appointment procedure)	see section 18(2)
section 21 (umpires)	see section 21(5)
section 24 (removal of arbitrators)	see section 24(2)
section 32 (preliminary point of jurisdiction)	see section 32(3)
section 42 (enforcement of peremptory orders)	see section 42(3)
section 44 (powers in support of arbitral proceedings)	see section 44(4), (5)
section 45 (preliminary point of law)	see section 45(3)
section 50 (extension of time for making award)	see section 50(2)
section 56 (power to withhold award)	see section 56(4)
sections 67, 68 (challenging the award)	see section 70(2), (3)
section 69 (appeal on point of law)	see sections 69(2), (4), 70(2), (3)

(3) The arbitration application must also state
- (a) whether it is made *ex parte* or on notice and, if made on notice, must give the names and addresses of the persons to whom notice is to be given, stating their role in the arbitration and whether they are made respondents to the application;
- (b) whether (having regard to rule 15) the application will be heard in open Court or in chambers; and
- (c) the date and time when the application will be heard or that such date has not yet been fixed.

(4) Every arbitration application which is used as an originating process shall be indorsed with the applicant's address for service in accordance with Order 6, rule 5.

Issue of application

5.—(1) This rule is to be read with the provisions of the High Court and County Courts (Allocation of Arbitration Proceedings) Order 1996[a] which allocates proceedings under the Arbitration Act to the High Court and the county courts and specifies proceedings which may be commenced or taken only in the High Court or in a county court.

(2) This rule does not apply to applications under section 9 of the Arbitration Act to stay legal proceedings.

(3) Any other arbitration application may be made—
- (a) in the Royal Courts of Justice, in which case it shall be issued out of the Admiralty and Commercial Registry;
- (b) in a district registry where there is a mercantile list, in which case it shall be entered into that list.

(4) Except where an arbitration application is issued out of the Admiralty and Commercial Registry, the Judge in charge of the list shall
- (a) as soon as practicable after the issue of the application, and
- (b) in consultation with the Judge in charge of the commercial list,
consider whether the application should be transferred to the Commercial Court or to any another list.

(5) Where an arbitration application is issued out of the Admiralty and Commercial Registry, the Judge in charge of the commercial list may at any time after the issue of the application transfer the application to another list, court or Division of the High Court, to which he has power to transfer proceedings.

(6) In considering whether to transfer an application, the Judges referred

(a) S.I. 1996/3215.

to in paragraphs (4) and (5) shall have regard to the criteria specified in article 4(4) of the High Court and County Courts (Allocation of Arbitration Proceedings) Order 1996[a] and the application shall be transferred if those Judges so decide.

(7) In this rule "Judge in charge of the list" means—

    (a) a Commercial Judge, where the arbitration application is issued out of the Admiralty and Commercial Registry;

    (b) a Circuit mercantile Judge, where the arbitration application is entered in a mercantile list;

    (c) a Judge of the business list in the Central London County Court, where the arbitration application is commenced in the business list established at the Central London County Court by Order 48C of the County Court Rules 1981[b];

but nothing in this rule shall be construed as preventing the powers of a Commercial Judge from being exercised by any judge of the High Court.

Stay of legal proceedings

6.—(1) An application under section 9 of the Arbitration Act to stay legal proceedings shall be served—

    (a) in accordance with Order 65, rule 5, on the party bringing the relevant legal proceedings and on any other party to those proceedings who has given an address for service; and

    (b) on any party to those legal proceedings who has not given an address for service, by sending to him (whether or not he is within the jurisdiction) at his last known address or at a place where it is likely to come to his attention, a copy of the application for his information.

(2) Where a question arises as to whether an arbitration application has been concluded or as to whether the dispute which is the subject-matter of the proceedings falls within the terms of such an agreement, the Court may determine that question or give directions for its determination, in which case it may order the proceedings to be stayed pending the determination of that question.

(a) The criteria specified in article 4(4) are (a) the financial substance of the dispute in the arbitration, including the value of any claim or counterclaim; (b) the nature of the dispute referred to arbitration (for example, whether it arises out of a commercial or business transaction or relates to engineering, building or other construction work); (c) whether the proceedings are otherwise important and, in particular, whether they raise questions of importance to persons who are not parties, and (d) the balance of convenience points to having the proceedings taken in the Central London County Court Business List. Generally, where the financial substance of the dispute exceeds £200,000, the proceedings are to be taken in the High Court unless they do not raise questions of general importance to persons who are not parties.

(b) S.I. 1981/1687; the relevant amending instruments are S.I. 1994/1288 and 1996/3218.

Service of arbitration application

7.—(1) Subject to paragraphs (2) and (4) below and to rules 6(1) and 8, an arbitration application shall be served in accordance with Order 10.

(2) Where the Court is satisfied on an *ex parte* application that
- (a) arbitral proceedings are taking place, or an arbitration application has been made, within the jurisdiction; and
- (b) an arbitration application is being made in connection with those arbitral proceedings or being brought to challenge the award or to appeal on a question of law arising out of the award; and
- (c) the respondent to the arbitration application (not being an individual residing or carrying on business within the jurisdiction or a body corporate having a registered office or a place of business within the jurisdiction)
  - (i) is or was represented in the arbitral proceedings by a solicitor or other agent within the jurisdiction who was authorised to receive service of any notice or other document served for the purposes of those proceedings; and
  - (ii) has not (at the time when the arbitration application is made) determined the authority of that solicitor or agent,

the Court may authorise service of the arbitration application to be effected on the solicitor or agent instead of the respondent.

(3) An order made under paragraph (2) must limit a time within which the respondent must acknowledge service and a copy of the order and of the arbitration application must be sent by post to the respondent at his address out of the jurisdiction.

(4) Where an arbitration application has been issued, any subsequent arbitration application made by the respondent and arising out of the same arbitration or arbitration agreement may be served on the applicant in accordance with Order 65, rule 5 (ordinary service: how effected) and similarly any subsequent arbitration application by any party may be served at the address for service given in the first arbitration application or in the acknowledgement of service.

(5) For the purposes of service, an arbitration application is valid in the first instance
- (a) where service is to be effected out of jurisdiction, for such period as the Court may fix;
- (b) in any other case, for one month,

beginning with the date of its issue and Order 6, rule 8 shall apply with the substitution, in paragraphs (2) and (2A), of "2 months" for "4 months" and "6 months" for "12 months".

Service out of the jurisdiction

8.—(1) Service out of the jurisdiction of an arbitration application is permissible with the leave of the Court if the arbitration application falls into one of the categories mentioned in the following table and satisfies the conditions specified.

Nature of application	Conditions to be satisfied
1. The applicant seeks to challenge, or to appeal to the Court on a question of law arising out of, an arbitration award.	Award must have been made in England and Wales. Section 53 of the Arbitration Act shall apply for determining the place where award is treated as made.
2. The application is for an order under section 44 of the Arbitration Act (Court powers exercisable in support of arbitral proceedings). Where the application is for interim relief in support of arbitral proceedings which are taking (or will take) place outside England and Wales, the Court may give leave for service out of the jurisdiction notwithstanding that no other relief is sought.	None.
3. The applicant seeks some other remedy or relief, or requires a question to be determined by the Court, affecting an arbitration (whether pending or anticipated), an arbitration application or an arbitration award.	The seat of the arbitration is or will be in England and Wales or the conditions in section 2(4) of the Arbitration Act are satisfied.

(2) An application for the grant of leave under this rule must be supported by an affidavit
    (a) stating the grounds on which the application is made; and
    (b) showing in what place or country the person to be served is, or probably may be found,
and no such leave shall be granted unless it shall be made sufficiently to appear to the Court that the case is a proper one for service out of the jurisdiction under this rule.

(3) Order 11, rules 5 to 8 shall apply to the service of an arbitration application under this rule as the apply to the service of a writ.

(4) Service out of the jurisdiction of any order made on an arbitration application is permissible with the leave of the Court.

Affidavit in support of arbitration application

9.—(1) The applicant shall file an affidavit in support of the arbitration application which sets out the evidence on which he intends to rely and a copy of every affidavit so filed must be served with the arbitration application.

(2) Where an arbitration application is made with the written agreement of all the other parties to the arbitral proceedings or with the permission of the arbitral tribunal, the affidavit in support must
   (a) give details of the agreement or, as the case may be, permission; and
   (b) exhibit copies of any document which evidences that agreement or permission.

Requirements as to notice

10.—(1) Where the Arbitration Act requires that an application to the Court is to be made upon notice to other parties notice shall be given by making those parties respondents to the application and serving on them the arbitration application and any affidavit in support.

(2) Where an arbitration application is made under section 24, 28 or 56 of the Arbitration Act, the arbitrators or, in the case of an application under section 24, the arbitrator concerned shall be made respondents to the application and notice shall be given by serving on them the arbitration application and any affidavit in support.

(3) In cases where paragraph (2) does not apply, an applicant shall be taken as having complied with any requirement to give notice to the arbitrator if he sends a copy of the arbitration application to the arbitrator for his information at his last known address with a copy of any affidavit in support.

(4) This rule does not apply to applications under section 9 of the Arbitration Act to stay legal proceedings.

Acknowledgement of service by respondent

11.—(1) Service of an arbitration application may be acknowledged by completing an acknowledgement of service in Form No. 15A in Appendix A in accordance with Order 12 (as that Order applies by virtue of rule 9 of that Order).

(2) A respondent who
   (a) fails to acknowledge service within the time limit for so doing; or
   (b) having indicated on his acknowledgement of service that he does not intend to contest the arbitration application, then wishes to do so,

shall not be entitled to contest the application without the leave of the Court.

(3) The Court will not give notice of the date on which an arbitration application will be heard to a respondent who has failed to acknowledge service.

(4) The failure of a respondent to give notice of intention to contest the arbitration application or to acknowledge service shall not affect the applicant's duty to satisfy the Court that the order applied for should be made.

(5) This rule does not apply to—
   (a) applications under section 9 of the Arbitration Act to stay legal proceedings; or
   (b) subsequent arbitration applications.

Acknowledgement of service etc. by arbitrator

12.—(1) An arbitrator who is sent a copy of an arbitration application for his information may make
   (a) a request *ex parte* in writing to be made a respondent; or
   (b) representations to the Court under this rule,
and, where an arbitrator is ordered to be made a respondent, he shall acknowledge service within 14 days of the making of that order.

(2) An arbitrator who wishes to make representations to the Court under this rule may file an affidavit or make representations in writing to the Court.

(3) The arbitrator shall as soon as is practicable send a copy of any document filed or made under paragraph (2) to all the parties to the arbitration application.

(4) Nothing in this rule shall require the Court to admit a document filed or made under paragraph (2) and the weight to be given to any such document shall be a matter for the Court.

Automatic directions

13.—(1) Unless the Court otherwise directs, the following directions shall take effect automatically.

(2) A respondent who wishes to put evidence before the Court in response to any affidavit filed in support of an arbitration application shall serve his affidavit on the applicant before the expiration of 21 days after the time limited for acknowledging service or, in a case where a respondent is not required to file an acknowledgement of service, within 21 days after service of the arbitration application.

(3) An applicant who wishes to put evidence before the Court in

response to an affidavit lodged under paragraph (2) shall serve his affidavit on the respondent within 7 days after service of the respondent's affidavit.

(4) Where a date has not been fixed for the hearing of the arbitration application, the applicant shall, and the respondent may, not later than 14 days after the expiration of the time limit specified in paragraph (2), apply to the Court for such a date to be fixed.

(5) Agreed indexed and paginated bundles of all the evidence and other documents to be used at the hearing shall be prepared by the applicant (with the co-operation of the respondent).

(6) Not later than 5 clear days before the hearing date estimates for the length of the hearing shall be lodged with the Court together with a complete set of the documents to be used.

(7) Not later than 2 days before the hearing date the applicant shall lodge with the Court—

    (a) a chronology of the relevant events cross-referenced to the bundle of documents;

    (b) (where necessary) a list of the persons involved;

    (c) a skeleton argument which lists succinctly

       (i) the issues which arise for decision,

       (ii) the grounds of relief (or opposing relief) to be relied upon,

       (iii) the submissions of fact to be made with the references to the evidence, and

       (iv) the submissions of law with references to the relevant authorities,

and shall send a copy to the respondent.

(8) Not later than the day before the hearing date the respondent shall lodge with the Court a skeleton argument which lists succinctly

    (a) the issues which arise for decision,

    (b) the grounds of relief (or opposing relief) to be relied upon,

    (c) the submissions of fact to be made with the references to the evidence, and

    (d) the submissions of law with references to the relevant authorities,

and shall send a copy to the applicant.

Directions by the Court

14.—(1) The Court may give such directions as to the conduct of the arbitration application as it thinks best adapted to secure the just, expeditious and economical disposal thereof.

(2) Where the Court considers that there is or may be a dispute as to fact and that the just, expeditious and economical disposal of the application can best be secured by hearing the application on oral evidence or mainly on oral evidence, it may, if it thinks fit, order that no further evidence shall be filed and that the application shall be heard on oral evidence or partly on

oral evidence and partly on affidavit's evidence, with or without cross-examination of any of the deponents, as it may direct.

(3) The Court may give directions as to the filing of evidence and as to the attendance of deponents for cross-examination and any directions which it could give in proceedings begun by writ.

(4) If the applicant makes default in complying with these rules or with any order or direction of the Court as to the conduct of the application, or if the Court is satisfied that the applicant is not prosecuting the application with due despatch, the Court may order the application to be dismissed or may make such other order as may be just.

(5) If the respondent fails to comply with these rules or with any order or direction given by the Court in relation to the evidence to be relied on, or the submissions to be made by that respondent, the Court may, if it thinks fit, hear and determine the application without having regard to that evidence or those submissions.

Hearing of applications: open Court or in Chambers

15.—(1) The Court may order that any arbitration application be heard either in open court or in chambers.

(2) Subject to any order made under paragraph (1) and to paragraph (3), all arbitration applications shall be heard in chambers.

(3) Subject to any order made under paragraph (1), the determination of a preliminary point of law under section 45 of the Arbitration Act or an appeal under section 69 on a question of law arising out of an award shall be heard in open court.

(4) Paragraph (3) shall not apply to
  (a) the preliminary question whether the Court is satisfied of the matters set out in section 45(2)(b); or
  (b) an application for leave to appeal under section 69(2)(b).

Securing the attendance of witnesses

16.—(1) A party to arbitral proceedings being conducted in England and Wales who wishes to rely on section 43 of the Arbitration Act to secure the attendance of a witness may apply for a writ of subpoena ad testificandum or of subpoena duces tecum to the Admiralty and Commercial Registry or, if the attendance of the witness is required within the district of a district registry, at that registry at the option of the party.

(2) A writ of subpoena shall not be issued until the applicant lodges an affidavit which shows that the application is made with the permission of the tribunal or the agreement of the other parties.

Security for costs

17. Subject to section 70(6) of the Arbitration Act, the Court may order any applicant (including an applicant who has been granted leave to appeal) to provide security for costs of any arbitration application.

Powers exercisable in support of arbitral proceedings

18.—(1) Where the case is one of urgency, an application for an order under section 44 of the Arbitration Act (Court powers exercisable in support of arbitral proceedings) may be made *ex parte* on affidavit (before the issue of an arbitration application) and the affidavit shall (in addition to dealing with the matters required to be dealt with by rule 9) state the reasons

  (a) why the application is made *ex parte*; and

  (b) (where the application is made without the permission of the arbitral tribunal or the agreement of the other parties to the arbitral proceedings) why it was not practicable to obtain that permission or agreement, and

  (c) why the deponent believes that the condition in section 44(5) is satisfied.

(2) Where the case is not one of urgency, an application for an order under section 44 of the Arbitration Act shall be made on notice and the affidavit in support shall (in addition to dealing with the matters required to be dealt with by rule 9 and paragraph (1)(c) above) state that the application is made with the permission of the tribunal or the written agreement of the other parties to the arbitral proceedings.

(3) Where an application for an order under section 44 of the Arbitration Act is made before the issue of an arbitration application, any order made by the Court may be granted on terms providing for the issue of an application and such other terms, if any, as the Court thinks fit.

Applications under sections 32 and 45 of the Arbitration Act

19.—(1) This rule applies to the following arbitration applications:

  (a) applications for the determination of a question as to the substantive jurisdiction of the arbitral tribunal under section 32 of the Arbitration Act; and

  (b) applications for the determination of a preliminary point of law under section 45 of the Arbitration Act.

(2) Where an application is made without the agreement in writing of all the other parties to the arbitral proceedings but with the permission of the arbitral tribunal, the affidavits filed by the parties shall set out any evidence relied on by the parties in support of their contention that the Court should, or should not, consider the application.

(3) As soon as practicable after the affidavits are lodged, the Court shall

decide whether or not it should consider the application and, unless the Court otherwise directs, shall so decide without a hearing.

Applications for leave to appeal

20.—(1) Where the applicant seeks leave to appeal to the Court on a question of law arising out of an arbitration award, the arbitration application shall identify the question of law and state the grounds on which the applicant alleges that leave should be granted.

(2) The affidavit in support of the application shall set out any evidence relied on by the applicant for the purpose of satisfying the Court of the matters mentioned in section 69(3) of the Arbitration Act and for satisfying the Court that leave should be granted.

(3) The affidavit lodged by the respondent to the application shall
   (a) state the grounds on which the respondent opposes the grant of leave;
   (b) set out any evidence relied on by him relating to the matters mentioned in section 69(3) of the Arbitration Act, and
   (c) specify whether the respondent wishes to contend that the award should be upheld for reasons not expressed (or not fully expressed) in the award and, if so, state those reasons.

(4) As soon as practicable after the lodging of the affidavits, the Court shall determine the application for leave in accordance with section 69(5) of the Arbitration Act.

(5) Where leave is granted, a date shall be fixed for the hearing of the appeal.

Extension of time: applications under section 12

21. An application for an order under section 12 of the Arbitration Act may include as an alternative an application for a declaration that such an order is not needed.

Time limit for challenges to or appeals from awards

22.—(1) An applicant shall not be taken as having complied with the time limit of 28 days referred to in section 70(3) of the Arbitration Act unless the arbitration application has been issued, and all the affidavits in support have been sworn and filed, by the expiry of that time limit.

(2) An applicant who wishes
   (a) to challenge an award under section 67 or 68 of the Arbitration Act; or
   (b) to appeal under section 69 on a question of law arising out of an award,

may, where the time limit of 28 days has not yet expired, apply *ex parte* on affidavit for an order extending that time limit.

(3) In any case where an applicant seeks to challenge an award under section 67 or 68 of the Arbitration Act or to appeal under section 69 after the time limit of 28 days has already expired, the following provisions shall apply:

(a) the applicant must state in his arbitration application the grounds why an order extending time should be made and his affidavit in support shall set out the evidence on which he relies;

(b) a respondent who wishes to oppose the making of an order extending time shall file an affidavit within 7 days after service of the applicant's affidavit, and

(c) the Court shall decide whether or not to extend time without a hearing unless it appears to the Court that a hearing is required,

and, where the Court makes an order extending the time limit, the respondent shall file his affidavit in response to the arbitration application 21 days after the making of the order.

PART II

Application of this Part

23.—(1) This Part of this Order applies to any application to the Court to which the old law applies and, in this rule, "the old law" means the enactments specified in section 107 of the Arbitration Act 1996[(a)] as they stood before their amendment or repeal by that Act.

(2) This Part of this Order does not apply to proceedings to enforce an award—

(a) to which Part III of this order applies; or

(b) by an action on the award.

(3) References should be made to the other provisions of these rules (except Parts I and III of this Order) for the procedure for any application not expressly provided for in this Part.

Matters for a judge in court[(b)]

24.—(1) Every application to the Court—

(a) to remit an award under section 22 of the Arbitration Act 1950[(c)]; or

---

(a) 1996 c.23.
(b) Rule 24 restates Order 73, rule 2 which was amended by S.I. 1979/522, 1983/1181 and 1986/632. Rule 1 of Order 73 was revoked by S.I. 1983/1181.
(c) 1950 c.27.

(b) to remove an arbitrator or umpire under section 23(1) of that Act; or

(c) to set aside an award under section 23(2) of that Act, or

(d) to determine, under section 2(1) of the Arbitration Act 1979[a], any question of law arising in the course of a reference,

must be made by originating motion to a single judge in court.

(2) Any appeal to the High Court under section 1(2) of the Arbitration Act 1979 shall be made by originating motion to a single judge in court.

(3) An application for a declaration that an award made by an arbitrator or umpire is not binding on a party to the award on the ground that it was made without jurisdiction may be made by originating motion to a single judge in court, but the foregoing provisions shall not be taken as affecting the judge's power to refuse to make such a declaration in proceedings begun by motion.

Matters for judge in chambers or master[b]

25.—(1) Subject to the foregoing provisions of this Order and the provisions of this rule, the jurisdiction of the High Court or a judge thereof under the Arbitration Act 1950 and the jurisdiction of the High Court under the Arbitration Act 1975[c] and the Arbitration Act 1979 may be exercised by a judge in chambers, a master or the Admiralty register.

(2) Any application
  (a) for leave to appeal under section 1(2) of the Arbitration Act 1979, or
  (b) under section 1(5) of that Act (including any application for leave), or
  (c) under section 5 of that Act,
shall be made to a judge in chambers.

(3) Any application to which this rule applies shall, where an action is pending, be made by summons in the action, and in any other case by an originating summons which shall be in Form No. 10 in Appendix A.

(4) Where an application is made under section 1(5) of the Arbitration Act 1979 (including any application for leave) the summons must be served on the arbitrator or umpire and on any other party to the reference.

Applications in district registries[d]

26.—(1) An application under section 12(4) of the Arbitration Act 1950

(a) 1979 c.42.
(b) Rule 25 restates Order 73, rule 3 which was amended by S.I. 1979/522, 1979/1716 and 1983/1181.
(c) 1975 c.3.
(d) Rule 26 restates Order 73, rule 4 which was amended by S.I. 1987/1423.

for an order that a writ of subpoena ad testificandum or of subpoena duces tecum shall issue to compel the attendance before an arbitrator or umpire of a witness may, if the attendance of the witness is required within the district of a district registry, be made at the registry, instead of at the Admiralty and Commercial Registry, at the option of the applicant.

Time limits and other special provisions as to appeals and applications under the Arbitration Acts[a]

27.—(1) An application to the Court—

(a) to remit an award under section 22 of the Arbitration Act 1950; or

(b) to set aside an award under section 23(2) of that Act or otherwise, or

(c) to direct an arbitrator or umpire to state the reasons for an award under section 1(5) of the Arbitration Act 1979,

must be made, and the summons or notice must be served, within 21 days after the award has been made and published to the parties.

(2) In the case of an appeal to the Court under section 1(2) of the Arbitration Act 1979, the summons for leave to appeal, where leave is required, and the notice of originating motion must be served and the appeal entered, within 21 days after the award has been made and published to the parties.

Provided that, where reasons material to the appeal are given on a date subsequent to the publication of the award, the period of 21 days shall run from the date on which the reasons are given.

(3) An application, under section 2(1) of the Arbitration Act 1979, to determine any question of law arising in the course of a reference, must be made, and notice thereof served, within 14 days after the arbitrator or umpire has consented to the application being made, or the other parties have so consented.

(4) For the purpose of paragraph (3) the consent must be given in writing.

(5) In the case of every appeal or application to which this rule applies, the notice of originating motion, the originating summons or the summons, as the case may be, must state the grounds of the appeal or application and, where the appeal or application is founded on evidence by affidavit, or is made with the consent of the arbitrator or umpire or of the other parties, a copy of every affidavit intended to be used, or, as the case may be, of every consent given in writing, must be served with that notice.

(6) Without prejudice to paragraph (5), in an appeal under section 1(2)

(a) Rule 27 restates Order 73, rule 5 which was amended by S.I. 1979/522, 1986/632 and 2289.

of the Arbitration Act 1979 the statement of the grounds of the appeal shall specify the relevant parts of the award and reasons, or the relevant parts thereof, shall be lodged with the court and served with the notice of originating motion.

(7) Without prejudice to paragraph (5), in an application for leave to appeal under section 1(2) of the Arbitration Act 1979, any affidavit verifying the facts in support of a contention that the question of law concerns a term of a contract or an event which is not a one-off term or event must be lodged with the court and served with the notice of originating motion.

(8) Any affidavit in reply to an affidavit under paragraph (7) shall be lodged with the court and served on the applicant not less than two clear days before the hearing of the application.

(9) A respondent to an application for leave to appeal under section 1(2) of the Arbitration Act 1979 who desires to contend that the award should be upheld on grounds not expressed or fully expressed in the award and reasons shall not less than two clear days before the hearing of the application lodge with the court and serve on the applicant a notice specifying the grounds of his contention.

Applications and appeals to be heard by Commercial Judges[a]

28.—(1) Any matter which is required, by rule 24 or 25, to be heard by a judge, shall be heard by a Commercial Judge, unless any such judge otherwise directs.

(2) Nothing in the foregoing paragraph shall be construed as preventing the powers of a Commercial Judge from being exercised by any judge of the High Court.

Service out of the jurisdiction of summons, notice, etc.[b]

29.—(1) Subject to paragraph (2), service out of the jurisdiction of
   (a) any originating summons or notice of originating motion under the Arbitration Act 1950 or the Arbitration Act 1979, or
   (b) any order made on such a summons or motion,
is permissible with the leave of the Court provided that the arbitration to which the summons, motion or order relates is governed by English law or has been, is being or is to be held within the jurisdiction.

(2) Service out of the jurisdiction of an originating summons for leave to enforce an award is permissible with the leave of the Court whether or not the arbitration is governed by English law.

(a) Rule 28 restates Order 73, rule 6 which was amended by S.I. 1979/522.
(b) Rule 29 restates Order 73, rule 7 which was amended by S.I. 1979/1542, 1980/2000, 1983/1181, 1987/1423 and 1994/1975.

(3) An application for the grant of leave under this rule must be supported by an affidavit stating the grounds on which the application is made and showing in what place or country the person to be served is, or probably may be found; and no such leave shall be granted unless it shall be made to appear to the Court that the case is a proper one for service out of the jurisdiction under this rule.

(4) Order 11, rules 5 to 8, shall apply in relation to any such summons, notice or order as is referred to in paragraph (1) as they apply in relation to a writ.

PART III

Application of this Part

30. This Part of this Order applies to all enforcement proceedings (other than by an action on the award) regardless of when they are commenced and when the arbitral proceedings took place.

Enforcement of awards[a]

31.—(1) This rule applies to applications to enforce awards which are brought in the High Court[b] and such an application may be made in the Royal Courts of Justice or in any district registry.

(2) An application for leave under—
    (a) section 66 of the Arbitration Act 1996;
    (b) section 101 of the Arbitration Act 1996;
    (c) section 26 of the Arbitration Act 1950[c]; or
    (d) section 3(1)(a) of the Arbitration Act 1975;
to enforce an award in the same manner as a judgment or order may be made *ex parte* in Form No. 8A in Appendix A.

(3) The Court hearing an application under paragraph (2) may direct that the application is to be served on such parties to the arbitration as it may specify and service of the application out of the jurisdiction is permissible with the leave of the Court irrespective of where the award is, or is treated as, made.

(a) Rule 31 restates Order 73, rule 10 which was amended by S.I. 1978/1066, 1979/35, 1716 and 1980/2000.
(b) Article 2(1)(c) of the High Court and County Courts Jurisdiction Order 1991, S.I. 1991/724, and the High Court and County Courts (Allocation of Arbitration Proceedings) Order 1996, S.I. 1996/3215, enable applications under section 26 of the Arbitration Act 1950 and under sections 66 and 101(2) of the Arbitration Act 1996 to be brought in the county courts as well as in the High Court.
(c) Section 26 was amended by the Administration of Justice Act 1977 (c.38), section 17(2), the County Courts Act 1984 (c.28), Schedule 2 paragraph 22 and S.I. 1991/724.

(4) Where a direction is given under paragraph (3), rules 11 and 13 to 17 shall apply with the necessary modifications as they apply to applications under Part I of this Order.

(5) Where the applicant applies to enforce an agreed award within the meaning of section 51(2) of the Arbitration Act 1996, the application must state that the award is an agreed award and any order made by the Court shall also contain such a statement.

(6) An application for leave must be supported by affidavit—
  (a) exhibiting
      (i) where the application is made under section 66 of the Arbitration Act 1996 or under section 26 of the Arbitration Act 1950, the arbitration agreement and the original award or, in either case, a copy thereof;
     (ii) where the application is under section 101 of the Arbitration Act 1996, the documents required to be produced by section 102 of that Act;
    (iii) where the application is under section 3(1)(a) of the Arbitration Act 1975, the documents required to be produced by section 4 of that Act;
  (b) stating the name and the usual or last known place of residence or business of the applicant and of the person against whom it is sought to enforce the award respectively,
  (c) stating as the case may require, either that the award has not been complied with or the extent to which it has not been complied with at the date of the application.

(7) An order giving leave must be drawn up by or on behalf of the applicant and must be served on the respondent by delivering a copy to him personally or by sending a copy to him at his usual or last known place of residence or business or in such manner as the Court may direct.

(8) Service of the order out of the jurisdiction is permissible without leave, and Order 11, rules 5 to 8, shall apply in relation to such an order as they apply in relation to a writ.

(9) Within 14 days after service of the order or, if the order is to be served out of the jurisdiction, within such other period as the Court may fix, the respondent may apply to set aside the order and the award shall not be enforced until after the expiration of that period or, if the respondent applies within that period to set aside the order, until after the application is finally disposed of.

(10) The copy of the order served on the respondent shall state the effect of paragraph (9).

(11) In relation to a body corporate this rule shall have effect as if for any reference to the place of residence or business of the applicant or the

respondent there were substituted a reference to the registered or principal address of the body corporate.

Nothing in this rule shall effect any enactment which provides for the manner in which a document may be served on a body corporate.

Interest on awards

32.—(1) Where an applicant seeks to enforce an award of interest, the whole or any part of which relates to a period after the date of the award, he shall file a certificate giving the following particulars—

(a) whether simple or compound interest was awarded;

(b) the date from which interest was awarded;

(c) whether rests were provided for, specifying them;

(d) the rate of interest awarded, and

(e) a calculation showing the total amount claimed up to the date of the certificate and any sum which will become due thereafter on a *per diem* basis.

(2) The certificate under paragraph (1) must be filed whenever the amount of interest has to be quantified for the purpose of obtaining a judgment or order under section 66 of the Arbitration Act (enforcement of the award) or for the purpose of enforcing such a judgment or order by one of the means mentioned in Order 45, rule 1.

Registration in High Court of foreign awards[a]

33. Where an award is made in proceedings on an arbitration in any part of Her Majesty's dominions or other territory to which Part I of the Foreign Judgments (Reciprocal Enforcement) Act 1933[b] extends, being a part to which Part II of the Administration of Justice Act 1920[c] extended immediately before the said Part I was extended thereto, then, if the award has, in pursuance of the law in force in the place where it was made, become enforceable in the same manner as a judgment given by a court in that place, Order 71 shall apply in relation to the award as it applies in relation to a judgment given by that court, subject, however, to the following modifications:

(a) for references to the country of the original court there shall be substituted references to the place where the award was made; and

(b) the affidavit required by rule 3 of the said Order must state (in addition to the other matters required by that rule) that to the best of the information or belief of the deponent the award has, in pursuance of the law in force in the place where it was made,

(a) Rule 33 restates Order 73, rule 8.
(b) 1933 c.13.
(c) 1920 c.81.

become enforceable in the same manner as a judgment given by a court in that place.

Registration of awards under the Arbitration (International Investment Disputes) Act 1966[a][b]

34.—(1) In this rule and in any provision of these rules as applied by this rule—

"the Act of 1966" means the Arbitration (International Investment Disputes) Act 1966;

"award" means an award rendered pursuant to the Convention;

"judgment creditor" and "judgment debtor" mean respectively the person seeking recognition or enforcement of an award and the other party to the award.

(2) Subject to the provisions of this rule, the following provisions of Order 71, namely, rules 1, 3(1) (except sub-paragraphs (c)(iv) and (d) thereof) 7 (except paragraph (3)(c) and (d) thereof), and 10(3) shall apply with the necessary modifications in relation to an award as they apply in relation to a judgment to which Part II of the Foreign Judgments (Reciprocal Enforcement) Act 1933 applies.

(3) An application to have an award registered in the High Court under section 1 of the Act of 1966 shall be made by originating summons which shall be in Form No. 10 in Appendix A.

(4) The affidavit required by Order 71, rule 3, in support of an application for registration shall—

(a) in lieu of exhibiting the judgment or a copy thereof, exhibit a copy of the award certified pursuant to the Convention; and

(b) in addition to stating the matters mentioned in paragraph 3(1)(c)(i) and (ii) of the said rule 3, state whether at the date of the application the enforcement of the award has been stayed (provisionally or otherwise) pursuant to the Convention and whether any, and if so what, application has been made pursuant to the Convention, which, if granted, might result in a stay of the enforcement of the award.

(5) There shall be kept in the Admiralty and Commercial Registry under the direction of the Senior Master a register of the awards ordered to be registered under the Act of 1966 and particulars shall be entered in the register of any execution issued on such an award.

(6) Where it appears to the Court on granting leave to register an award or an application made by the judgment debtor after an award has been registered—

(a) 1966 c.41.

(b) Rule 34 restates Order 73, rule 9 which was amended by S.I. 1968/1244, 1977/1955, 1979/1716, 1982/1111 and 1987/1423.

(a) that the enforcement of the award has been stayed (whether pro-visionally or otherwise) pursuant to the Convention, or

(b) that an application has been made pursuant to the Convention, which, if granted, might result in a stay of the enforcement of the award,

the Court shall, or in the case referred to in sub-paragraph (b) may, stay execution of the award for such time as it considers appropriate in the circumstances.

(7) An application by the judgment debtor under paragraph (6) shall be made by summons and supported by affidavit.

Registration of awards under the Multilateral Investment Guarantee Agency Act 1988[a][b]

35.   Rule 34 shall apply, with the necessary modifications, in relation to an award rendered pursuant to the Convention referred to in section 1(1) of the Multilateral Investment Guarantee Agency Act 1988 as it applies in relation to an award rendered pursuant to the Convention referred to in section 1(1) of the Arbitration (International Investment Disputes) Act 1966.".

6.   After Form No. 8 in Appendix A there shall be inserted the form in Schedule 1 to these Rules.

7.   After Form No. 15 in Appendix A there shall be inserted the form in Schedule 2 to these Rules.

Hearsay evidence

8.   For Order 38, rules 20 to 34, there shall be substituted the following—

"Application and interpretation

20.—(1) In this Part of this Order the "1995 Act" means the Civil Evidence Act 1995[c] and any expressions used in this Part of this Order and in the 1995 Act have the same meanings in this Part of this Order as they have in the Act.

(2) In this Part of this Order:
"hearsay evidence" means evidence consisting of hearsay within the meaning of section 1(2) of the 1995 Act;
"hearsay notice" means a notice under section 2 of the 1995 Act.

(3) This Part of this Order applies in relation to the trial or hearing

(a) 1988 c.8.
(b) Rule 35 restates Order 73, rule 9A which was added by S.I. 1988/1340.
(c) 1995 c.38.

of an issue or question arising in a cause or matter and to a reference, inquiry and assessment of damages, as it applies to the trial or hearing of a cause or matter.

Hearsay notices

21.—(1) A hearsay notice must
   (a) state that it is a hearsay notice;
   (b) identify the hearsay evidence;
   (c) identify the person who made the statement which is to be given in evidence;
   (d) state why that person will (or may) not be called to give oral evidence; and
   (e) if the hearsay evidence is contained in a witness statement, refer to the part of the witness statement where it is set out.

(2) A single hearsay notice may deal with the hearsay evidence of more than one witness.

(3) The requirement to give a hearsay notice does not apply to
   (a) evidence which is authorised to be given by or in an affidavit; or
   (b) a statement which a party to a probate action desires to give in evidence and which is alleged to have been made by the person whose estate is the subject of the action.

(4) Subject to paragraph (5), a party who desires to give in evidence at the trial or hearing of a cause or matter hearsay evidence shall
   (a) in the case of a cause or matter which is required to be set down for trial or hearing or adjourned into Court, within 28 days after it is set down or so adjourned or within such other period as the Court may specify, and
   (b) in any other case, within 28 days after the date on which an appointment for the first hearing of the cause or matter is obtained, or within such other period as the Court may specify,
serve a hearsay notice on every party to the cause or matter.

(5) Where witness statements are served under rule 2A of this Order, any hearsay notice served under this rule shall be served at the same time as the witness statements.

Power to call witness for cross-examination on hearsay evidence

22.—(1) Where a party tenders as hearsay evidence a statement made by a person but does not propose to call the person who made the statement to give evidence, the court may, on application, allow another party to call and cross-examine the person who made the statement on its contents.

(2) An application under paragraph (1) shall be made on notice to all other parties no later than 28 days after service of the hearsay notice.

(3) Where the court allows another party to call and cross-examine the person who made the statement, it may give such directions as it thinks fit to secure the attendance of that person and as to the procedure to be followed.

Credibility

23.—(1) If
   (a) a party tenders as hearsay evidence a statement made by a person but does not call the person who made the statement to give oral evidence, and
   (b) another party wishes to attack the credibility of the person who made the statement;
that other party shall notify the party tendering the hearsay evidence of his intention.

(2) A notice under paragraph (1) shall be given not later than 28 days after service of the hearsay notice.

Powers exercisable in chambers

24. The jurisdiction of the Court under rules 20 to 23 may be exercised in chambers.".

9. Nothing in rule 8 shall apply to proceedings
   (a) in which directions have been given, or orders have been made, as to the evidence to be given at the trial or hearing, or
   (b) where the trial or hearing has begun
before 31 January 1997.

Miscellaneous amendments

10. Order 29, rule 11(2)(a)[a] shall be amended by substituting for the words "as insurer" the words "an insurer".

Mackay of Clashfern, C.,
Stephen Brown, P.,
Rattee, J.,
Colman, J.,
Bell, J.,
Dated 19 December 1996   *Jean Ritchie.*

(a) Order 29, rule 11 was added by S.I. 1970/944 and amended by S.I. 1980/1010 and 1986/2892.

SCHEDULE 1

Arbitration application

No.8A
(O.73, r.4(1))

Guidance notes for Applicants

---

1. You should read the following notes carefully before completing the attached form. The form can be used to either:

    (a) make an application in existing proceedings;
    or
    (b) begin proceedings (as an originating document).

    Notes 2 and 4 are relevant to an application as at 1(a); Notes 3 and 4 are relevant to an application as at 1(b).

---

2. No acknowledgement of service is required if the form is being used to make an application in existing proceedings. You should delete the notes relating to returning an acknowledgement of service. But you must still complete the address boxes at the end of the form as appropriate.

Service

3. (a) A completed acknowledgement of service must be served with the arbitration application. Notes for guidance attached to that form will tell you how to fill it in.

    (b) The application **may not** be served more than 1 month from the date of issue **unless**:
    it is to be served on a party outside England and Wales,
    or
    the time for service has been extended by the Court

    (c) You must write in the appropriate time limit for returning the acknowledgement of service. The relevant number of days should be given in the box below paragraph 6 of the notes about service.

    (d) If you are an applicant acting in person and you reside at an address which is not in England and Wales, you must give an address for service which is within the Court's jurisdiction.

4. Detach the guidance notes before this form is served.

Arbitration application

In the High Court of Justice   19   No

**Queen's Bench Division
Commercial Court**

District Registry Mercantile List   use black ink and capital
letters

---

1.   (i) In an arbitration application between

Applicant

and

Respondent

of

Respondent

of

Respondent

of

(ii) and in the matter of an (anticipated) arbitration between

Claimant

Respondent(s)

(iii) The arbitrator(s) to whom notice of this application is given are:

*give name of any
arbitrator(s) listed
above as respondents
      or
give full names
and addresses
where not named as
respondents*

Hearing
(delete (i) or (ii) as applicable)

2. (i) This application is made on notice (ex parte).

(ii) The hearing of this application will take place in court (chambers)

on

at   o'clock,

(or on a date to be fixed)

at *(specify court)*

Grounds for application and details of what is being claimed

The grounds for making the application and details of what is being claimed should be set out either in the box below or on a separate sheet attached to this application. The details should include those required by Order 73.

(Set out below the grounds and details of your claim)

The applicant seeks an order for the costs of this application against:

(Set out below the name of the person(s) against whom costs are sought)

Dated ....

Returning the acknowledgement of service
(see also "Notes for arbitrators", at paragraph 5 below)

1. If you are   (a) named as a respondent to this application, and
               (b) served with a copy of this application

you should complete and return the accompanying acknowledgement of service to the court office which issued it. **You have only a limited time in which to do this.** Full details of the time allowed are set out in the notes for guidance to the form of acknowledgement. **Whether or not you complete the form, and how you complete it, if you decide to do so, will affect your right:**

- **to contest the application; and**
- **to be kept informed of any hearing or future hearings,**

2. If you **complete the form of acknowledgement** and **indicate that you intend to contest the application**, you will **be notified of all hearing dates** relating to this application and **will be entitled to put your case to the Court**. If you wish to put evidence before the Court in response to any affidavit filed by the applicant in support of the application, you must serve your affidavit on the applicant within 21 days after the time limited for acknowledging service (see time for acknowledging below).

3. If you **complete the form of acknowledgement** but **do not indicate that you intend to contest the application**, you will be notified of all hearing dates relating to the application but, unless the court gives permission, you **will not be allowed to put your case to the Court**. The Court will make whatever order it feels is just in the circumstances. If, after returning the acknowledgement, you decide you **do** wish to contest the application, you must **ask the Court's permission to do so**.

4. If you **do not return** the form of acknowledgement, you will **not be entitled to contest** the application, **or be notified of any hearing dates relating to it**. If you **fail to return** the form of acknowledgement within the time allowed for the purpose (see the notes for guidance on the form of acknowledgement) you must ask the Court's permission to return the form of acknowledgement after the proper time. Unless the Court gives permission, you will not be allowed to put your case to the Court. The Court will make whatever order it feels is just in the circumstances.

Notes for arbitrators

5. If you were or are an arbitrator in the arbitration which gave rise to this application and you are named as a respondent to the application, paragraphs 1 to 4 above apply to you as to any other respondent.

6. If you were or are an arbitrator in the arbitration which gave rise to this application and you are **not** named as a respondent, the application has been sent to you for your information. You need not complete or return the acknowledgement. You may, if you wish, file an affidavit or make representations in writing to the Court. If you wish to do this, you should do so as soon as practicable. You should send a copy of the document which you have sent to the Court to all parties to the arbitration application. Alternatively, you may apply to be made a respondent to the application. Any such application should be made to the Court in writing.

(write in 14 days, or where application is to be served out of the jurisdiction the time limit set by the Court)

The time limit for the respondents to

acknowledge service is ☐ **days**

> **This summons was issued by**
>
> **of**
>
> **(Applicant) (Solicitor for the applicant)**

(Complete only if you are an applicant acting in person and you reside at an address which is outside the Court's jurisdiction)

Applicant's address for service within the jurisdiction is

SCHEDULE 2   Rule 7

No. 15A

Acknowledgement of Service of
Arbitration Application   (O.73, r.11(1))

Guidance notes for the Applicant

Read these notes carefully

The notes explain what you have to do before this form is sent to ("served" on) the respondent

---

Form heading

You must fill in the heading of the form with:

• the number allocated to the application

• the name of the appropriate High Court Division, for example, Queen's Bench Division, (Commercial Court), or if the arbitration application was issued in a District Registry, the name of the District Registry, and

• the names of the parties (the "title") as they appear on the application.

Part 3   Please leave blank for respondent to complete

Part 4
Return address
Write in the full address of the District Registry or office in the Royal Courts of Justice to which the form should be returned.

On the reverse of acknowledgement form (Applicant's (Applicant's solicitor's) details.)
Fill in your name and address to which papers about the case should be sent.
Detach these guidance notes before the form is sent to the respondent.

**Acknowledgement of Service of
Arbitration application**

Guidance notes for the Respondent

Read these notes carefully.

They will help you to fill in the form attached and tell you what other steps you need to take.

Act quickly.

You have only a limited time to return the form.

Help and advice

You can get help and legal advice from:

• a solicitor, or

• a Citizens' Advice Bureau.

They will also tell you if you qualify for help with your legal costs ("legal aid").

Staff at any District Registry or office in the Royal Courts of Justice (Strand, London) will help you to fill in the form.

Time for returning the form

You have **14 days** from the day you receive the arbitration application to **return the completed form to the court**. The day on which the 14 day period begins depends on how you received the application (how it was "served" on you).

If the application was:

• handed to you personally, the 14 days begins on the day you were given the application;

• delivered by post, the 14 days begins 7 days from the date of the postmark;

• put through your letter box, the 14 days begins 7 days from the day this was done.

If you are a limited company and the application was delivered by post, the 14 days begins:

- on the second working day from the date of the postmark if first class post was used;

- on the fourth working day from the date of the postmark if the second class post was used.

Note: You may have less than 14 days to return the form in certain kinds of proceedings where an early hearing date has been fixed. If in doubt, seek advice.

If the arbitration application was served on you at an address outside England and Wales, the application will tell you how long you have to return the acknowledgement form.

Filling in the form

Read these notes carefully

They will help you to fill in the form opposite and tell you what other steps you need to take.

> **You can use the same form of acknowledgement for two (or more) respondents provided the form makes this clear and they all wish to reply in the same way.**

If you are **under 18 or suffering certain mental disorders** ("under disability") you must ask another person to act for you. That person can be any friend or relative who is over 18 and not a co-defendant in the same claim. But they must act on your behalf with the help of a solicitor. **The solicitor must fill in the form of acknowledgment.**

Part 1 Write in your full name. If your name was incorrect on the summons, add the words "sued as" followed by the name stated on the application.

If you are: a person trading in a name other than your own, write in your name followed by the words "trading as" and the name under which you trade;

a partner in a firm, write in your name followed by the words "a partner in the firm of" and the name of the firm. **If you are sued as a partner but are not, say so.**

Part 2 Tick the appropriate box to show whether you intend to contest the application, the claim for costs, or neither. Read note 2 below.

Part 3 Unless your solicitor is filling in the form on your behalf, you must sign the form and give an address to which court documents should be sent, and any reference, telephone or fax numbers. If you are being sued as an individual (that is in your own name rather than of your firm or company) the address you give must be one in England and Wales. If you are a **limited company**, the form may be filled in by an **authorised officer** who must state his position in that company, or a solicitor. A solicitor may give his firm's address, an authorised officer must give the registered or principal office of the company.

What to do when you have filled in the form

1. Return the form

Detach these guidance notes and send or take the acknowledgement form to the office in the Royal Courts of Justice or the District Registry which issued the application.

2. Preparing your defence

If you are a respondent and wish to contest the application, you must set out your reasons in an affidavit (a sworn statement). You must send a copy of the affidavit to the applicant, the court and the other respondents. You must do this not more than 21 days after the last day for returning the acknowledgement of service, that is, 14 days after service.

If you are an arbitrator who is not named as a respondent, you may apply to be made a respondent or make representations to the court. If you wish to make representations, you may do so informally in writing or in an affidavit. You must send a copy to the court and all other parties as soon as practicable after you receive the application.

Acknowledgement of service of originating summons
Arbitration application

In the High Court of Justice   19   NO
Queen's Bench Division
Commercial Court
Mercantile List
District Registry   Use black ink and capital letters

Respondent

Applicant

Part 1   (Your)(Respondent's) full name

Part 2   (Do you) (Does the respondent) intend to contest:

the application?   ☐

the claim for costs (if applicable)?   ☐

or neither?   ☐

Part 3   I acknowledge that (I have) (the respondent has) been served with a copy of the arbitration application.

Signed   Date
Respondent (Solicitor for the respondent)(Authorised officer)

Address to which papers about this case should be sent.

Solicitor's ref.		Telephone no.		Fax no.	

Part 4 When completed this form should be returned to:

Applicant's (Applicant's solicitor's) details

Address to which papers about this case should be sent.

Solicitor's ref.		Telephone no.		Fax no.	

EXPLANATORY NOTE

(This note is not part of the Rules)

These Rules amend the Rules of the Supreme Court so as—
- (a) to substitute a new Order 73 (Applications relating to Arbitration) which provides for the bringing of applications under the Arbitration Act 1996 *(rules 2 to 7)*;
- (b) to provide a procedure for giving hearsay notices under the Civil Evidence Act 1995 *(rules 8 and 9)*;
- (c) to make a minor amendment to order 29, rule 11(2) *(rule 10)*.

UNCITRAL NOTES ON ORGANIZING ARBITRAL PROCEEDINGS[1]

The list of matters for possible consideration in organizing arbitral proceedings as published by the United Nations in 1996 is set out below:

1. Set of arbitration rules

If the parties have not agreed on a set of arbitration rules, would they wish to do so

2. Language of proceedings

(a) Possible need for translation of documents, in full or in part
(b) Possible need for interpretation of oral presentations
(c) Cost of translation and interpretation

3. Place of arbitration

(a) Determination of the place of arbitration, if not already agreed upon by the parties
(b) Possibility of meetings outside the place of arbitration

4. Administrative services that may be needed for the arbitral tribunal to carry out its functions

5. Deposits in respect of costs

(a) Amount to be deposited
(b) Management of deposits
(c) Supplementary deposits

1 Published by United Nations, Vienna 1996.

6. **Confidentiality of information relating to the arbitration; possible agreement thereon**

7. **Routing of written communications among the parties and the arbitrators**

8. **Telefax and other electronic means of sending documents**

   (a) Telefax
   (b) Other electronic means (e.g. electronic mail and magnetic or optical disk)

9. **Arrangements for the exchange of written submissions**

   (a) Scheduling of written submissions
   (b) Consecutive or simultaneous submissions

10. **Practical details concerning written submissions and evidence (e.g. method of submission, copies, numbering, references)**

11. **Defining points at issue; order of deciding issues; defining relief of remedy sought**

    (a) Should a list of points at issue be prepared
    (b) In which order should the points at issue be decided
    (c) Is there a need to define more precisely the relief or remedy sought

12. **Possible settlement negotiations and their effect on scheduling proceedings**

13. **Documentary evidence**

    (a) Time-limits for submission of documentary evidence intended to be submitted by the parties; consequences of late submission
    (b) Whether the arbitral tribunal intends to require a party to produce documentary evidence
    (c) Should assertions about the origin and receipt of documents and about the correctness of photocopies be assumed as accurate
    (d) Are the parties willing to submit jointly a single set of documentary evidence
    (e) Should voluminous and complicated documentary evidence be presented through summaries, tabulations, charts, extracts or samples

14. **Physical evidence other than documents**

    (a) What arrangements should be made if physical evidence will be submitted
    (b) What arrangements should be made if an on-site inspection is necessary

15. Witnesses

- (a) Advance notice about a witness whom a party intends to present; written witnesses' statements
- (b) Manner of taking oral evidence of witnesses
  - (i) Order in which questions will be asked and the manner in which the hearing of witnesses will be conducted
  - (ii) Whether oral testimony will be given under oath or affirmation and, if so, in what form an oath or affirmation should be made
  - (iii) May witnesses be in the hearing room when they are not testifying
- (c) The order in which the witnesses will be called
- (d) Interviewing witnesses prior to their appearance at a hearing
- (e) Hearing representatives of a party

16. Experts and expert witnesses

- (a) Expert appointed by the arbitral tribunal
  - (i) The expert's terms of reference
  - (ii) The opportunity of the parties to comment on the expert's report, including by presenting expert testimony
- (b) Expert opinion presented by a party (expert witness)

17. Hearings

- (a) Decision whether to hold hearings
- (b) Whether one period of hearings should be held or separate periods of hearings
- (c) Setting dates for hearings
- (d) Whether there should be a limit on the aggregate amount of time each party will have for oral arguments and questioning witnesses
- (e) The order in which the parties will present their arguments and evidence
- (f) Length of hearings
- (g) Arrangements for a record of the hearings
- (h) Whether and when the parties are permitted to submit notes summarising their oral arguments

18. Multi-party arbitration

19. Possible requirements concerning filing or delivering the award

Who should take steps to fulfil any requirement

It must be remembered that the UNCITRAL Notes are primarily aimed at international arbitrations and where an arbitral institution may provide all or part of the administration. The notes are also appropriate for arbitrations under civil law jurisdictions as well as common law. The requirements of the Arbitration Act 1996 do not apply to the UNCITRAL Notes.

INDEX

Throughout the index, the suffix "n" after a page number indicates a reference to the notes on that page. The suffix "&n" indicates a reference to both the main text and the notes on that page.